GAINING GROUND

GAINING GROUND

*Tailoring Social Programs
to American Values*

CHARLES LOCKHART

UNIVERSITY OF CALIFORNIA PRESS
BERKELEY   LOS ANGELES   LONDON

University of California Press
Berkeley and Los Angeles, California

University of California Press, Ltd.
London, England

© 1989 by
The Regents of the University of California

Library of Congress Cataloging-in-Publication Data

Lockhart, Charles, 1944–
    Gaining ground.
    Bibliography: p.
    Includes index.
    1. United States—Social policy—1980–   .
2. Human services—United States.   3. Social values.
I. Title.
HN59.2.L63   1989   361.6'1'0973   88-29594
ISBN 0-520-06437-2 (alk. paper)

Printed in the United States of America

1   2   3   4   5   6   7   8   9

To my father and the memory of my mother
and
for J.M.D., M.G., and J.G.

Contents

Preface

My interest in public social provision can be traced to the late 1970s, when three close friends were stricken with serious, lengthy illnesses. In each case, treatment cost more than limited insurance and moderate incomes could bear. Under these circumstances the anxieties of illness can wreak as much damage to the soul as illness does to the body; it is particularly difficult to retain a sense of self-respect when some of the authorities to whom one turns for healing act as though it were morally reprehensible not to have sufficient savings to cover catastrophic medical bills. At the time, the Texas economy was booming, and this coincidence exacerbated my sense of the unfairness of my friends' plight. Furthermore, as a member of a political science faculty with an abiding interest in Western European politics, I knew that my friends and others like them would have suffered less severely had they been living in almost any other advanced industrial society.

The experiences of my friends were hardly unusual. Every day the lives of good people are shattered by social hazards over which they have little control: illness, disability, unemployment, divorce. Nonetheless, as a society we have yet to develop sufficiently thorough efforts to protect people from incluctable social hazards. Thus responsible, productive citizens who might reasonably be viewed as assets to their communities sometimes find themselves in dire straits through nothing more than bad luck.

At the time of my friends' illnesses I was completing some work on the management and resolution of international conflicts. Thereafter, I tried my hand for a while at studying the variety of responses made by contemporary advanced industrial societies to common social hazards. But it was difficult for me to distract my attention at length from the American case. Was there no hope for improvement? I began to formulate a response to this question in late 1982. A leave during the 1983–84 academic year gave me a chance to put together a rough manuscript of this book.

In the autumn of 1984 I discovered Charles Murray's *Losing Ground: American Social Policy, 1950–1980*. Aspects of his interesting analysis of the relations between Americans and public social programs reinforced my own views, though in terms of policy prescriptions he and I stand a long way apart. Murray's suggestions would, I believe, make the plight of many vulnerable people even more difficult. But Murray's policy prescriptions are not the only conclusions one could reasonably derive from an analysis similar to his. There are ways of regaining the ground that we have lost. Thus while I have my differences with Murray, I greatly respect his book, and my obvious play on his title reflects these two distinct reactions.

I have learned a good deal about social policy over the last five years. I want to mention those who have helped me while absolving them of any responsibility for gaps in my learning. Early on in my work I benefited from the help and encouragement of two colleagues at Texas Christian University (TCU), Gregg Franzwa and Richard Galvin. I appreciate as well a leave TCU granted during the 1983–84 academic year. My leave was spent at the Harvard University Center for European Studies. I am grateful to Alexander George and Robert Jervis for their help in placing me there. Peter Hall went out of his way to assist me, and I owe the basic outline of this book to a series of conversations with him in the autumn of 1983. I am thankful as well for kindly assistance from Chris Allen, Jennifer Schirmer, and Rosemary Taylor. Abby Collins and Kirsten Morris of the Center's administrative staff were also extremely helpful. In the spring of 1984 I sat in on Hugh Heclo's seminar on the welfare state. I am extremely grateful for the experience, and I benefited immensely from interaction with seminar members including Jeff Rubin, Ronald Samuels, Steven R. Smith, Peter S. Stamus, and Adam Swift. Others in Cambridge who have been helpful then or since include Douglas Hibbs, Ellen Immergut, Eric Nordlinger, Theda Skocpol, and especially Margaret Weir.

In the several years since my return to Texas a number of people have been particularly helpful. Gary Freeman has been unstinting in his assistance and encouragement. And Jennifer Hochschild, whose work provided me with crucial inspiration earlier on, read the manuscript on multiple occasions. Others who have been generous in their assistance include John Ambler, Larry Biskowski, Charles Cardwell, Jim Fishkin, Jim Gerhardt, Russell Juelg, Julie Manworren, Marcia Melton, and Charlene Urwin.

Finally, I appreciate particularly the understanding I have received from my wife, Jean Giles-Sims. Working on this manuscript has meant much separation from both her and our daughter Andrea. I can only hope that the manuscript will contribute to good in excess of the difficulty that it has caused.

Introduction

Social policy questions present Americans with a cruel dilemma. From practical experience most of us realize that we are likely to confront certain hazards, such as illness or aging, against which private personal resources are an inadequate defense. Thus it is generally clear that the conditions of contemporary life necessitate some forms of public social programs. Yet when we think abstractly about the appropriate nature of public institutions, concepts like individualism and self-reliance seem to undermine the legitimacy of extensive public programs aimed at insulating vulnerable citizens from threatening contingencies.[1]

This dilemma takes particularly severe forms in discussions of extensive public programs for the poor.[2] In such instances, hesitancy based on abstract principles is reinforced by skepticism about the legitimacy of the needs these recipients evince. An excellent statement of this skepticism is provided by Charles Murray in *Losing Ground: American Social Policy, 1950–1980* (Basic Books, 1984). Life is tough, Murray asserts, and the characteristics that people need to successfully cope with adversity—discipline and morality—must be carefully taught and nurtured. Most importantly, Murray argues that the social programs developed from the mid-1960s through the early 1970s provided few incentives for recipients to work hard or otherwise act responsibly. Instead, these programs exacerbated the plight of the poor by creating disincentives for responsible activity.

For Murray the destructive consequences of recent social programs are both material and moral. Whether the poor are materially better or worse off as a result of these programs is a hotly contested matter, and one I will leave to others.[3] Regardless of Murray's accuracy on the material consequences, he gives eloquent voice to the value concerns that public social provision is apt to engender in American political culture. To the degree that social programs carry the message—to the poor or to society generally—that impoverished citizens bear little or no responsibility for their predicaments, they carry a message at odds with some of the most cherished values of American political culture, beliefs in extensive if not equal opportunity and in human dignity through disciplined self-reliance. These conflicting messages, of course, sometimes accurately describe life situations: a child born into a severely impoverished household bears no responsibility for this event. In such cases American beliefs about opportunity are apt to be stretched to their limits, if they are applicable at all.

But Murray strikes home when he argues that the notion that people are not responsible for all that happens to them can be subtly transformed into the proposition that the poor are to be relieved from the arduous tasks involved in alleviating their conditions. Since the mid-1960s, he charges, the designers of American social programs have been too unwilling to insist on conscientious effort from poor persons in school classrooms, in families, on the streets, and in the labor market. In the related terms of Lawrence Mead, the practices of American public social provision have been too permissive.[4]

I do not share Murray or Mead's views on many matters, but I nonetheless suspect that they are correct on this point. Recent social programs—especially those focused on the poor—have been disinclined to elicit levels of personal responsibility from program recipients similar to those valued in the culture generally. As a consequence, we have on one hand a clear and widely recognized need for public social programs, and we have on the other widespread dissatisfaction with the ways we now go about some aspects of public social provision.

My purpose in this book is to suggest a way of escaping, or at least reducing, the problems of this dilemma by tailoring public social programs to prominent values of American political culture. Most of the ideas that I apply to the plight of victims of various social hazards are not new in and of themselves—as Richard Burn noted two hundred years ago, "Almost every proposal which hath been made for the reformation of the poor laws hath been tried in former ages and found ineffectual."[5] My desired contribution lies rather in the arrangement of somewhat familiar ideas into a package that emphasizes certain implications largely ignored by other analysts. It is widely argued, for instance, that the United States represents a less encouraging environment for social programs than do many other advanced industrial societies. Apart from public education, whose special status I will discuss later, American performance with respect to social programs has been aptly characterized as "laggard."[6] Whether we consider the range of programs introduced or the proportion of gross national product spent on such programs, the United States trails many other advanced societies.

Throughout various explanations of American hesitancy with respect to social programs, two broad factors are frequently mentioned. First, some scholars hold that the values central to American political culture differ from those prevailing in some other advanced societies and are less supportive of social programs. The precise nature of these differences is disputed, but the attitudes of American elites are distinct from those of elites in other advanced societies.[7] Second, most analysts agree that the highly decentralized character of American political structures hampers the development of programs opposed by specific interests. The federal government, split among branches, finds coordinated action difficult. State and local governments are, through federalism, unusually active. And American political parties are weak, while interest groups are exceptionally diverse and unrestrained. Thus, all in all, central direction is difficult, and veto points are common and easily used. Programs that affect narrow groups, however, tend to slip through this structure more easily than social programs affecting broad segments of the population.[8] This is particularly the case when the groups are well financed and organized and can draw on spokespersons exhibiting expertise and social position. In such an unsupportive environment we might reasonably expect that both successful strategies for developing social programs and appropriate program design features would differ from their counterparts in other advanced societies.

These difficulties notwithstanding, one American social program is well developed even by the standards of other advanced societies. In 1986 social security spending on pensions for the elderly, survivors, and disabled persons was $194 billion, 20 percent of the federal budget or about 5 percent of the gross national product (GNP).[9] The national commitment to social security illustrates that Americans *are* willing to support social programs that respect prevailing values; it also exemplifies the pliable nature of American core values and the capacity of American political institutions, even in the realm of social policy, to adapt to changing conditions.[10]

My thesis runs as follows: The development of social programs in America has been and will probably continue to be difficult, but social programs that fit nicely with the political culture are more likely to be successful than those that fit poorly. As the astute program executives of social security saw, one way to achieve an acceptable fit is to distribute program benefits in accordance with individual investments, that is, benefits are earned through the exertion of constructive effort and stored as effort-related credits in individual accounts. In enunciating this investments model, the architects of social security couched the program in innovative nuances of familiar American values. They well understood the value of creating a public image—in some respects a mythology—that avoided associations with socialism or the welfare state.[11] In so doing, they largely succeeded in creating a new form of public policy, one that has brought respectability to at least a segment of American social provision.[12]

Today the investments theme is an established principle of American political culture. As such, it could be explicitly extended to a broader range of episodic problems. Moreover, the design features of social security could be adapted for the development of social merging programs directed at reducing poverty. Rather than imposing particular activities on the recipients of public assistance (workfare), social merging programs could offer benefits that would facilitate and supplement recipients' concurrent efforts at self-support. By linking benefits to the recipients' efforts, social merging programs could both supplant most current public assistance programs and dispel popular perceptions of recipients as people who are getting something for nothing.[13] It is imperative that we take advantage of these opportunities for constructive emulation.

For, while public social provision is a necessary accoutrement of advanced industrial societies, much contemporary American social program practice is markedly and needlessly at odds with important values of American political culture.

In developing my investments model, I use the language of rights—socioeconomic rights—rather than refer to socialism or the welfare state. Some people may question the appropriateness of discussing programs generally associated with the political left in terms of rights of any kind. The reservation runs that those on the left wave the term *rights* for rhetorical purposes but do not respect rights as ideals to be upheld in crucial situations.[14] But I have no hesitancy in linking individual rights to social programs. As I will argue in part 1, socioeconomic rights are the most recent of several steps in the extension of the Anglo-American tradition of individual rights. The types of rights encompassed by this tradition have grown over the last three centuries,[15] and different types of rights are not completely compatible. But socioeconomic rights, as we shall see, do not break new ground in this respect.[16] And if my thesis is correct, efforts to minimize the distance between socioeconomic rights and American core values are essential to the full realization of the rights in question.

My argument thus begins with an examination of the status of socioeconomic rights with respect to American values. The central question here is, To what degree is meeting the basic needs addressed by socioeconomic rights through such rights compatible with American values? In chapters 1 through 4, I develop a cautiously optimistic response to this question.

On this foundation, I establish in part 2 of this book what I call the investments approach to social programs. The central question here is, How can American social programs be designed to better serve both basic human needs (thereby realizing socioeconomic rights) and other values of American political culture (thereby acquiring greater political viability)? Following the example of Alexander George's work with focused comparison,[17] I present limited case studies of three programs: social security, Aid to Families with Dependent Children (AFDC), and Medicare. These three programs highlight distinctive features of exceptional importance: social security illustrates a limited but generally encouraging example of the investments approach; AFDC exemplifies a disturbing program that fits neither American values nor the needs of its beneficiaries; and Medicare turns our attention to the special problems private providers create. Each program is examined in terms of a standard series of questions developed in part 1, with particular attention on the implications of current practice for tailoring revitalized programs to American values.

With respect to the scope of this study, four points deserve emphasis here. First, while I sometimes draw on the experiences of other nations, this is not a comparative study. Other advanced industrial societies have broader experience with social programs, and surely we could learn something from their experience. But the United States is widely regarded as exceptional,[18] and what works elsewhere may not work here. The converse is true as well, and my analysis, directed at the peculiarities of the American situation, is not intended as applicable to or appropriate for advanced societies generally.

Second, I restrict my analysis to income earning and income maintenance with a secondary focus on medical-care provision that enables me to contrast the easier tasks of transfer payments with the less enviable trials of providing for unpredictable and expensive social services. In passing, I point out several implications of my arguments for housing and education programs, but neither these nor the provision of transportation or legal services are addressed by my policy recommendations. Of course, social policy inevitably creates problems of "harmonization" with other policy areas,[19] and several such issues arise as prominent concerns in later chapters.

Third, I want to point out how recent American social policy innovations relate to my own thinking. Limiting the out-of-pocket expenses of Medicare patients through catastrophic medical-care insurance is consistent with the spirit of my proposals on medical care in chapter 8 although the Medicare measure affects a relatively small proportion of the population. In contrast, the welfare reform measure signed by President Reagan in October 1988 does not represent a sharp change from current practice and is insufficiently bold to break the grip of the problems I discuss in chapter 6.

Fourth, I cannot but acknowledge that even if basic needs receive the more thorough and effective public support that I recommend, socioeconomic inequities will persist. A more equitable distribution of the material resources required to satisfy basic needs would diminish the suffering, deprivation, and anxiety many Americans experience when disturbing contingencies befall them. But much unfairness about the organization of work will remain, and dreary jobs will not be transformed into meaningful work. These obvious difficulties will not vanish; nor will the "hidden injuries of class" by which many burdens of failure are carried by the children of the poor.[20]

Part One

Socioeconomic Rights and American Values

One

Patterns of
Resource Inadequacy and
American Values

Craig was five when his father died in an automobile accident. Since the accident involved only his father's car, which skidded on an icy patch of roadway, there were no suits for damages. At the time of the accident Craig's parents had little in the way of savings or other assets, and the father's life insurance coverage was quite modest. Craig's father was in his mid-twenties and had been a high school teacher for several years. Craig's mother had never worked, apart from summer jobs in high school and between her two years of college. Grandparents from both sides of the family offered assistance of various kinds: emotional support, food, child-care, and money.

As survivors of a member of the labor force, Craig and his mother might each expect to receive social security benefits from Old Age, Survivors, and Disability Insurance (OASDI). The amount of these monthly support checks would depend on the father's earnings history. Under current rules Craig would receive benefits until he finished high school. The same benefits would be accorded to Craig had his father been permanently and totally disabled rather than killed in the accident, or had Craig's parents divorced prior to the accident so long as Craig had not been formally adopted by a stepfather.

But under slightly different circumstances, social security would not protect Craig. For example, suppose Craig's father had not yet worked long enough to earn social security survivor's eligibility for his family. Or suppose that Craig's father had contracted an illness that forced him to stay home from work for several months. No general public program provides protection against this contingency. (State workers' compensation programs cover only job-related illnesses and injuries.) Rather, Craig's fate would depend on whether his father's employer provided for paid sick leave and private group medical insurance. Or suppose the crisis was that Craig's father had been indefinitely laid off from work. The family would then have to rely on state unemployment compensation, which provides benefits of limited duration.

As a final example of the inadequacies of current programs, consider Darlene, a two-year-old whose father deserted Darlene's mother during pregnancy. Darlene's mother, like Craig's mother, is young and has no experience or work skills that would command good wages in the labor market. Further, Darlene's extended family cannot afford to offer assistance other than intermittent childcare. With no savings and no family support to fall back on, Darlene and her mother will qualify for public assistance from Aid to Families with Dependent Children (AFDC), more commonly known as "welfare." Like workers' compensation and unemployment insurance, AFDC benefits follow general federal guidelines but vary markedly from one state to another and even within states. Generally, eligibility for AFDC provides access to Medicaid benefits, food stamps, and limited public housing assistance.

AFDC benefits provide crucial support, but the recipients pay a price, for welfare, unlike social security, is not considered an earned right but a form of public charity. Because eligibility for welfare is not based on prior contributions but on need, many Americans— including many welfare recipients—view being on welfare as a sign of disgrace, a mark of failure in a land of opportunity, an affront to personal dignity. And surviving on the largesse of public charity rather than on one's personal accomplishments sets recipients apart from the members of—and thus membership in—mainstream society.

Let us suppose that Darlene's mother is determined to be off welfare and to be self-supporting as soon as possible. Once she finds a job, the AFDC benefits will begin to disappear. The specific income levels at which benefits are withdrawn vary from state to state, but the following pattern is typical. For several months the first few dollars of earnings that Darlene's mother makes each week do not affect AFDC benefits. Thereafter, an allowance is made for work-related expenses—child-care, for example- -but above that allowance each three dollars of earnings reduces benefits by two dollars. After four months nearly all earnings above limited work-related expenses reduce benefits dollar for dollar, and earnings above modest cutoff points lead to the cessation of AFDC and Medicaid benefits. If earnings subsequently drop below the cutoff points, benefits are not reinstated until the family again reaches a designated level of destitution. If Darlene's mother is typical of many AFDC recipients, she will manage to obtain independence from welfare, perhaps more than once.[1]

I could add variations to these predicaments, but two points should already be clear. First, Craig and Darlene's needs for food, clothing, housing, child-care, and medical care remain about the same regardless of the scenario we pick. While a few children have exceptional medical-care or dietary needs, generally what varies from one scenario to another is not the child's needs but the availability of public and private resources to meet those needs. Second, no matter which scenario we pick, we cannot reasonably blame Craig or Darlene for ending up in a situation that may or may not provide resources to meet their basic needs. All these disruptive incidents—death, illness, layoffs, desertion—are well beyond the children's control.

While these points are clearest in a discussion of the plight of young children, they apply to all citizens of advanced industrial societies. Because we no longer live in an era of economically self-sufficient homesteaders, individuals' needs for public policy protection from certain social hazards are greater than they were a century ago. We can no longer look to the model of the society that prompted the liberal tradition—the society that grew out of Locke and Adam Smith's ideas. The gradual transformation of America into an advanced industrial society has left us more, not less, vulnerable to social hazards.

Wage Dependency and Vulnerability

Through the first half of the nineteenth century America was a nation of farmers, shopkeepers, and small businessmen living in small towns.[2] Capitalism was local and commercial, rather than national and industrial, and the family was a self-sustaining economic unit. Family members worked largely within the confines of the household, on the family's land, or in the family's shop or other small business. Gradually, however, technological development and increases in economic centralization and differentiation combined to erode households' self-sufficiency. More people began to work outside the family for wages or salary. And as needs came to be more commonly supported by participation in the labor market, fewer families held their own land or other businesses. Today, only a small fraction of Americans owns household-sustaining property. The vast majority of us, including many professional and managerial people, are dependent for our livelihoods on selling our labor in the market.

Wage dependency creates the preconditions for wage vulnerability. Any disruption in wages threatens a worker's ability to meet basic needs. And many disruptions to participation in the labor market—disabling injury, aging, recession, plant closings due to loss of international competitiveness—lie beyond the control of an individual worker. Even households in the top quintile of income distribution are not immune to such hazards. Only the very wealthiest households can sustain themselves over lengthy periods without labor market participation and without recourse to outside assistance, such as public social programs.[3]

Other trends characteristic of advanced industrial societies reinforce the problems of wage dependency and vulnerability. As people go to work for others, they tend to move from rural to urban environments, and urban settings afford fewer opportunities for household production of food and shelter. Additionally, the nuclear family, itself an adaptation to urban industrial society,[4] has been splintered by desertion and divorce, events that often leave women and their children without a source of adequate income. New households based on remarriage, sibling ties, and friendships have reduced some, but by no means all, of these difficulties.[5] Finally, as life expectancies increase well beyond society's conception of the duration of people's economic usefulness, a growing proportion of elderly people find themselves excluded from regular participation in the labor market.

In addition to these trends associated with wage dependency and vulnerability, the prices of customary and essential services have far outpaced normal income levels. The rural household of the early nineteenth century was largely self-sufficient not only with respect to basic goods but also with respect to services. For example, home remedies were the rule for illness or injury, in part because of the expense of hiring a physician, particularly the cost of transportation, but in part because a professional healer could not always be expected to achieve results more encouraging than those of a layperson.[6]

Today, in contrast, the efficacy of sophisticated medical services is far superior to lay remedies, and people who cannot acquire access to the most crucial of these services cannot successfully claim full membership in contemporary society. Indeed, in a wage-dependent economy, individuals rely heavily on medical care to cure the illnesses or injuries that disrupt their ability to earn a living. Yet while medical care is increasingly important, it is also extremely expensive, beyond the reach of most people's incomes. The fortunate have their medical bills paid for by private insurance or public social programs; the unfortunate often go without even the most basic care.

In sum, an intrinsic characteristic of advanced industrial societies is that families are no longer independent economic units. In light of the family's loss of self-sufficiency, modern societies have created social programs to provide a measure of protection for their citizens. In the United States, as in other advanced industrial societies, these social programs are intended to cushion people against episodic disruptions of income as well as to sustain people whose economic resources are persistently insufficient.

Patterns of Resource Inadequacy

Resource inadequacy refers to two related but distinct problems: episodic financial shortfalls and persistent poverty. These are not hard-and-fast categories. Some households are beset by both problems at once, and others experience alternating periods of each. But this distinction highlights two general patterns of social distress that require different public policy responses.

Episodic resource inadequacy results from a particular event or crisis—childbirth, illness, aging, unemployment, divorce—that overwhelms a household whose income is usually well above the

poverty line. Suddenly, the household's income is disrupted or expenses for necessary goods and services (most often medical) exceed its income. These episodes sometimes drive households into
poverty, but often the shortfall is covered by savings, private or
public insurance, changes in household membership, or the entry
of unemployed household members into the work force.

In contrast, poverty is characterized by an ongoing low level of
income and wealth. In this sense, poverty is a time- and culture-
bound circumstance. A standard of living that we would deem impoverished in the United States in 1988 might well be superior to
that of a nineteenth-century American family or a present-day
Mauritanian family—neither of which would be considered impoverished by its own culture's standards.[7]

By current American norms, about four households in ten experience at least one year of poverty in the course of a decade.[8]
Households impoverished by contemporary American standards
generally suffer from both material and cultural disadvantages vis-
à-vis more mainstream households. Three of these households experience poverty-level incomes in more than one year during the
decade, and roughly one in ten falls below the poverty threshold
for the entire decade. For every household that is impoverished all
or much of the time, then, there are many more that experience
poverty intermittently, frequently spending years only barely beyond outright destitution.

Episodic Inadequacy and Social Insurance

With the exception of aging, the conditions that trigger episodic
resource inadequacy are unpredictable and, as a rule, people beset
by such problems are not blamed for their difficulties. Unemployment was once an exception to this rule, even when dismissal was
caused by macroeconomic forces, but this tendency seems to be
changing. Nor is blame usually cast in situations that may reasonably be seen as the consequences of purposive action (divorce,
childbirth), although in specific instances such acts may be deemed
irresponsible or negligent.

That such episodic problems call for social insurance to prevent
beleaguered citizens from falling into poverty is an idea that has
taken hold across the world.[9] Indeed, in comparison to many

Western European societies, the United States has been laggard in accepting the concept of social insurance and in implementing this concept through public social programs. Nonetheless, even here social insurance now has an extensive history and public support and government funding for specific programs are high.[10]

The essential task of social insurance is to widely distribute, over time and a broad population, much of the cost of individual crises. Though programs vary widely, several principles are common to all. First, the more short-lived the hazard, the more easily it may be handled. Lengthy episodes can be accommodated so long as they are relatively rare or their annual costs are either relatively low or balanced by high contributions. (Longer life expectancies, which create longer periods of retirement for a larger proportion of the population, upset this balance and are now posing serious difficulties for social insurance programs like social security.) Second, social insurance programs must have some mechanism by which potential beneficiaries contribute to the support of the system. Such contributions take various forms: labor, service in the armed forces, and payment of income or payroll taxes. Third, programs must establish guidelines and formulas for distributing the resources to beneficiaries. Typically, social insurance programs redistribute resources horizontally (across an individual's life cycle) rather than vertically (from rich to poor). Although some vertical redistribution occurs,[11] cross-strata reallocation is neither the primary objective nor consequence of these programs.

In the United States the largest social insurance program by far is social security (OASDI); smaller insurance programs include: Medicare, railroad retirement, black lung payments, workers' compensation, unemployment insurance, and veterans' benefits.[12] If we measure American public provision against the programs of many other advanced societies, universal medical-care insurance and general child-care assistance are the most obvious gaps in American social policy.

One explanation for these gaps is the widely accepted notion that American political culture supports a peculiarly strong preference for market as opposed to public solutions to social problems. In this cultural climate private insurance flourishes, but it is inherently unable to meet all the basic needs of many individuals and remain profitable. For example, there are no realistic private counterparts for public benefits for dependent children, support for single-parent households, and unemployment insurance. And profitability requires that private insurance contracts for illness, disabling injury, retirement, or death pose limitations on eligibility or on the size and duration of benefits. Further, contributions are generally risk-rated, with participants who face the greatest risks paying the highest premiums. But because individual risk and ability to pay are often inversely related, those with the greatest need for insurance are also those least likely to be able to afford it.

Among those fortunate enough to have private insurance, there are wide variations in the breadth and depth of coverage. Many professionals, managers, and unionized industrial workers acquire fairly thorough private coverage through group insurance. But large portions of the population do not belong to such groups and do not have the resources to purchase individual policies.[13] Even people who succeed in obtaining, say, private medical insurance find that exclusionary riders, deductibles, and coinsurance and copayment provisions may leave them personally liable for substantial medical costs. Similarly, workers covered by private retirement pensions often discover that inflation, not to mention fund mismanagement or the demise of the sponsoring firm, cuts deeply into the value of their pensions. Other difficulties arise when workers change employers.[14] Sickness, disability, and life insurance are less troubling in these regards, but good coverage can be quite expensive.

Some of the deficiencies of private insurance are amenable to reform through legislative pressure and initiatives. But the ultimate responsibility for meeting the needs of vulnerable citizens is apt to remain a public matter.

Poverty and Social Merging

Poverty associated with varying degrees of material and cultural disadvantages, the second pattern of resource inadequacy, is not so obviously constructed of discrete problematic episodes. Relatively few households are perpetually impoverished, but many face lengthy spells of poverty or near poverty.[15] Thus the distinction made earlier between problems arising from income disruption and problems stemming from occasional need for expensive services is rather irrelevant to the plight of households for which even fairly modest expenses can pose a continuing problem.

Nor do the needs of the poor lend themselves to traditional social insurance solutions. People in poverty are not generally coping well with their material needs, and they require both intangible and material resources in order to merge with more materially successful portions of society. As I will detail in subsequent chapters, it is possible to link this infusion of resources to a beneficiary's contributions, but it is generally less feasible to make public benefits a reward for *prior* contributions as is the case with social insurance. Rather, the crux of social merging involves concurrent self-help contributions: people near the bottom of the socioeconomic ladder receive benefits that facilitate and supplement their own efforts to increase their material resources in socially acceptable ways, with the ultimate goal of merging with the socioeconomic mainstream.

In contrast to the essential task of social insurance programs—spreading the costs of episodic individual problems—the basic task for merging programs is to improve people's long-term incentives, opportunities, and capacities for meeting basic needs in socially acceptable and personally dignified ways. This is a more demanding enterprise than providing social insurance, but the progress made in the last 150 years by advanced societies offers hope of further reducing the proportion of their citizens who cannot meet basic needs.

The United States does not now have prominent social programs whose primary efforts are focused on merging objectives. Instead we have a series of programs that provide resources for basic needs to people with little or no income and wealth at the time of application. These means-tested public assistance programs include AFDC, Supplementary Security Income (SSI), Medicaid, food stamps, general assistance, veterans' pensions, housing assistance programs, and basic educational opportunity grants.[16] Throughout the 1980s the largest public assistance income maintenance program, AFDC, has had 10–11 million beneficiaries a year (largely single women and their children), slightly less than a third as many as social security. These recipients received $13–15 billion in benefits annually—a bit less than one-thirteenth the amount spent on social security in the early 1980s.[17] And overall

AFDC expenditures have remained fairly constant, while social security outlays have risen sharply from year to year.

According to the measures used by the federal government, at any given time roughly 30 to 35 million Americans experience poverty. But there is significant turnover among the poor, and "the poor" are not a homogeneous group. Indeed, one may wonder whether a single label—the poor—adequately describes the life situation of all Americans whose income and wealth are at the lowest levels.[18] In the sociological literature we find two contending schools of thought. What we could call the attitudinalist position is exemplified by the analyses of Edward C. Banfield.[19] For him, the predicament of lower-class people is miserable, not because they are sound persons without opportunities, but because they are flawed individuals who cannot take advantage of constructive opportunities. Banfield attributes this improvidence to an individual's inability to delay gratification, to a general incapacity to take the future into account. Accordingly, he faults social policies aimed at this underclass for creating unrealistic expectations and for encouraging flawed individuals to continue, indeed to expand, their improvidence.

In contrast, Herbert J. Gans offers a situationalist interpretation of the plight of the poor.[20] Gans describes the poor as generally sound people who face unusually discouraging circumstances beyond their control. Where Banfield sees improvidence, Gans contends that what constitutes rational action for severely disadvantaged people may differ sharply from what is rational for middle-class citizens. Specific forms of public intervention, he argues, may provide the resources and skills the poor need to overcome some of the social disadvantages they suffer.

Few views about the impoverished are capable of bridging these two schools of thought. But if we acknowledge the obvious—that the poor, like other large social groups, includes both miscreants and relatively sound persons—our attention shifts from speculating about the character of these persons as a class to trying to understand how individuals end up in one category rather than another. For instance, what life experiences set apart the underclass that Banfield discusses? What kinds of disadvantages are germane and how frequently do these experiences arise? Such investigations belie many popular generalizations about the poor. For example, minorities do not constitute a majority of the poor, although some minorities are disproportionately represented. And the vast majority of low-income Americans either work, sometimes full-time,[21] or have compelling reasons for not working. Most members of this latter group, which constitutes well over half of the total, are single mothers and their children; in smaller numbers are the elderly, the physically disabled, and the blind. It is this group that holds a near monopoly on the receipt of public assistance supported by the federal government. The working poor, in contrast, receive little or no public assistance and their number includes higher proportions of single persons, childless couples, and two-parent families.

More importantly, it does not appear that attitudes alone are responsible for poverty. Across the socioeconomic spectrum most Americans profess nearly identical attitudes toward matters such as work and family obligations.[22] Realizing what these attitudes call for does vary markedly, owing to a variety of subtle psychological factors as well as obvious sociological factors that are beyond an individual's control.[23] Thus we might reasonably ask that social programs encourage responsible activity. For instance, we should expect them to support the efforts of the disadvantaged to merge with mainstream society or, at the very least, programs should not foster the growth of an underclass that makes no sustained effort to live by the values of mainstream society.

Unfortunately, American means-tested programs not only fail to support merging objectives, they may actually discourage them. In chapter 6 I will examine this issue in detail, but for now two points are of particular relevance. First, public assistance programs rarely emphasize improving incentives, opportunities, and capacities for constructive activities among impoverished people. With the exception of basic educational opportunity grants for needy college students,[24] public assistance programs are designed to provide subsistence-level material support for specific categories of impoverished people.

Second, the major means-tested income maintenance program, AFDC, is not limited to persistently poor people. There is substantial turnover among recipients, and leaving or joining the program often hinges on discrete events, such as a change in household composition or finding or losing a job. In this, AFDC addresses episodic resource inadequacy, similar to the forms of insurance discussed earlier.[25] Equally important, AFDC and allied programs (most notably Medicaid) contain significant financial disincentives for recipients to improve their lot in the work force.[26] The strength of these disincentives has led some policy analysts to assert that these means-tested programs are functioning as poverty-maintenance devices, perhaps with the latent purpose of social control by regulation, rather than as social merging programs.[27]

Although expenditures for AFDC are but a fraction of those allocated to social security, the United States does spend an unusually high proportion of its income-maintenance budget, about 12 percent, on means-tested programs. Only a few other industrial nations come close on this score.[28] One disputed interpretation of this statistic is that the United States has a larger proportion of low-income persons.[29] An alternative interpretation proceeds from the fact that we spend a smaller proportion of gross national product on social insurance forms of income maintenance than do other advanced societies.[30] Perhaps, then, we rely on means-tested programs to meet some needs that other societies address through social insurance. Whether or not this interpretation explains the discrepancy, it raises the notion that a change in the balance of social insurance and means-tested programs might be beneficial. As a concept, social insurance seems truer to American values of self-reliance and individual effort. Social insurance programs, therefore, are more likely to be perceived as fair and would be less politically vulnerable than our present means-tested programs.

From this analysis of resource inadequacy problems, we may conclude that American public policy could be strengthened in three ways. First, because the concept of social insurance is fairly widely accepted and works reasonably well in the American context, social security should be expanded to cover a broader range of both hazards and people. Specifically, people overwhelmed by episodic crises would be covered by social insurance rather than having to apply for means-tested public assistance programs. Second, we need to devise programs that improve the opportunities available to disadvantaged people and provide the incentives and training they need to take advantage of these opportunities. Third, we need some type of income-maintenance and medical program to provide for those people who cannot on their own join the mainstream because of mental illness or retardation, addiction to various substances, chronic and disabling physical afflictions, and criminality or other serious psychological deficits.[31] Policy recommendations concerning the first two of these enterprises constitute the final goal of this book.

Public Programs and American Values

It is frequently argued that the United States lags behind other advanced industrial societies in public social provision because a broad social policy agenda conflicts to a peculiar degree with core American values. Samuel P. Huntington identifies six such values: liberty, equality, individualism, democracy, the rule of law under a constitution, and concerns for limited and local government.[32] In the next three chapters I will expand this set a bit, but already we see the crux of the problem. In Huntington's terms, these core values collectively provide American political culture with an antistatist tinge that makes ambitious state programs directed against resource inadequacy difficult to achieve. This view is consistent with Donald J. Devine's earlier thesis about the Lockean character of the American political culture.[33]

Nonetheless, there is an undeniable pragmatic, or operational, strand running through American political culture.[34] Anxiety about and instances of vulnerability to various social hazards lead most Americans to support public programs such as national health insurance. Thus in pragmatic affairs liberalism, in the contemporary American sense of the term, predominates, and herein American political culture rather resembles the cultures of other advanced societies.[35] Pragmatic liberalism, however, repeatedly clashes with America's more abstract or ideological principles, which are the domain of the antistatist values of classical liberalism (Locke and Adam Smith).

An alternate analysis of the disjunctions in American values, presented by Jennifer L. Hochschild, observes that with respect to assessments of fairness, or distributive justice, Americans tend to apply different principles to particular domains of life.[36] Concepts of distributive justice tend to be more egalitarian within the family (the socializing domain) and within the realm of public issues (the political domain) than in the workplace (the economic domain). Situations that cross domains (for example, cases in which participants can be viewed both as fellow members of the labor force and as fellow citizens) frequently provoke confused responses.

It is not clear, however, that the mass culture is especially relevant for the character of American public programs. Various political scientists and sociologists argue that the values of the American elite have been particularly influential in directing American social policy and shaping public opinion.[37] Scholars generally agree on the distinctive character of elite values in the United States, but some question whether all segments of the elite are adequately characterized by Huntington's antistatist collection of values.[38] In general, American bureaucrats are less homogeneous than their European counterparts (broader recruitment patterns), while American politicians are more homogeneous than the Europeans (no leftist parties). Finally, the attitudes of many American bureaucrats and legislators are more favorable to state involvement in social provision than Huntington's description of core values would suggest.

Three assumptions about American political culture inform my analyses and recommendations. First, Huntington's list of core values provides a useful starting point, although it needs to be expanded and the multiple and frequently conflicting meanings of these values must be enunciated. But basically we must accept antistatism as setting some limitations on American public policy.

Second, this collection of values does not form an internally coherent ideology relatively impervious to change. Rather, these values are loosely defined, ambiguous, and inconsistent. In Huntington's words, "Defined vaguely and abstractly, these ideas have been relatively easily adapted to the needs of successive generations."[39]

Third, because these core values are adaptable, a capable and determined group of elites could today—following the example of the originators of social security—reshape American political institutions.[40] In particular, the early Social Security Board successfully distinguished social security from public assistance and placed social security in the category of earned rights, similar to public education, rather than gratuitous public benefits. This emphasis on earned benefits challenged the near stranglehold that self-reliance had previously held with respect to human dignity. Especially against the macroeconomic forces of the Great Depression, a contributory system of earned benefits came to be seen as a dignified way for individuals to cope with social hazards beyond their control.

The central implication of public social programs is that market distribution is flawed in some respects. This implication leads us to an inquiry about the nature of distributive justice. Wholehearted proponents of laissez-faire argue that free markets represent a natural evolution and that although one may wish to fiddle marginally with distribution, the topic of justice is as irrelevant to a discussion of distribution as to a discussion of mountain lions killing deer.[41] But I want to approach the topic of distributive justice through the concept of socioeconomic rights, rights to basic material resources that sustain human activity.[42] And these rights both reinforce and pose problems for other values of importance to the American cultural context, most notably for negative liberty and economic efficiency.

Before I turn to the matter of distributive justice, the compatibility of socioeconomic rights and two core values can be mentioned quickly and then set aside. There is no inherent incompatibility between socioeconomic rights and the rule of law under a constitution. A particular conception of socioeconomic rights or a particular manner of realizing socioeconomic rights through public programs might be incompatible with the U.S. Constitution. But since 1937, when the Supreme Court held that social security fell within Congress's powers to tax and appropriate funds, there have been no general challenges to the constitutionality of social programs and the rights they create. Additionally, there is no incompatibility between socioeconomic rights and procedural democracy in Huntington's sense of popular control of government. Throughout advanced industrial societies systems of multiple political parties competing in frequent elections held under rules of universal adult suffrage coexist with socioeconomic rights. With these two points behind us, let us examine the compatibility of socioeconomic rights and American conceptions of distributive justice.

Two

Socioeconomic Rights and American Conceptions of Distributive Justice

Social programs shielding people from selected hazards now have a history of slightly over a century, but only since the 1940s have the benefits these programs provide been commonly considered beneficiary rights.[1] In the postwar period this view has been most clearly enunciated in the United Kingdom. Increased British social solidarity during the war years, while not without its limits, facilitated William Beveridge's effort to gain recognition of standard, minimum social program benefits as rights of citizenship. While the character of British social program benefits has changed over the years, the idea of benefits as a class of rights, socioeconomic rights, has flourished both in Britain and throughout industrial societies generally.[2] This trend has been more pronounced in the "corporatist democracies" than in other nations,[3] but even the United States has shared in this tendency. The status of some American program benefits as rights marks something of a watershed in the nation's history, denoting a period in which distributive justice has been affirmed as a value and as a phenomenon distinct from market distribution.[4] The nature of a just distribution may vary with the good being distributed. After examining how social program benefits might be called rights, I will discuss a particular concept of socioeconomic rights tailored to American beliefs about just distributions for the goods these benefits entail.

Socioeconomic Rights in Theory

Following Joel Feinberg, I construe rights as a certain type of claim. *Claims* are cases meriting consideration, and *rights* are claims "whose recognition as valid is called for by some set of governing rules or moral principles."[5] Legal rights are recognized by rules of positive law, and existing social program benefits may be thought of as rights in this sense. But Feinberg extends the category of rights beyond existing statute: moral rights are claims "the recognition of which is called for—not (necessarily) by legal rules—but by moral principles or the principles of an enlightened conscience" (p. 277). For Feinberg, entitlements represent a different dimension of rights than do claims. If I have a legal right to retirement benefits, Feinberg explains, this right merges an entitlement *to* benefits with a claim *against* anyone who might obstruct my receipt of them, a recalcitrant social security administrator perhaps.

Let us set positive law aside for a while and not rest claims for socioeconomic rights on the convenience that throughout advanced societies many such rights are found in law. Instead, we may turn to the logical, empirical, and normative underpinnings that give validity to claims for such rights. I start from the premise that the sophisticated sorts of conscious agency which are the distinguishing features of human life hinge on both freedom and well-being.[6] Since well-being is just as important a prerequisite for this agency as freedom is, the two deserve coequal status as rights. More broadly, "Any consistent moral code, whatever it might be, is going to have to recognize certain kinds of capacity and needs among persons that will have to be fulfilled if persons are to be able to pursue the ideals enshrined in any moral code."[7] That freedom is both a prerequisite to a distinctively human life and a right of humans is widely accepted in Western thought. That securing well-being through meeting basic material needs should hold a similar status is a more recent and, particularly in the American context, a more controversial point.[8]

Support for the inclusion of resources aimed at basic human needs among people's rights is not hard to come by, however. Food, clothing, shelter, medical care, and education may be viewed as prerequisites to the exercise of rights of a more distinguishingly human character—free expression. Precedence and priorities come

into sharper focus when one ponders the order in which people
would give up rights under duress.[9] Voicing one's opinion is surely
a more distinguishingly human activity than is eating, but it is not
a more basic need and is unlikely to be the preference of many
forced to choose between speaking freely and eating.

Arguments supporting coequal status for rights to freedom and
well-being confront at least four sorts of practical difficulties. First,
free speech and eating are usually not perceived as inhibited by the
same forces. Locke taught us to regard the state as a perpetual
source of danger to free expression. His predecessor, Hobbes,
stressed the threats that our peers pose to freedom of action. While
these threats are generally less obvious and brutal today than those
envisioned by Hobbes, in most advanced societies informal social
pressures—fears that voicing one's opinion will offend one's associates—are probably a more frequent problem than state intervention. Yet the state and one's associates rarely impose similar
pressures with respect to eating, particularly for citizens or ac-
quaintances on the brink of starvation. ("Let them eat cake!") The
liberal tradition has held that the distribution of material resources
is now and ought to be governed largely by *impersonal* market
forces. While many still hold this view, others see conscious human
design and manipulation behind market forces.[10] An extensive market system necessarily creates wage dependency and vulnerability
for many as well as highly asymmetrical reward distributions.
And other social practices such as intergroup prejudices exacerbate the disadvantages with which some have to cope in attempt-
ing to meet basic material needs through the market.

Bernard Williams makes an interesting case that it is immoral
for society, especially a society wealthy in material resources, to
follow practices that leave some of its members' basic needs un-
met.[11] The purpose of basic goods, Williams argues, is straightforward. For example, medical care is for healing the sick and injured, not just the sick and injured who are rich; medical care that
enriches the provider at the expense of those who need but cannot
pay for treatment is an artificial perversion of the concept of healing. For Williams any differences in the treatment humans receive
in regard to medical needs should be supported by reasons that are
relevant (sick or well) as opposed to irrelevant (rich or poor). But
in America arguments revealing the human hand behind market

distribution have been stymied by the inertia of the "invisible hand" theory in the political culture.

A second issue raised by arguments for the coequality of rights to freedom and well-being involves conflicting value hierarchies. Robert Nozick, for example, uses the same Kantian point of departure as Williams—that humans must be ends in themselves rather than means—to deny any individual's right to welfare or duty to help others with their material needs.[12] For Nozick, the individual's freedom not to be treated as a means to another's ends is a paramount value. Grudgingly, he allows for taxes used to finance local police and national defense, purposes that sustain freedom in the long run, but he deems taxes to ensure basic material resources for the unfortunate to be inappropriate constraints on human agency. From this perspective, any claim to such resources runs afoul of the superior and incompatible claims of personal freedom.

Henry Shue proposes instead that we use a priority principle to distinguish among basic rights (food), nonbasic rights (public education), cultural enrichment (Shakespeare over Stallone), and preference satisfaction (Haagen Dazs over Sealtest).[13] No one's liberty, according to Shue, should extend to the area of preference satisfaction if others are thereby blocked from meeting basic needs. Your yacht should not come at the expense of my starvation.

Nozick's position also introduces a third problem for the coequality of freedom and well-being: the difficulties involved in providing freedom and well-being are different. Here we need to distinguish negative rights—the rights associated with negative liberty or freedom from external constraint—from positive rights, the rights to resources that enable individuals to engage in activities previously beyond their reach.[14] Free speech is a negative right; eating is a positive right.

Negative and positive rights are widely held to differ in the demands they make on public policy and the obligations they place on other citizens. The negative civil-political rights now broadly recognized among advanced societies are thought by many to require only forbearance on the part of others; whereas, positive socioeconomic rights are said to require some form of active cooperation or help. For example, allowing a destitute malcontent to praise socialism on a city street corner requires no positive acts of cooperation. But if he is to receive expensive medical care, others will have to contribute, either directly or through the tax system. Suppose, however, that irate citizens attack this soapbox orator. Then, maintaining his freedom of speech will require the intervention of the police and possibly the courts and prisons, all public institutions supported by taxes. Or suppose that he needed medical care for an injury he had sustained while in the army. Then we could say that had the state not called him into service, no cooperation to help him overcome his current malady would now be necessary.[15] These latter examples blur the distinctions between positive and negative rights and their characteristic balance of government activity and citizen obligation.

Other considerations distinguish negative and positive rights. Negative rights, products of the natural rights of the seventeenth century, may be seen as focusing on procedures, as, in effect, tools of procedural or formal justice; whereas positive rights may be described as products of the twentieth-century human rights movement and as concerned with outcomes or substantive justice.[16] To ensure the rights to freedom, then, all we need to do is identify a set of procedures—a uniform legal code, for instance—as appropriate. But to ensure well-being we would need to examine whether all individuals have the resources (money to hire an attorney) to make use of the code.

Even for those who do not insist that, as a result of these distinguishing provision problems, positive and negative rights differ in kind, differences in degree are important. For instance, the financial burdens that police, courts, and prisons place on the state are small in comparison to those arising from social programs. Additionally, some have argued that it is "easier to state a negative right without reference to degree than a positive one"[17]—although the degrees of, say, free speech are also uncertain and frequently controversial. Among the limits we place on this negative right are restrictions on slanderous speech and statements that exacerbate a "clear and present danger," as well as the perennial injunction against yelling "Fire!" in a crowded theater.

A fourth problem for the coequality of rights to freedom and well-being is posed by the following argument.

Negative rights are generally only valuable to those whose rights they are if they are able to do or have that which the right involves, for example to walk. If they cannot or do not, then a merely negative right could be useless. A positive right, on the other hand, will not normally be of much help to someone who already has what such a right would require others to help supply him with. A negative right, then, can be useless and a positive one redundant. And if negative rights are all we grant, then we may expect the poor and unadvanced to be disgruntled, while if we insist on positive rights as well, the wealthy and powerful might similarly be unhappy. [Narveson, "Human Rights," p. 177]

In other words, rights to expressive freedom and basic resources benefit different groups and rely on varying concepts of liberty. In the United States, a nation steeped in the tradition of negative liberty, negative rights have been more thoroughly supported than positive rights. The well-known association between political participation and socioeconomic status, particularly strong in the United States in the absence of large-scale working-class organization, reinforces the dominance of negative rights of interest to the politically active, materially comfortable portion of society.[18]

The Reagan administration's recent attacks on social programs and through them, socioeconomic rights, are not the first instances of the powerful resisting the extension of opportunities they already possess as rights to a broader section of society.[19] In London at the turn of the nineteenth century, wealthy and politically powerful citizens who could afford private security forces denounced a proposal to establish a public police force as an infringement on liberty.[20] The nineteenth-century British struggle over the extension of political rights also exemplifies this pattern. Suffrage was extended to some middle-class males in the 1830s, but universal male suffrage was opposed by many in the socioeconomic elite who, enjoying extensive political privileges, had no use for political rights.[21] Time and again elites have argued that severe, even civilization-destroying consequences would follow the extension of rights to the masses, whom the elites depicted as too flawed to exercise any new rights in a constructive fashion.[22] Clearly, extensions of political and socioeconomic rights are quite different matters, but the constancy of the opposition's themes is noteworthy. On the subject of socioeconomic rights, in the United States today we again hear the privileged decrying the character of those less fortunate than themselves. Distinctions between negative and positive rights thus derive not only from abstractions and theoretical premises but also from the material interests of different groups.

In sum, rights to freedom and well-being differ in the typical fashions through which they are constrained, their relative positions in conflicting value hierarchies, the manners of their provision, and their primary beneficiaries. Depending upon one's philosophical perspective, these differences are modest, amounting to minute variations of degree, or so sharp as to be contradictory in their implications. No set of conceptual tools can bridge the gap between philosophical positions supportive of rights to well-being and those hostile to such rights, but I believe some headway can be made.

Let us begin, then, from the relatively uncontroversial logical-empirical position that well-being is a prerequisite to human agency and is a coequal of freedom in this regard; that is, well-being and freedom are each necessary but not alone sufficient. Then we must ask, What sort of moral right to well-being might be persuasively argued, particularly in the hostile American context? As Maurice Cranston suggests, "the standard way of justifying a moral right is to demonstrate that it has been earned."[23] Let us see what we can make of this. It is not unreasonable to assume that a society can agree on the rough limits of basic material needs within the context of its time and culture. Federal guidelines about dietary needs and the proportion of household budgets appropriately allotted to these needs represent a working attempt to do this.[24] Some aspects of these needs are universal, like the need for protein, while others are time or culture bound, such as what sources of protein—fish or fowl or insects—are suitable. With respect to these needs, let me suggest a rule: Those who contribute to the product of society shall in return have secured the resources for meeting these needs. Stated differently, justice in the distribution of basic goods resides in reciprocity: goods in return for contributions. This formulation of earning rights fits the dominant "work ethic" in the United States. Those who consciously strive to help themselves and their households by working should receive in return for their efforts the goods necessary for meeting basic material needs.

Such a formulation raises the issue of how to measure contributions to the social product. Somewhat reluctantly, I propose to use

GNP, or more simply, paid labor, as the index of the social product. In moral terms this is a needlessly restrictive conception, for the social product may be reasonably thought to imply the result of more than earnings-generated labor. Parents assuredly contribute to the social product by rearing children, homemakers contribute through their household activity, and hospital volunteers and struggling artists contribute as well. But even though many of these contributions are as or more important than some activities of the paid labor force, within American political culture at this point in time, only income-producing work has a realistic chance of being accepted as earning socioeconomic rights. Since my purpose is to show how systematic social program protection can be compatible with existing American values, I have made the pragmatic choice: Those who contribute to the social product earn rights to support for basic needs in the face of social hazards. (The choice of GNP as an index of the social product also raises the issue of how paying jobs can be made available to all those who want to contribute and thus earn socioeconomic rights. I devote considerable attention to this matter in chapters 6 and 8.)

The principle of reciprocity in the earning of socioeconomic rights must be complemented by provisions to extend socioeconomic rights on the basis of need to people who are physically unable to work and to those who should not work, including children.[25]

This linkage between rights to resources and duties to produce creates a tight fit between my conception of socioeconomic rights and Cranston's first test of human rights: practicality. The means for providing the resources these rights entail are generated at least in part by earning the rights. The conception also meets another of Cranston's tests for human rights: paramount importance. The benefits these rights bestow are not aimed at equalizing income or assuring that everyone has a videorecorder. Instead they focus on those basic material resources that by general agreement are deemed to be prerequisites to full human agency.

The conception of socioeconomic rights I am proposing, however, departs from Cranston's third criterion, universality, in two respects. First, the resources to be provided would vary from one society to another. I would not expect Tanzania to support basic needs in the same way the United States might. As Michael Walzer says: "rights beyond life and liberty . . . do not follow from our common humanity; they follow from shared conceptions of social goods; they are local and particular in character."[26] In fact, the underlying justifications for rights—life and liberty included, Walzer notwithstanding—may be of little interest beyond the frontiers of Western culture. There are ways of recognizing human dignity apart from rights.[27] Second, these socioeconomic rights would be extended only to participants in the paid labor force. They do not arise simply from being human, and they are thus not human rights, nor even what Beveridge called citizen rights. They are, with exceptions, producers' rights. Again, such restrictions are based on a pragmatic assessment of the kind of socioeconomic rights American political culture will support.

Though distributed somewhat more narrowly than Walzer's counterparts, such socioeconomic rights do fit his conception of independent spheres of justice and autonomous distributive criteria for these spheres.[28] Holding modest consequences for the essential character of many spheres of social life, my suggestion is a fairly conservative one. For instance, the market remains the primary device for production and distribution decisions. Although the latter are constrained with respect to basic resources, a wide range of goods and services would continue to be distributed through the market. And matters such as the criteria for office or the relative autonomy of family and religious life would remain largely unaffected. It is generally the case that changes in one feature of an interdependent social system will have repercussions for other features, and it is not clear how far the ripples of these socioeconomic rights would reach or how high their crests might be. It does seem unlikely that they will precipitate anything remotely resembling simple equalities.

Practical Applications

This conception of socioeconomic rights does not allow for private claims of one individual randomly on another or others. The indigent malcontent on the street corner has, by virtue of these rights, no immediate claim on the money in the pockets of passersby for his medical care.[29] He does, under certain circumstances involving prior or concurrent contributions to the social product, have a valid claim—a right—to a portion of the resources that government has already removed (or might remove) from the social product and authoritatively allocated to the support of such problems. That is, contributions to production develop a claim against the public allocation process, not directly or randomly against other citizens. Government, in turn, derives the resources to be allocated to meeting basic needs by taxes approved by elected officials. As I will argue later, payroll taxes are a particularly appropriate vehicle.

Second, these socioeconomic rights do not involve simply redistributing resources vertically from rich to poor. Significant socioeconomic leveling seems unlikely in the United States, and the egalitarian results of any such efforts would likely be short-lived. But the principal intention and result of programs based on this conception of socioeconomic rights is horizontal redistribution, the shifting of resources over an individual's life cycle to meet episodic social hazards.[30] In this, my proposals follow the example of social security and most existing social insurance programs.

Three categories of social hazards would trigger resource assistance. First are episodic needs for income maintenance and medical care that result from disabling injuries or illnesses, childbirth, and aging. In these cases the conditions can be defined physiologically, and resources in the form of income maintenance and group medical insurance can usually be productively applied. Social security now provides reasonably adequate substitute income for a large portion of our aging and disabled populations. But current retirement eligibility and benefit rules create government funding problems.[31] SSI covers additional cases of both retirement and long-term disability less generously, and except for social security recipients (Medicare) and the extremely poor (Medicaid) the medical-care aspects of illness, childbirth, and non-work-related short-term disability remain uncovered. (Workers' compensation provides assistance with respect to job-related injuries.) Under a theory of socioeconomic rights, then, the category of physiological hazards covered by social insurance would be expanded.

Unemployment represents a more troublesome hazard. Income maintenance during short periods of unemployment (say, up to a month) could be covered by social insurance in nearly the same fashion as income maintenance for short-term illness or injury. But chronic or extended unemployment and resulting resource inadequacy present problems beyond income maintenance, and traditional unemployment insurance does not address the fundamental difficulties:

Social insurance, however, has not been effective in correcting long-term chronic poverty. The contribution/benefit orientation of a social insurance system automatically leaves uncovered those who cannot contribute and pays small benefits to low contributors. . . . For this reason, social insurance programs can do little to alleviate existing poverty, however effective they may be in preventing households from falling into poverty if their normal flow [of income] is interrupted.[32]

But once we are willing to credit concurrent contributions, not just past ones, this obstacle to full participation is overcome. Public programs that offer earned benefits while expanding incentives, opportunities, and capacities for self-support are the sorts of enterprises we should turn to for helping impoverished households merge with the socioeconomic mainstream. Just as students learn from daily application and earn their grades and scholarships, so too the unemployed who attend meaningful training programs could earn maintenance benefits. This emphasis on training and education to facilitate labor market participation nicely reflects Americans' traditional tendency to rely on education, frequently as an alternative to other social programs. Additionally, disadvantaged individuals who are employed might thereby earn specific social-merging program benefits that would supplement their market rewards.

Problematic episodes that shatter ties between a household's dependents and their major wage earner form a third hazard category. These episodes more obviously raise troubling issues about the manner of vesting socioeconomic rights than do the two preceding categories. As social programs have expanded in this century, it has become general practice that they serve households. For example, many programs provide the primary beneficiary with additional allowances based on the number of dependent household members—a characteristic that no doubt contributes to Ronald Dworkin's perceptions of program benefits as policies rather than rights.[33] But when the wage earner through whom benefit eligibility has been derived breaks off from the household, eligibility issues arise. Children, as a group that our society thinks should not work, are already covered by my conception of socio-economic rights. But eligible workers also leave behind noneligible working-aged adults—generally unemployed or marginally employed spouses, most of whom are women and many of whom are parents as well. Since their situations represent problematic episodes of a severity similar to those introduced above, I will later argue that some forms of earned protective response need be made available to them.

In practice, then, the socioeconomic rights I am proposing draw on five principles. First, social programs ought—as much as possible—to be based on reciprocity; those who contribute to the social product may in turn draw on that product when social hazards confront them. Second, social program assistance should generally be aimed at supplementing recipient households' efforts at self-support. Third, programs should be inclusive; while programs need not benefit recipients equally, those who face a social hazard for which benefits are accorded and have made whatever prior or concurrent contribution is required should have similar access to programs. Fourth, we should rely insofar as possible on social insurance for meeting the needs of those confronting various social hazards. And fifth, social merging programs that incorporate features similar to those of social insurance are preferable to public assistance efforts.

Socioeconomic Rights and Distributive Justice

Any notion of socioeconomic rights amounts to at least a partial concept of distributive justice. The concept I have introduced is partial, covering only the most basic material resources. In examining how this concept compares with American beliefs about distributive justice, I will draw heavily on Jennifer L. Hochschild's *What's Fair? American Beliefs About Distributive Justice* (Harvard University Press, 1981).

Hochschild conducted in-depth interviews with a small number of respondents, who differed in income and other background characteristics, in order to probe Americans' thoughts about the fairness of the existing distribution of income and other resources.

From these interviews, Hochschild distinguished three domains of life—social (family, school, local community), economic or workplace, and political—and several criteria of substantive justice: strict equality, need, investment, results, ascription, and procedural principles such as lotteries or free consent. While some respondents had consistent conceptions of distributive justice, most of her respondents held beliefs that changed from one domain to another. Briefly, egalitarian criteria—strict equality, need, and investment in the form of effort—prevailed in the social domain; differentiating criteria—investment, results, ascription, and procedures such as free consent or social Darwinism—were applied in the economic domain; and egalitarian criteria were used with respect to most areas of public life—including matters of welfare and social policy.

Hochschild's central discovery is that the nature of the domain, rather than the respondent's socioeconomic status, ideology, or other characteristic is the primary determinant of judgments of fairness. But some of her subsidiary findings are equally interesting for my purposes. Her respondents suffer considerable ambivalence about their beliefs in part because, despite liberalism's separation of the political and economic domains, many issues of well-being relate to both. For instance, in some situations her respondents were uncertain whether to apply the differentiating norms of the marketplace (treating a person as a fellow worker) or the egalitarian norms of the political domain (treating a person as a fellow citizen). Additionally, while respondents initially trotted out fairly standard tenets of classical liberalism, as the conversations continued they frequently offered more egalitarian views.

Specifically, most respondents supported selected public efforts—providing jobs being the most popular—to alleviate poverty, which they tended to perceive as a consequence of societal structure. Rich and poor alike, they "support much more equality than they realize, as long as it is couched in terms of need, investments, or results—anything except equality per se."[34] This conclusion presents some interesting challenges to any proposals concerning socioeconomic rights. One might expect to find public opinion generally favorable toward public social provision, but only as long as the policy is not based on the most general and obvious moral appeal—economic redistribution in accordance with the equality of basic human material needs.

No comparable study has been made of elite values and attitudes, and available studies offer contradictory interpretations of
elite beliefs.[35] There is reason to imagine that public-sector elites
apply egalitarian beliefs similar to those Hochschild's respondents
apply to the political domain; however, there is also reason to suspect the limited utility of addressing appeals for equality to elites.[36]
So the importance of relating socioeconomic rights to other values
probably holds with respect to American elite culture as well. Accordingly, my conception of socioeconomic rights makes minimal
reference to egalitarian appeals and relies instead on other criteria
of distributive justice—such as investments and need—that enjoy
wider support. In particular, the notion of earned rights to basic
resources fits the American elite's preferences for rewarding work
and reducing relative inequalities through securing minimum
thresholds.[37] In order to reveal the points of conflict and compatibility between this conception and the various norms of distributive justice examined by Hochschild, let us consider a series of
norms that start from an egalitarian position and become progressively more differentiating.

Strict Equality

My conception of socioeconomic rights does not realize strict
equality either procedurally or subtantively. Procedurally, not all
people are treated equally because the necessity to earn benefits by
labor-market participation is set aside for people who are physically unable to work or whom society would not have work. Further, people who do not contribute in acceptable ways fail to earn
these rights. This deviation from strict equality is a practical political necessity required to bridge the worlds of inquiry and power.
One consequence of this insistence on earning rights through active participation is that some people will slip through the safety
net or socioeconomic floor that social programs would provide, either because they are unwilling to cooperate, or fail to understand
how to cooperate, or perhaps never hear of the opportunity.[38]

Substantively, the most obvious deviation from the criterion of
strict equality lies in the restriction of these socioeconomic rights
to basic material resources. My proposals for social programs
make no effort to achieve substantive equality by redistributing resources from rich to poor. While the social merging proposals in-

volve greater vertical redistribution, the focus of these rights is restricted to basic material goods, which means that the limits of this
redistribution are reached rather quickly. The experience of other
advanced industrial societies that have extensive social programs
is that horizontal, or life-cycle, redistribution predominates over
vertical.[39]

Need

In its substantive focus, my conception of socioeconomic rights is
needs-driven: it aims to provide for the most basic, universal human needs when problems of resource inadequacy arise. Of course,
a host of nonmaterial needs, the need for love or companionship,
lie beyond the scope of these rights and beyond the capacity of
modern bureaucratic governments.

More importantly, procedurally, need alone does not, in most
cases, activate the provision mechanism. The basic material needs
of those who do not contribute to the social product lie beyond the
protective umbrella these rights offer. Only those who cannot contribute or for whom contribution is deemed undesirable are entitled to the benefits of these rights on the basis of need.

Investments

Hochschild distinguishes two categories of investments. One com-
prises more or less infinitely renewable investments that everyone
or nearly everyone can make: effort is one such investment. The
second category—specific forms of education or training, for example—includes activities or resources not equally available to all,
and renewal is neither always possible nor always necessary.

Investment in the sense of effort in the labor force lies at the
heart of my conception of socioeconomic rights. While many unpaid and voluntary efforts are assuredly no less important contributions to society, as a practical matter it is not likely that our
political culture will consider such efforts on a par with income-
generating work. This same distinction between paid and unpaid
labor is used in calculating eligibility and benefit levels for social
security, and it seems prerequisite to ensuring the political viability
of broader social programs.

Since socioeconomic rights are to be earned through participation in the paid labor force, the efforts made by individual workers

must be measured and recorded. Again, social security provides a model: a system of individual accounts of monetary contributions arising from payroll-tax deductions.

Individual investments in the form of advanced education, Hochschild's second category, are relevant to socioeconomic rights in that such activities tend to enhance one's ability to contribute to the social product. But investments of this sort also pose problems for my conception. For in contrast to effort and exertion, which we may expect of all able-bodied adults, an advanced degree lies beyond the reach of many people. Since the needs that socioeconomic rights address are essential and universal, it would be unfair to demand that these rights be earned by achievements that only a few can realize. So while this type of investment is to be encouraged, it is unacceptable as a criterion for the distribution of crucial basic resources.

Results

Hochschild equates the criterion of results with market achievement. In her view market achievement is to some degree attributable to factors neither so impersonal nor natural as libertarians suggest. Rather, the results of market forces represent in part the relative capacity of different individuals or groups to use government—an artificial device for libertarians—to define property, delimit appropriate employer or employee activities, or constrain markets (as through tariffs).[40] The criterion of results then represents a mixture of what others refer to variously as achievement, merit, and desert; results in this sense also include the distributive consequences of such factors as the favorable market position that inherited wealth provides, advantages similar to, only more subtle than, the use of government by the working class to enhance material well-being through social programs. This definition of *results* might be seriously problematic in a work of abstract philosophy,[41] but for our purposes it has no importantly deleterious effects.

Other scholars do not see market operations as appropriately categorized by a principle of distributive justice that focuses on outcomes.[42] For them the market represents an example of procedural justice in the form of free consent. This consent emphasizes a natural, impersonal, and noncoercive perspective on market operations.[43]

For our purposes, we may accept Hochschild's criterion of results as an end-oriented principle designed to justify the consequences of a system of distribution dominated by varying market influences. Both social programs and subsequent notions that these programs realize socioeconomic rights have developed as a result of the disturbing consequences market allocation has held for basic human needs.[44] In the United States results offer the stiffest competition, in terms of the breadth and depth of their popular appeal, to my preferred criterion of exertion-type investments as a principle of distributive justice for basic material goods. In part this popularity stems from the contention of market proponents that free markets allocate rewards in proportion to contributions. However, it is indisputable that market success is not directly proportional to investments in the form of exertion and effort. Oligopolies or monopolies with respect to indispensable inherited resources and asymmetries in the distribution of narrow capacities skew the relation between effort and market rewards. For the very wealthy, minimal efforts may reap enormous rewards; for the very poor, extensive effort may not return sufficient material goods to support a household.[45]

Under my conception of socioeconomic rights, the distribution of those basic resources essential to well-being, and therefore human agency, would be insulated from market allocation. Rather these resources would be distributed in a fashion consistent with our cultural norms—Americans should not have to turn to crickets for protein—according to exertion in creating the social product that is used to supply those resources. Exertion in this sense is a criterion for distribution that both lies within the reach of all and satisfies the familiar principle of desert being determined by effort. Nonessential goods and services, in contrast, will continue to be distributed by the results of market performance.

Ascription

The distinction between those who can and cannot contribute to the social product is appropriately viewed as an ascriptive criterion for it rests on time- and culture-bound conventions. Only fairly recently, for instance, have we expected youths of fifteen to be in school. And some societies might be more inclined to include child-rearing among contributions to the social product. But I have used these distinctions to determine only the manner—exertion or need—of entitlement, not whether or in what amounts basic resources should be distributed. On these latter questions ascription is irrelevant: the conditions one is born into (gender, race, social class) should not affect one's right to basic resources.

It is extremely difficult, however, to ensure this type of equality by means of public programs in a society afflicted with sexism and racism. Even programs that are broadly inclusive, operating without regard to sexual or racial differences, cannot assure these results. Those who have suffered the most from sexism or racism are apt to be among those with the lowest stocks of personal resources—both material and intangible—to apply to meeting their needs in conjunction with supplemental public programs. I will return to this problem in chapters 4 and 6.

Procedures

The preceding five criteria—equality, need, investments, results, and ascription—for distributive justice each focus on achieving a desirable outcome. Other criteria place their faith in a procedure—procedural justice—and allow the outcomes to fall as they may.[46] A lottery, for instance, may be perceived as a fair way to distribute discrete goods (tickets to a championship game) when the demand vastly exceeds the supply. But when the goods to be distributed are basic resources—surplus food, public housing—a lottery seems less fair in that its procedures ignore characteristics of individuals that by substantive criteria—need—might be thought relevant to the distribution of the goods. No procedural system for distributing scarce material resources—lottery, free consent, social Darwinism, Pareto optimality, or competition—can ensure the sorts of outcomes with respect to basic needs that my concept of socioeconomic rights demands.

Socioeconomic Rights and American Beliefs

From this comparison of my conception of socioeconomic rights and various norms of distributive justice, two salient points emerge. First, we have in effect arrived at an altered rationale for this con-

ception: namely, consistency with the most rigorous generally applicable form of earning such rights. Persons who exert the relevant sorts of effort to produce the resources required to fulfill basic
material needs will, quid pro quo, be entitled to adequate sustaining resources. For those few who are unable, or in the case of children for whom society considers such contributions premature,
need alone will entitle persons to benefits.

Second, we have seen that these rights rest on criteria compatible with Americans' beliefs about distributive justice in the social
and political domains, in which other people are viewed as family
members or fellow citizens. Socioeconomic rights in effect link
these two domains, and such linkage may be long overdue given
the demise of the family as a self-sustaining economic institution.
In the economic domain, where Americans typically apply investment, results, ascription, and differentiating procedures, my proposal for socioeconomic rights would create difficulties were it to
include a wide range of nonessential material goods (yachts, for
instance). But since these socioeconomic rights extend only to
those material goods that support basic needs, they do not threaten
marketplace norms. Further, an investments approach meshes
with the work-ethic principle of effort and reward.

This conception of socioeconomic rights earned through a specific type of exertion might well be unnecessarily stringent for
other cultures. The United Kingdom follows a citizens' rights notion that until the Thatcher government was applied so liberally in
the area of medical care as to approximate a human rights conception. It is doubtful that such a practice would be supported in the
United States. But in the process of moderating politically dangerous enthusiasm for meeting human needs, we must avoid as well
the terrors of the workhouse that might befall an exertion-oriented
conception of socioeconomic rights.[47] I will devote attention to this
problem in later chapters. For the moment let us turn to the consequences this conception of socioeconomic rights holds for related
values.

Three

Implications for Prominent American Values

Distributive justice is not a value that has commanded exceptional attention in postcolonial American society. Prior to the last half century only a small portion of American political commentators distinguished distributive justice even implicitly from the results of market operations. And as the distinction has become more widely accepted, distributive justice has come into increasingly prominent conflict with the values that the American political culture has long considered the primary virtues of market operations: freedom and economic efficiency.[1] In this chapter I will examine the consequences that my conception of socioeconomic rights holds for six prominent American values: liberty, economic efficiency, equality, democracy, community and social solidarity, and human dignity. I will attempt to tease out the contradictions within and tradeoffs among these values. In doing so I am mindful of our limited capacity to explain the effects of social phenomena, such as specific public programs, on society.[2]

Liberty

Let us follow Isaiah Berlin in differentiating positive and negative liberty, and let us also adopt C. B. Macpherson's dissection of three aspects of positive liberty.[3] First is the freedom to participate in political decision making; these political rights are compatible with, but distinct from, negative liberties, or civil rights. Second, and according to Macpherson at the heart of the concept of positive liberty, is developmental liberty, the freedom to be one's own master, to act on one's conscious purposes, and to develop and apply one's capacities and abilities. Unfortunately, developmental liberty is often transmogrified into the third aspect, a distorted form of liberty by which those who think they know human truth more perfectly than others coerce others to act accordingly.

The importance of negative liberties—freedom from external constraints on speech, press, and association—in American history is partially responsible for the characterization of the United States as a nation in which individualism reigns. In the Lockean tradition, American political culture generally holds government to be the principal external threat to liberty. But as Hobbes reminds us, the actions of individuals may pose threats to fellow citizens, in which case government is expected to step in to help. Marketplace operations may also be seen as infringements on liberty, though America has been more reluctant than other advanced industrial societies to adopt this view.

There are potential clashes between my conception of socioeconomic rights and Americans' negative liberties in at least four areas: participation would be compulsory, rather than voluntary, for all members of the paid labor force; increased payroll taxes would further reduce discretionary income; the professional autonomy of physicians and perhaps other providers of essential services might be restricted; and program beneficiaries could be subject to certain requirements. Let us take up each of these in turn.

The kinds of social insurance programs I am proposing require the compulsory participation of all members of the labor force so that the costs are spread as widely as possible. Compulsory participation would also preclude the individual and societal problems that arise when people decline optional enrollment but are subsequently beset by social hazards.[4] Yet compulsory participation in a program addressing hazards that may never afflict some participants seems a poor fit with the aspects of negative liberty that Americans denote with the term individualism.[5]

Nonetheless, there was no widespread public protest when Supplementary Medical Insurance (SMI—Part B of Medicare) to cover physicians' bills was changed from an option that social security recipients had to explicitly elect into an automatic enrollment that recipients had to explicitly decline. Indeed, the change in procedure was made because more than 95 percent of recipients were opting to pay the extra monthly premium for the additional coverage.[6] In general, the opposition to compulsory social insurance has come not from the general public but from employers, private insurance companies, and the American Medical Association (AMA), with the AMA being the most persistent in its resistance.[7]

As to the cost of social insurance programs, certainly increased payroll taxes would reduce workers' discretionary income and the freedom of choice that it supports.[8] To the degree that new taxes were progressive they might be all the more obnoxious in that those least likely to receive benefits—high-income taxpayers—would be required to pay a disproportionate share of the costs. Such complaints, however, always arise in any discussion about the American tax system. On this count, the theoretical constraints posed by socioeconomic rights are no different than those posed by the overall revenue-gathering system.

The practical importance of progressive taxes is unclear, for we cannot precisely discern how regressive or progressive the current American tax system is.[9] What is the overall effect of various federal, state, and local levies: income taxes, property taxes and assessments, sales and excise taxes, and taxes on estates and inheritances? Suppose we assume that the overall system is moderately progressive and that the well-off do pay more heavily for social programs that serve the poor. Does this mean that our tax system places unfair constraints on the liberties of the well-off?

Surely some vertical redistribution takes place, but, as noted in chapter 1, a substantial portion of social program benefits involves horizontal rather than vertical redistribution. The social merging programs I am suggesting would create some vertical redistribution, as does the current AFDC program, but social insurance does not involve much vertical redistribution since a good portion of today's taxes for social insurance programs will be returned to a worker in benefits as he or she encounters social hazards. Thus constraints on current income are the means of providing a citizen with freedom in subsequent situations.

Further, while socioeconomic rights do make substantial demands on government budgets, one cannot say that cutting social program expenditures would reduce taxes or the constraints on liberty that they represent. The savings might simply be shifted to defense or other programs, as has occurred to some degree during the Reagan administration. It is also reasonable to ask, as I will in the next section, whether the developmental liberty that socioeconomic rights create offsets the constraints to negative liberty that taxes pose.[10]

As to how socioeconomic rights might challenge the liberties of providers of basic services, possible restrictions on physicians are the most commonly discussed. In Britain's National Health Service (NHS), American providers see fearful restrictions on income and professional autonomy. It is possible, however, to ensure broad access to medical services without following the British model. In the Federal Republic of Germany, for example, a system of decentralized private organizations operates within federal guidelines to secure socioeconomic rights to medical care.[11]

The fourth type of constraint on negative liberty concerns various restrictions on the recipients. For instance, programs that distribute basic goods in kind—food stamps and some housing programs—offer recipients less freedom to choose goods than do transfer-payment plans. Public assistance programs such as AFDC and related efforts in other nations in some instances dictate constraints on personal activities, including household membership.[12]

In summary, socioeconomic rights pose or can pose several problems for negative liberty. Libertarians who place negative liberty above all other values and tolerate conflicting concerns only reluctantly can never be expected to exhibit any enthusiasm for socioeconomic rights nor, in many instances, for social programs.[13] But the libertarian position is an extreme one, even in America, and we need not end our inquiry here because libertarians object to the way in which socioeconomic rights infringe on negative liberty. Rather we need to focus our attention on the breadth and depth of the problems socioeconomic rights pose for negative liberty—that is, whose liberty is constrained and how severely—as well as on what practical measures can be taken to reduce these difficulties.

In this vein neither the compulsory character of social insurance nor its characteristic life-cycle redistribution has by and large created problems for participating citizens. Instead, these issues have been used by professional groups such as the AMA as stalking horses for other concerns. The public may, however, protest if the level of benefits from social insurance programs drops and payroll deductions continue to rise.

The tradeoff of reduced discretionary income against social program benefits has been more problematic for public assistance programs than for social insurance, particularly when vertical redistribution is widely perceived as failing to facilitate improvements in recipients' lives. The investments approach attempts, through social merging efforts, to overcome this problem by assuring that, to the widest degree possible, recipients of these programs earn their benefits by contributing to their self-support in socially approved ways. All other restrictions on recipients could be reduced, for they are not inherent to socioeconomic rights.

This leaves us with the most politically troublesome problem that socioeconomic rights pose for negative liberty: the freedom of private service providers, doctors in particular. But we need look no further than Medicare to see that socioeconomic rights can be implemented in ways that allow providers relatively high incomes and considerable professional autonomy. Unfortunately, the British NHS, which does restrict providers, has so dominated the thinking of the AMA and other American medical organizations that they have exerted their considerable political resources—money, organization, and social position—toward blocking the development of all social programs intended to realize basic socioeconomic rights without stopping to differentiate among proposals according to the degree of threat to their interests.

Developmental Liberty

By *developmental liberty,* I am referring to situations in which the application of external resources, tangible or intangible, opens up to a person new choices or opportunities that would otherwise not exist and that encourage the development of individual human potential.[14] In practice, the fostering of developmental liberty involves devising ways by which limiting circumstances may be overcome—ignorance or indigence set aside—so that choices may be expanded. Here, governments often play a constructive role through infusions of resources that enable people to engage in choices denied them by market distribution. Developmental liberty thus comes at some expense to negative liberty (taxes on discretionary income) of either the same or similar people at other points in time (social insurance) or of different and generally more prosperous people (public assistance or social merging). Among social scientists and the public at large, one hears diverse assessments of this tradeoff.[15]

Americans have generally been supportive of developmental liberty as applied to public education, though this support is generally expressed in terms of meritocratic equality of opportunity rather than developmental liberty.[16] Indeed the United States has been more inclined than most other industrial societies to attack problems of resource inadequacy through education (and the upward social mobility that it presumably provides) than through programs that directly upgrade the material resources of desperate households. My emphasis on self-help in socioeconomic rights, particularly in terms of acquiring better preparation for the labor market, fits well with these American predispositions. Beyond the realm of public education, however, the United States has generally been less supportive of developmental liberty, perhaps seeing in it troubling egalitarian manifestations of equal results. The British, in contrast, are quick to point out that the NHS contributes to citizens' liberty by healing and allowing normal activity as well as by relieving citizens of some of the costs and anxieties associated with medical care under market circumstances.[17]

In contrast to what we found in the case of negative liberty, socioeconomic rights mesh nicely with the spirit of and the more prosaic material contributions to developmental liberty. Social programs that supply basic material goods and services such as education and medical care during difficult periods can open or re-open constructive avenues of activity. Of course, human development also requires intangible support, love and encouragement from others, for example. But social programs can help, and the basic resources they provide are more essential to developmental liberty than those directed through the police, courts, prisons, and defense programs. Nonetheless, we must be mindful that while basic resources are necessary, they are not sufficient for socially constructive developmental liberty. Food stamps may help to keep an impoverished child alive, but development can take ugly turns if the child grows up in a destructive family environment, faces stultifying prejudice from society, or receives social program support of a form that stifles self-actualization.

As I pointed out above, the tradeoffs between negative and developmental liberty appear to be less bothersome to Americans in the case of social insurance than in programs designed to address persistent problems of social disadvantage. Self-interest may well play a part in this: most Americans expect to make use of social security, while far fewer expect to rely on AFDC. But the difference also rests on the public's perceptions of the recipients and on the style of redistribution. Social insurance recipients are viewed as sound people facing episodic problems involving life-cycle redistribution, while public assistance recipients are often viewed as persons of dubious character on the fringes of society who take resources from others. Here, the investments approach may be salutary in changing both the nature of programs directed at disadvantage and the public's perceptions of program recipients. People who receive benefits from social merging programs in return for their contributions to the social product are legitimized in a way that recipients of current public assistance are not.

Economic Efficiency

In order to be politically viable, any concept of socioeconomic rights must limit its conflict with economic efficiency. Specific issues include the consequences of socioeconomic rights on work incentives, savings patterns, risk taking, and international competitiveness.

A prominent American view is that existing social programs reduce work incentives and productivity generally.[18] The three principal arguments are that a system of extensive social programs: (1) emboldens organized mainstream labor to press for wage increases and other demands, because workers know they will be protected during strikes or interludes of unemployment; (2) reduces workers' motivation, since increased earnings will be taxed to the benefit of others; and (3) discourages people from accepting jobs that pay about the same amount as might be obtained through generous social programs, especially if those jobs are dirty, dangerous, dreary, or degrading in other ways.

If we look overseas, we have no trouble finding evidence that casts doubts on each of these contentions. In Sweden, for example, the extensive realization of socioeconomic rights accompanies high levels of productivity and strong work incentives;[19] the Federal Republic of Germany is frequently mentioned in this context as well. Lester Thurow finds little relationship between economic efficiency and economic equality, and Harold Wilensky finds that state spending on social programs is positively associated with levels of productivity.[20]

Whether these patterns are relevant to the United States is a question that admits no easy answer, and the evidence is quite mixed.[21] For example, from 1900 to 1980 aggregate labor trends among men exhibit little change except for a decline in labor-force participation among men of retirement age, retirement presumably as a result of social security; women, again except those of retirement age, have dramatically increased their participation in the labor force across the same period.[22] The negative income tax experiments conducted in stages in several locations in the 1970s, however, show moderate declines in hours worked by people, particularly women, whose income levels were assured.[23] Overall, the rate of growth in American productivity has declined since social programs were expanded in the 1960s, but this association may be attributed to any number of confounding variables.[24]

In a society as atomized or individualistic as the United States, it does not seem unreasonable to suggest that particular forms of social programs represent threats to work incentives for people trapped in low-paying jobs, often called the secondary labor market.[25] Characteristically, such jobs not only return low wages and few fringe benefits but also tend to be subject to frequent termination on short notice. Often dreary, dirty, or dangerous, this sort of work does not lead to pay raises, job security, or promotion in rank or responsibilities.

Popular perceptions of the secondary labor market show vestiges of the notion of two races or two species, a conception prominent in early-nineteenth-century Britain.[26] The superior class comprised property-owners, and they were motivated by desires for profit, or what we might call positive reinforcement. In contrast, "the poor," or the class that had to work for a living, was alleged to be motivated by the threat of punishment, that is, by adversive control, such as the prospect of starvation.

Today most Americans have to work for a living, but no one would suggest that professionals, paraprofessionals, white-collar workers, or skilled manual workers are primarily motivated by adversive control. For while their jobs are imperfect in many ways, they do afford varying measures of positive reinforcement: good wages, a sense of personal pride, and the development of personal expertise, among others. But for people at the bottom of the income and job-status distributions, it may well be reasonable to suppose that adversive control remains an important factor in decisions about work and therefore that some forms of social programs reduce work incentives. If so, what is called for is a long-range effort to revitalize these incentives through positive reinforcement rather than adversive control. But in the near term we should also question the wisdom of social programs that, like the policy initiatives of the mid-1960s through the mid-1970s, tended to provide benefits without asking for specific forms of constructive activity in return.

The effects of existing social programs on work incentives seem to reflect distinct program features. Wilensky, for instance, argues that retirement pensions provide a powerful incentive for developing a regular work history—a thesis consistent with the aggregate labor trends cited above.[27] But current American practices with respect to AFDC and unemployment insurance may be destructive of work incentives. Even the disability aspect of social security may be more problematic in this regard than are pensions for the elderly.[28] Overall, social insurance programs aimed at clearly episodic problems are less troublesome with respect to work incentives than programs aimed at social disadvantage, although both types of programs may improve the payoffs for socially undesirable activities.[29]

The effort requirement introduced in chapter 2 reduces the work-incentive problems posed by some existing social programs. By facilitating labor-market participation and supplementing its rewards, thereby making household support both necessary and more feasible, the investments approach positively reinforces desirable activity, unlike most current social programs for working-aged adults.

A second criterion of economic efficiency is the personal savings rate. Martin Feldstein, among others, argues that since American social insurance programs operate on a pay-as-we-go basis, they create no funds that can be used for investment.[30] Further, he maintains that social insurance discourages relatively prosperous citizens from accumulating personal savings to protect themselves against social hazards. Feldstein's first point is accurate, but its significance in this context hinges on the second: Would Americans save more and would the nation have more capital for productive investment if there were less social program support? The historical evidence suggests that the answer is no. The personal savings rate, expressed as a proportion of gross national product was 16 percent in 1973, the same as in the 1920s, before any national social insurance programs existed.[31] Nor does Henry J. Aaron's analysis of American savings patterns in the last fifty years reveal any discernible trends in personal savings.[32]

Even if we assume that Americans would start to save more, we cannot be sure what proportion of the new savings would be available for capital formation rather than locked into collectibles or real estate. We may also wonder whether productivity-enhancing investments would rise with the savings rate. If Americans saved more, they would purchase less, and if social programs reduced their benefits, consumer demand would also drop. Thus the combination of higher savings and lower social benefits might dampen demand to the point that American producers would see little motive to invest in improved domestic capital stock. In that case public policy could structure incentives to channel savings in specific directions and to stimulate domestic capital investment, but such incentives are fully independent of funding for social programs, neither following from reductions in social programs nor requiring such reductions as a preliminary step.[33]

A third aspect of economic efficiency involves business's attitudes toward risk taking. Production costs (including payroll taxes for social insurance programs), the incentives of workers, and the availability of capital all affect the willingness of American entrepreneurs and corporate managers to take risks with new enterprises or to expand or modernize existing facilities. In the United States, indeed, business enjoys an unusual independence in risk-taking decisions. Whereas French state managers and Swedish labor officials may routinely participate in corporate investment decisions, American businesses expect relative autonomy in their decision making. The prospect of government "interference" regarding worker safety or environmental impacts makes American private managers hesitant to invest capital in a new enterprise. Similarly, a restive or powerful workforce, or the perception of one, tends to curtail risk-taking.

For this reason, American businesses are wary of social programs that strengthen labor's hand.[34] In offering substantial benefits to limited segments of the working-age population without a clear quid pro quo, programs like unemployment insurance and AFDC could be interpreted as counterproductive. But this does not mean that economic benefits must be denied to vulnerable individuals in order to allow business managers to feel more confident about risking capital. Rather, it suggests that we try to provide these basic benefits in a way that will be less troubling to business. Again, the investments approach to socioeconomic rights is designed to address this concern.

Increasingly, economic efficiency is discussed in the context of global economic competitiveness. Once, American businesses argued that if social programs were inevitable, uniform national programs were preferable to interstate variations that would put some businesses at a disadvantage.[35] Today they envision the United States as a relatively homogeneous unit competing with other advanced industrial societies, and they ask whether national social programs may hamper the competitive position of American products and services. Among the potential dangers cited are deleterious effects on work incentives, additions to labor costs, depletion of capital, and constraints on business managers' willingness to take risks due to uncertainties about such problems.[36]

As noted earlier, however, the United States spends a smaller percentage of gross national product on social programs than do most other industrial societies. Thus any lack of competitiveness of American products cannot be attributed to anomalous social program costs. Nonetheless, one might argue that reducing social program costs might increase the competitiveness of American products or that reducing future increases in social program costs might improve the competitiveness of American products over time.

Such arguments, however, exceed our understanding of the practical consequences of existing social programs and alternatives to them. There is simply no clear consensus among economists or other analysts about the macroeconomic costs and benefits of social programs. Recent debates about deregulation suggest that business managers perceive social programs as conflicting with their interests—and perhaps with economic efficiency too. The perceptions of this exceptionally influential group carry significant political weight, but we have no way of objectively judging whether they are accurate.

Despite these uncertainties, two points seem indisputable. First, social programs are merely one factor contributing to work incentives, savings patterns, risk taking, and international competitiveness. And if social programs were shown to impinge on the realization of economic efficiency, it might be possible to counterbalance this effect by other actions. For example, changes in management style might enhance work incentives, and various tax-reform strategies have been proposed to stimulate savings.

Second, we can easily see that some formulations of socioeconomic rights are more inconsistent with economic efficiency than others. On this criterion my proposal seems less disruptive than, say, the guaranteed-income approach of the Nixon and Carter administrations. Again, anticipated conflicts between socioeconomic rights and core American values may be reduced by careful design of social insurance and social merging programs.

Equality

Equality is a value frequently set in juxtaposition to both negative liberty and economic efficiency.[37] We may usefully distinguish between equality of results, which has not achieved considerable support in theory or in practice among Americans, and equality of opportunity, which in limited senses, at least, has become a core American value.

The essence of the relationship between socioeconomic rights and equality of results was presented in chapter 2. Because equality of results remains a controversial value in American political culture, my proposal for socioeconomic rights is based on a limited conception of this principle, one designed to minimize the conflict with negative liberty and economic efficiency. My contention that people who contribute to the social product from which basic resources are derived have rights to these resources beyond what market allocation provides entails a reduction in the relative inequalities of some results. But both the manner of assuring certain minimums for those at the bottom of the socioeconomic hierarchy and the means of rewarding efforts at self-help fit reasonably well with American political culture.[38] Beyond these basic resources, for which distributive justice demands allocation on the basis of effort, market or other means of distributing tangible and intangible resources are acceptable; my proposal for socioeconomic rights does not attempt what Michael Walzer calls simple equality or roughly equal shares of resources.[39]

As we have seen, these limited socioeconomic rights involve some sacrifice of liberty by some persons to meet the needs of others. While the United States has engaged in a variety of practices that sacrifice liberty to achieve greater equality of selected results,[40] the nation has characteristically done so grudgingly, complaining all the way, and frequently implementing the redistributive mechanisms in a hostile manner inimical to the abstract intent of achieving greater equality of results. By requiring contributions to the social product as a prerequisite to recipient status, I intend to make more palatable such tradeoffs between liberty and equality. Like beneficiaries of social security and public education, recipients would be entitled to benefits in return for constructive activity. And the requirement that effort be exerted in the paid labor market brings equality of results within the bounds of economic efficiency as well.

In contrast to equality of results, limited senses of equality of opportunity have achieved considerable support, in both theory and practice, within the United States. One aspect of this value is procedural fairness, the use of performance-related criteria rather than sex, race, or age in the distribution of work or educational opportunities, unless such native characteristics are directly relevant to performance.[41] While the historical record of American practice leaves a lot to be desired and our progress has been slow and painful, it is probably appropriate to identify this aspect of equality of opportunity as part of the American creed.

The most obvious shortcoming in this regard evinced by existing social programs involves race. Because social security and other public insurance programs serve a broad cross-section of the population, while AFDC and public assistance programs have a disproportionate number of minority recipients, many socioeconomically comfortable Americans view public assistance as an "us-versus-them" issue. If programs created to help our most economically vulnerable citizens are to acquire greater political viability, they must be designed to emphasize inclusiveness, serving minorities as an indistinguishable aspect of serving a much broader and more representative constituency.

A second aspect of equality of opportunity relates to differences in developmental opportunities, or the equality of life chances.[42] Obviously procedural fairness will not in itself equalize opportunity among youngsters who attend private preparatory schools and the children of migrant farmworkers. Nor can efforts to equalize life chances by giving disadvantaged youngsters extra preschool or afterschool activities put them on a par with children whose lives are richer in the developmental experiences and role models that foster abilities to compete successfully for educational and occupational positions. Related efforts to give preferential consideration to school or job applicants who have disadvantaged backgrounds have been highly controversial.

The sources of resistance to efforts to realize greater equality of life chances are several: such efforts necessarily constrain negative liberty and procedural fairness, and they sometimes unnecessarily abridge other values as well; and racism and related forms of prejudice predispose some constituencies to oppose any form of affirmative action. While conservatives in the late 1970s and 1980s made a constructive contribution in emphasizing the desirability of eliciting greater responsibility from people who sought social protection or assistance, conservative thinkers have balked at fathoming the full array of problems that profound social disadvantage presents.

The socioeconomic rights that I have suggested are necessary, but far from sufficient, for improving the life chances of the disadvantaged. Government programs can and should provide food for hungry children, but social programs cannot supply these children with the supportive parents, peers, and school environments that encourage intellectual and emotional growth.[43]

The situation in the case of episodic social hazards is more encouraging, for here benefits serve to mitigate the effects of problematic episodes in the lives of those who generally cope relatively well. In such cases equality of opportunity greatly resembles developmental liberty, with socioeconomic rights expanding the opportunities of those whose fortunes, were they limited to private means, would be more restricted.

Though socioeconomic rights lead us in the direction of greater equality of life chances, these rights are not forceful facilitators of this value. And they are of less help in cases of disadvantage than when applied to episodic problems. But in the process of lending minimal support to equalities of results and opportunities, these socioeconomic rights reflect some of the tension inherent in our nation's troublesome commitment to two incompatible values, negative liberty and equality.

Democracy

In the late eighteenth century democracy was rescued from political obscurity and given a representational structure. Civil rights— to speech and assembly, for example—were gradually established, and in the nineteenth and early twentieth centuries political rights were added.[44] The distinguishing features of democracies of this sort were depicted by Joseph Schumpeter as procedures involving periodic elite competition within widely accepted guidelines.[45] Civil rights formed the background rules of political competition, and the exercise of political rights—roughly one person, one vote— determined winners and losers.

As more recent empirical studies have revealed, this conception of democratic practices harbors several inadequacies. For one, levels of political information and participation are not as high as the conception of electoral competition suggests. For another, this description largely overlooks how elected and appointed officials reach public decisions. Additionally, the focus on democracy as a process of selected procedures tends to downplay the outcomes— who gets what—and the values or ends those outcomes support.

Specifically, empirical studies show that individual information and participation levels are associated with socioeconomic status as well as membership in politically minded groups—unions and other interest groups, political parties, churches.[46] And whereas the electoral competition conception of democracy focuses on individuals who are organized into parties at elections, in practice we see a range of groups, many of which are well-organized and backed by extensive financial resources, relevant expertise, and impressive social connections, and which are active during and in between elections, lobbying public bodies to support their interests.[47]

These findings have led some to argue that average citizens are only marginally involved in contemporary democracies.[48] And even their interests are represented largely by groups reflecting a limited portion of the citizenry and subject to the iron law of oligarchy.[49]

If contemporary democracy involves such modest participation on the part of the citizenry, what makes it democratic? An increasingly prominent answer focuses on a substantive matter: the values a polity realizes. By this line of thought a polity cannot rightfully be considered a democracy by procedures alone, particularly if these procedures appear to benefit primarily a socioeconomic elite. Rather, a democracy must uphold certain ends, including a conception of distributive justice whose policy outcomes benefit the population broadly. In essence, there is an implicit tradeoff: the price elites pay for encouraging political ground rules and mild competition is sharing material payoffs with the many who do not participate as regularly or thoroughly as elites in the expressive freedoms of procedural democracy. This tradeoff fits the suggestion, mentioned in chapter 2, that negative (civil-political) rights may be useless from the perspective of the masses, while positive (socioeconomic) rights are redundant for the elite.[50] The presence of each in contemporary democracies thus provides something for everyone, or nearly so; in effect, the "subsistence rights" of feudalism have been recovered.[51] By this reformulation democracy involves the realization of three types of rights, shared in varying degrees by different groups: civil rights, or rights *against* the state; political rights, or control *of* the state; and socioeconomic rights, or claims *on* the state.[52]

What we have here are alternative conceptions of the contemporary meaning of democracy. By one, democracy is appropriately a procedural matter, and extraprocedural considerations of who gets what are external or anterior, rather than inherent, to the meaning of democracy. Charles A. Beard, for instance, argues that the American system of democracy was designed to leave "the fundamental private rights of property anterior to government and morally beyond the reach of popular majorities."[53] The alternative view acknowledges some substantive essence to democracy: regardless of procedures, in a democracy political outcomes realize certain other values, among them protecting citizens from the social hazards created by wage dependence and vulnerability.

Socioeconomic rights have little place in the property-rights-as-anterior conception, for they entail constraints on negative liberty—taxes—and perhaps also on economic efficiency—taxes or regulation more generally—that effectively dissolve the special anterior status of exclusionary private property rights. Nonetheless, all contemporary democracies, including the United States, have for some while treated the screen protecting property rights as permeable in at least some instances.

To a considerable degree this desanctification of property rights stems from wide experience suggesting that if the pursuit of property is left relatively unhindered by the state, a tiny proportion of the population ends up with most of it,[54] while the vast majority of people have insufficient wealth to endure common social hazards. To meet these needs, life-sustaining public entitlements—to some a new form of property[55]—have been fashioned. Such programs have increased the legitimacy of the state for many, but they restrict the traditional property rights of the few. Naturally, these restrictions elicit resentment and protest from proceduralists and members of the propertied minority.[56]

Community and Social Solidarity

Individualism has such a hold on American society that the values of community or social solidarity have received relatively scant attention. Most often a sense of national community or social solidarity has appeared in response to foreign threats or natural disasters. This form of social solidarity is not unusual, but other societies, frequently with organic pasts, have been able to transcend community based solely on such threats, and social programs have been relevant to these achievements. For instance, while the British criticize nearly innumerable specifics of their National Health Service, they nevertheless derive a sense of community and comfort from its existence. And the Swedes have made some progress in reducing income differentials through solidaristic approaches to wages.[57]

But Sweden has a tradition of state paternalism, and American individualism may prohibit similar social program contributions in the United States.

Yet we often hear discussions these days of Americans' yearning for a sense of community.[58] Individualism, it seems, fails to fulfill personal needs for fellowship and a sense of meaning derived from contributing to broadly recognized values. Historically most American experience with community has been local and voluntary, but other aspects of social solidarity are relevant to national scales of action, for example, exhibiting concern for fellow citizens' medical-care needs by establishing a national program.

Whether public programs can, outside of wartime, engender social solidarity against the background of the individualistic American political culture is unclear. Up to now the categorical character and political vulnerability of American public assistance has often made these programs sources of divisiveness. More promising is the example of social security, which suggests that Americans are willing to support an involuntary social insurance program that is broadly inclusive. It does not, therefore, seem foolish to hope that socioeconomic rights that are inclusive and generally compatible with American political culture might further the values of community and social solidarity.

Human Dignity

Rights are a relatively new means for achieving human dignity, but they have become indispensable to the American conception. One's capacity for self-esteem stems from the possession of rights that others must respect.[59]

During the nation's first century, the civil and political rights associated largely with negative liberty were sufficient supports for dignity for much of the American population. Most people were born into relatively large families and lived in households that owned life-sustaining property. The traditional American conception of human dignity thus came to be closely associated with self-reliance. The dignified American lived free from both predatory government tyranny and supportive government paternalism.

Self-reliance, however, was not well suited to the industrial America that began to develop between the Civil War and the Great Depression. During the progressive era a few state governments tried to adjust public policy to fit the changing character of American society,[60] but no general progress with respect to wage dependence and vulnerability was made until the 1930s, when worldwide economic calamities led the Roosevelt administration to propose the New Deal. It is well worth remembering that the programs initiated by FDR were largely designed to cope with the nation's immediate problems, rather than to inaugurate a competing concept of human dignity.

But the creators of social security, a relatively insignificant part of the overall effort, used the concept of individual accounts of earned rights to give social security a special status and dignity among American efforts at public social provision. In contrast to public assistance that was applied to indigency, social security benefits were earned throughout the beneficiary's working life. Individual workers paid taxes into a personal account that provided a right to draw on the program's trust fund when aging disrupted wages.

The creators of social security may rightly be faulted for sacrificing the immediate well-being of the needy elderly and others during the depression years in order to develop a long-term social insurance program that was in fact and in symbolism different from public assistance.[61] Benefits were not paid out until 1940, and the program initially provided extremely modest benefits to a limited number of people. However, the concept of individually earned rights enabled Americans for the first time to view public social provision within the realm of dignified human activity.

In the half century since the New Deal, Americans have increasingly come to reject as too restrictive the traditional conception of human dignity. Through the example of social security, we have come to see dignity in planned participation in earned public entitlements that offer protection from social hazards. Put another way, earned rights are now viewed as a dignified way to cope with the social hazards caused by wage dependency. Dignity is no longer afforded solely by self-reliance; it can also be achieved through public benefits earned by conscientious efforts at self-help.

Conclusions

For several core American values—negative liberty, the procedural or property-rights-as-anterior sense of democracy, and the equa-

tion of human dignity with self-reliance—my conception of socioeconomic rights poses incompatibilities. These conflicts are significant insofar as these values have been central to American political
culture. So long as these values inspire a following, the realization
of socioeconomic rights will require some sacrifice and compromise, but not the complete subjugation of these core values. These
socioeconomic rights broaden certain facets of democracy and human dignity; they also entail compulsory participation in social insurance programs, some restrictions on discretionary income, and
some limits on the income and professional autonomy of some private service providers.

Thus Americans who place great importance on selected aspects
of negative liberty, or particular conceptions of property rights and
human dignity, will not be enthusiastic about socioeconomic rights.
And the American population may well include a larger proportion of such people than some other advanced industrial societies
contain. But these values are no longer the sole constituents of
American political culture, especially when the discussion turns
from abstract theories to practical affairs.

On the relationship between socioeconomic rights and economic efficiency, empirical uncertainty precludes any easy assessment of the seriousness, even the existence, of incompatibilities.
Reputable scholars using different data and methods offer contradictory conclusions. Nonetheless, two points seem clear. First,
regardless of the actual effects of social programs on work incentives, propensity to save, willingness to invest, or American competitiveness, there are widespread perceptions that such effects are
negative. Any programs created to implement socioeconomic rights
must therefore be designed to reduce perceptions of conflict between public social provision and economic efficiency. Toward this
end, programs that emphasize personal investments of effort and
self-help are preferable to, say, a guaranteed-income system.

Second, all measures of economic efficiency are affected by a
constellation of factors. If social programs are shown to reduce,
for instance, the propensity to save, we can probably manipulate
other aspects of public policy—tax policy—to counter this effect.
These manipulations will require careful thought and difficult
choices, for values do conflict. But we should not see the issue as
an all-or-nothing decision.

Among values less central to American political culture than negative liberty or economic efficiency, we have discussed several that are compatible with socioeconomic rights: developmental liberty, equality of results and opportunity, the triple-rights-conception of democracy, community and social solidarity, and the contemporary conception of human dignity. In most cases, however, basic socioeconomic rights admit only limited or partial realizations of these values so as not to impinge severely on core values. For example, socioeconomic rights will reduce the inequality of some results but cannot enforce equality of results without threatening the fundamental principles of liberty. The realization of these secondary values also depends on the nature of particular programs; a social insurance program, for example, much more clearly realizes the contemporary conception of human dignity than does a public assistance program like AFDC.

Would the cumulative impact of all these conflicting influences produce a situation preferable to current patterns of public social provision in the United States? Despite the incompatibilities I have mentioned, implementing basic socioeconomic rights would neither broaden nor intensify fundamental value conflicts inherent in the American creed. Further, socioeconomic rights offer possibilities for moderating other value conflicts. More-comprehensive social insurance would reduce reliance on vertical redistribution; earned rights would enhance work incentives; the supplementary character of benefits would encourage working and saving; strong work incentives would facilitate managerial risk-taking; and the clear association between beneficiary status and self-help would afford a new measure of dignity to social provision.

Were American political culture based on an internally coherent and relatively fixed ideology, the inconsistencies we have examined would represent impressive obstacles to the implementation of socioeconomic rights. But the values of the American culture have a heuristic openness that permits new nuances to emerge as empirical conditions change. Moreover, the core set of values contains internal inconsistencies. It has been through gradual shifts in the meaning and emphasis of core values that American institutions have been able to accommodate changing circumstances, such as the transformation from rural commercial capitalism to advanced industrial capitalism. In some instances, as in the case of social security, institutions even lead the way in the evolution of American values.

A set of basic socioeconomic rights tailored to American political culture would not, we may conclude, produce value conflicts novel in kind or degree. The crucial problems, to which I now turn, are practical ones.

Four

Practical Problems:
Complexity and Compliance

The implementation of basic socioeconomic rights in the United States would require intricate practical support. While such private initiatives as employer-sponsored pension plans have a role to play, public social programs lie at the heart of the matter.[1] Here, two sets of issues seem particularly problematic in the American context: the complexities entailed by large-scale social action and the difficulties of motivating compliance from all parties.

Coping with Complexity

Three distinct problems deserve our attention: selected difficulties arising from the necessity for action, limits and related harmonization issues, and the conflicts between the centralized bureaucracy needed to administer public social programs and the American preference for limited and local government.

Pitfalls Associated with
Complex Social Action

All large-scale efforts, public or private, must overcome institutional inertia, human fallibility, unanticipated changes in the social environment, and the like.[2] While such problems are in no way peculiar to public social policy, their negative effects have had an exceptionally high political profile among these programs. One may explain this dissatisfaction by referring to Americans' general

skepticism about social programs or to Americans' frustration
with these programs' failure to decisively eradicate poverty. Whatever the explanation, it is clear that public social programs have
attracted exceptional attention for rather unexceptional difficulties
in managing complexity.

To minimize both the actual difficulties and the perception of
such difficulties, my proposals for social insurance and other programs stick fairly closely to activities that our country already en-
gages in and does fairly well. Rather than suggesting that we
emulate Western European nations that have well-developed reper-
toires of public decision-making and implementation strategies,
my proposals play to our proven strengths. We have encouraging,
albeit controversial and limited, experience with social insurance
funded by personal contributions to individual accounts. We have
as well a recent history of exceptionally heavy reliance on public
assistance, though few are excited by its success. We have relatively
modest experience with active labor-market efforts. Given our
relatively narrow range of successful practical experience, to suggest programs that would require dramatically different or ambitious machinery would be to invite serious practical difficulties.

Limits and Harmonization Issues

All rights have limits. In the United States we have a good deal
more experience analyzing the limits on First Amendment rights
than we do with those on socioeconomic rights. We have seen the
boundaries of protected speech vary over time, and we have argued
over troublesome instances in which freedom to assemble threatens other liberties or civic values.

Placing limits on basic socioeconomic rights raises questions
about the nature of human needs. A limit on the amount and type
of food necessary to sustain an individual could be based on a
physiological assessment, but food is a social good as well as a
source of nutrients. Thus basic everyday needs are in part defined
by conventional cultural patterns. In our country today a nutri-
tionally sound diet that featured insects as the primary source of
protein would not fulfill our sense of basic needs. Needs also have
a way of expanding into wants,[3] but there are no steadfast distinc-

tions between the two. For instance, are organ transplants or eso-
teric life-support systems needs or wants in our society?[4]

Additionally, as William Leiss points out, needs become less coherent in the high-intensity market settings of contemporary advanced societies. We continually reinterpret our concepts of needs
in light of market offerings. Further, he argues, in a consumer society people focus less attention on basic needs—food—than on
distinguishing features of the commodities—ease of preparation.
In combination, these two processes, the "fragmentation of needs"
and the "dissolution of commodities," orient our needs toward
what is available rather than what is customary or conventional.[5]

Despite these problems, our federal government has devised income guidelines that delineate the boundaries of poverty. These
boundaries have often been challenged, but disagreements will always exist over the limits of any right. Thus while socioeconomic
rights raise difficult questions about limits, these problems are different only in degree, not in kind, from those raised by civil or political rights. Further, we do not need unanimous agreement about
the limits of socioeconomic rights in order to realize some version
of them. Public opinion surveys in all advanced industrial societies,
including the United States, reveal disagreements on specific points
but considerable support for the general principle of providing security from common social hazards through such rights.[6]

Different types of costs are associated with low and high estimates of appropriate limits. Low estimates endanger the human
dignity and social membership status of vulnerable and disadvantaged citizens,[7] while high estimates demand more extensive resources and are more likely to overload the system and create
inequities between recipients of public social provision and the
lowest-paid self-supporting workers. At least in the short term
there can be little doubt that if socioeconomic rights are to be politically acceptable in the United States, low estimates about the
material limits of such rights are crucial. But benefits even more
limited than current AFDC payments could contribute effectively
to reasonable levels of household support if they were designed to
supplement household efforts at self-support and if external conditions facilitated self-support.

A related matter involves harmonizing social program practices with activities in other policy areas.[8] In the United States we have tended to isolate social programs rather than integrate them into broader public policy. But were we to use more-aggressive labor-market tactics in conjunction with social programs, households could rely more on efforts at self-support and less on transfer payments. The most obvious harmonization problems relate to general macroeconomic goals, particularly levels of unemployment and inflation.[9] We will return to these problems in chapters 5 and 6.

Preferences for Limited and Local Government

One element of Huntington's version of the American creed that I did not discuss in chapter 3 is the traditional American preference for limited and local government.[10] As a practical matter, any conception of American socioeconomic rights would require substantial activity by the federal government. This necessity clashes with traditional Lockean preferences for limited government, yet no advanced society—the United States included—has been willing to ignore its most vulnerable citizens for the sake of Lockean ideals. Rather the controversy focuses on the nature of the specific proportions or mechanisms of public social programs. Even some prominent libertarians acknowledge the appropriateness of using public programs to help vulnerable people whose needs market activities fail to address.[11]

In short, Americans prefer limited government, but this preference is generally wistful or abstract, rather than operational, and it does not inform everyday decisions. Indeed, in the absence of a powerful ideology and given the nation's transition from commercial capitalism to advanced industrial conditions, American wistfulness for limited government is anachronistic in practice.

Huntington also discusses Americans' preference for local government. Again, there is little doubt that this preference exists, as Tocqueville noted and other observers have since. Nevertheless, in a society in which centralization is the rule—big business, big labor, corporate agriculture, and big international adversaries—preferences for the predominance of local government are largely as wistful as the ones for limited government.[12]

At various times regional groups have exerted considerable influence to ensure a local voice in the administration of public social programs. In response to regional officials' desires to retain certain features of existing local practice, both the unemployment and public assistance portions of the Social Security Act of 1935 allow for state-level variations. Under these provisions, progressive Wisconsinites retained more-generous unemployment insurance features, while southerners delayed making equal public assistance payments to blacks.[13]

These precedents notwithstanding, there have been growing pressures for nationwide standardization in public social provision. Business groups, for example, favor standardization of the costs of employer contributions to ensure interstate competitiveness. And proponents of strong social programs see national standardization as both just and rational. Why, they ask, should recipients of a federal program like AFDC be subject to enormous variations in state-defined benefit levels? If program benefits sanctioned by positive law are rights or entitlements, then an individual's rights should not vary significantly as a result of place of residence.[14] The growing scope of social security, a program with no regional variations, has probably also contributed to perceptions that regional variations in national social program benefits are undesirable. Finally, regional variation and local discretion have been criticized by some as leading to systematic waste, by others as a tool for discriminating against some potential recipients.[15]

Finally, we must return again to the example of social security, a most highly centralized program that should have stirred the wrath of every American committed to limited and local government. Up until the politicization of the administration of social security in the 1970s, the program was widely regarded as exceptionally sound, fair, and efficient. Social security still enjoys great public confidence and support, even though it is intrusive (levying taxes on 90 percent of the labor force), large (consuming roughly 20 percent of the federal budget and 5 percent of GNP), highly centralized, and highly professionalized.

We should not use this example to advise public program planners to disregard the American preference for limited and local government. Social programs administered by sophisticated, centralized bureaucracies that allow little if any local discretion do pose some risks. But the histories of various American social programs suggest that these risks may be well worth taking, and that programs consonant with other American values will face less difficulty on this score.

Competing Interest Groups

Social programs, like other public policies, serve multiple and sometimes conflicting objectives, and conflicts among various groups seeking competing benefits from public social provision form another set of practical problems for the realization of socioeconomic rights.

At the top of any list of explicit objectives of public social provision would be helping the victims of social hazards; here the largest single constituency is the elderly. A related and frequently compatible objective of social programs lies in the contributions they make to macroeconomic policy. Since program benefits are usually spent or consumed directly and represent, to some degree, spending that would not otherwise occur, program expenditures encourage aggregate demand.[16] If such demand stimulates employment without fueling inflation, then the national economy as a whole prospers, and both public officials and the public generally enjoy the fruits of prosperity.

From the standpoint of the wealthy and powerful the resources that public social programs provide are redundant,[17] and elites have often fought the establishment or expansion of such programs. Nonetheless, the development of social programs can be interpreted as elite efforts to anticipate the problems of incorporating the working class into advanced societies.[18] For political leaders such programs offer opportunities to achieve their own ends either by building societal support or minimally reducing opposition. Whether or not social program platforms are productive means of electoral competition, political elites have at times perceived them in this fashion. Particularly in the United States it is probably appropriate to link social insurance programs to schemes of electoral competition and public assistance programs to concerns for placating potentially disruptive social groups.[19]

Under some circumstances the agendas of public elites and the needs of vulnerable citizens may overlap. For example, whichever political party increases pensions for the elderly may expect the votes of the elderly in the next election. But elite agendas, even when they call for social program development, may have objectives contrary to the interests of targeted recipients. For instance, Bismarck's pioneering social programs of the 1880s represented the carrot portion of a two-pronged strategy designed to reduce the political and economic influence of the left and to preserve the societal domination of a conservative state.[20] Similarly, contemporary American public assistance programs have been accused of being covert efforts to maintain a potentially disruptive population in a minimal, depreciating fashion that neutralizes recipients' political energies.[21]

Social programs also affect other particular groups: the public provision of medical care has increased the incomes of physicians and nursing homes; public housing programs benefit lending institutions, construction firms, landlords, and realtors; and public education benefits modern corporations and other employers with sophisticated personnel needs.[22] Beneficiaries such as these generally have interests distinct from those of the explicitly-targeted recipients of public social programs, and the former are generally better-organized, better-financed, and more experienced in gaining access to public decision makers. Policies fashioned to fit the political objectives of such groups may serve socioeconomic rights only incidentally and poorly. However, social provision policies that ignore the ends of these groups will probably face stiff resistance and low levels of compliance. For this reason, respect for the values of powerful groups is an important consideration in social program development. Social programs mean socioeconomic rights to some, but they mean income, profits, election success, or social control to others whose cooperation is necessary.

Reaching Potential Recipients

The young and the elderly draw, in different ways, more heavily on social provision programs than do middle-aged citizens. Serving these groups presents a variety of practical problems, to be sure, but these may be less serious than the difficulties of reaching potential recipients of the lowest socioeconomic status. The following generalizations may oversimplify a bit, but they suggest the kinds of practical problems that must be addressed.[23]

First, the lower a potential recipient's socioeconomic status, the less likely he or she is to know what benefits are available and how to apply for them.[24] Second, the more disadvantaged potential recipients tend to have poorer skills in dealing with the bureaucrats who serve as gatekeepers for social programs.[25] Third, the wider the gap in socioeconomic status between the professionals who deliver social services and recipients, the more both groups are apt to experience anxiety and reluctance about contact.[26] Fourth, persons in the lowest socioeconomic groups tend to be alienated by program features that represent the aspirations of mainstream culture but do not fit with their own experiences.[27] Finally, people lowest in the socioeconomic hierarchy tend to have less personal control over certain aspects of their activities, including those that relate to the objectives of social programs. For instance, their health may be threatened by a variety of environmental factors at work or at home over which they have little control.

One implication of these generalizations is that programs designed to ameliorate social disadvantage face more demanding tasks than do social insurance programs that cover episodic hazards.[28] A second implication is that public perceptions of a program's success are likely to be more negative if the socioeconomic status of recipients is relatively low. For instance, unemployment insurance—whatever its problems—has not been subject to the range and vehemence of criticism that AFDC—a form of unemployment support for the disadvantaged—has endured.

Some programs are also apt to face more difficulties in motivating recipient compliance. Compliance has been more of a problem in unemployment insurance programs than in pensions for the elderly. Murray's argument about the "unintended rewards" of unemployment benefits, the relief from drudgery that these benefits can bring, seems exaggerated.[29] But the incentives to use social programs to escape the unpleasant rigors of the market probably increase as these rigors increase—generally as we move down the socioeconomic ladder.

Guidelines for Action

Together the difficulties described in this chapter suggest that there
are clear limits on what government can successfully accomplish in
the field of public social provision. There are some meritorious
provision objectives that we cannot reasonably expect to fulfill.
And expectations for the United States should probably be narrower than those for nations in which popular orientations toward
government are more encouraging and public experiences in dealing with resource inadequacy problems are broader. In recognition
of the particularities of the American case, I propose four simple
guidelines for social programs designed to realize basic socioeconomic rights.[30]

First, these social programs should not expect or require dramatic changes in the activities of any of the actors—public officials, private service providers, recipients, and so on. Realizing
basic socioeconomic rights will require some important changes in
existing American practice, and incremental changes are not necessarily more apt to succeed than sharp ones.[31] Nonetheless, we
can reasonably expect that, when a worker who has disciplined
herself or himself to living within her or his income across a working life of four decades receives a pension, he or she will use the
pension to support her or his needs responsibly in retirement. But
asking for dramatic changes in recipients' activity may be asking
for trouble, as we learn when the public schools try to educate a
child whose home and peers provide little positive reinforcement
for doing well in school. In general, we can expect better outcomes
if public social policies do not require people to undertake new,
complicated activities that are incompatible with their cultural traditions, preferred life choices, or professional norms.

Second, social programs that require less complicated cooperation from actors—recipients, and public facilitators, or private
providers—are apt to be more effective than those requiring more.
Disbursing pensions to the elderly, for example, is easier than delivering medical care to the poor in part because the former can be
accomplished after a one-time enrollment on the pension distribution list, while the latter requires a series of cooperative endeav-
ors: the sick must consult health-care professionals whenever ill-

ness strikes, these professionals must be willing to provide care, and the recipients must follow their advice. To the degree that complicated cooperation is unavoidable, there are some benefits to centralizing its management and oversight within sophisticated professional bureaucracies.

Third, social programs are apt to produce more encouraging results if their design allows recipients, facilitators, and providers to keep their social status and personal dignity intact. Both specific design features and the general character of a program's targeting and visibility are at issue. A program, such as AFDC, that in effect penalizes efforts at self-support even as American culture creates expectations of self-support is incoherent and stigmatizing. And while there are exceptions, such as veterans' benefits, for which narrow targeting works, generally the more universal program targeting becomes, the less stigmatizing recipient status is apt to be. Broadly targeted programs also tend to have a better public image because elites are less likely to build destructive features into programs that serve broad constituencies. Additionally, inclusive programs that address the most frequent social hazards facilitate public empathy with the plight of program beneficiaries. The visibility of programs, particularly their visibility as social programs, is relevant here as well. Neither suburban commuters who make daily use of interstate highways explicitly constructed for defense purposes nor wealthy citizens whose tax breaks are presented as necessary prerequisites to economic recovery are perceived, by themselves or generally, as recipients of "welfare."

Fourth, social programs are more likely to achieve their objectives if all parties see the program requirements as consistent with desirable prior or concurrent activity. In broad terms, recipients need to know that benefit rights are earned by prior or concurrent contributions, and providers must feel that the services they are delivering meet contemporary professional standards.

Unfortunately, these four guidelines cannot be applied with equal ease (or sometimes even at all) in every instance. Social insurance programs directed toward episodic disruptions of income hold the greatest potential for fitting fairly well with all four. Such programs do not by nature require extensive changes in recipient activity; complicated cooperation can usually be left to centralized state bureaucracies; and rights are earned through prior, responsible activity that leaves the recipients' social status and self-respect unsullied.[32] Programs that entail the delivery of social services run afoul, minimally, of the second guideline. They require complicated cooperation from both recipients and relatively autonomous service providers, and many of these complications cannot be centralized.

Programs directed at persistent resource inadequacy face more difficult problems still. Generally these programs serve recipients of low socioeconomic status, and if they try to comply with the first two guidelines, they run afoul of the second pair and vice versa. That is, if a program does not ask recipients to substantially change their activities, then the general public is not likely to view recipients as engaging in responsible behavior, and recipients' social status, if not self-respect, is apt to suffer. The AFDC program has tried to cope with this dilemma in a variety of ways, but with no great success to date. If a program takes the contrary tack, it may well run into the problems associated with expecting dramatic behavioral changes and introducing forms of complicated cooperation.

The more general point is that modern governments, which necessarily rely on the impersonal operations of bureaucracies, are better suited to working with people's aspirations, opportunities, and capacities—as social insurance objectives generally allow—than for changing these factors, as programs targeted at severely disadvantaged recipients sometimes attempt to do. Program recipients nestled within the mainstream culture can usually take effective advantage of social programs to accomplish some objective they value—medical care, education, income maintenance—and to accomplish it in a socially approved way. But people located on the margins of society have greater difficulties, both with the bureaucratic mechanisms and the program objectives. Programs designed to help these people enter the mainstream may require complicated changes in recipients' activities; narrow targeting tends to stigmatize recipients; and efforts to link benefits to activities approved of by the mainstream public may seem insulting or menacing to recipients.[33]

Surely public programs can seek to ease the lives of socially disadvantaged citizens. But public efforts to "reform" the poor are frequently not necessary and, necessary or not, are only marginally productive.[34] Rather than imposing mainstream standards, public programs should try to work with whatever desires the disadvantaged have to merge with the socioeconomic mainstream by facilitating and supplementing their constructive efforts to do so. Little good can be expected of programs that force people into destitution in order to qualify for public social provision and that subsequently discourage their efforts at self-support.

Part Two

The Investments Approach to Social Programs

Introduction to Case Studies

In the preceding chapters I have examined several sets of obstacles to the establishment of basic socioeconomic rights and to the use of public social programs to realize these rights. I now want to apply these analyses to case studies of three existing programs. In turn, in chapter 8 I will integrate the conclusions of these case studies and detail a new approach—the investments approach— to American social provision.

The case studies presented here employ the focused comparison technique of Alexander George.[1] The following questions guide these studies:

Distributive Justice

What are the criteria for the distribution of benefits?

> Do they reflect effort or results and thus appeal to American concerns for human dignity and vertical equity?

> Do they reflect need? If so, are they categorical, thus raising concerns for horizontal equity? What mechanisms exist for certifying the need?

To what degree are benefits linked to the provision of basic goods?

To what degree does this program represent an attack on traditional property rights?

Negative Liberty and Individualism

Is the program compulsory or voluntary?

In what ways and roughly to what degree do the taxes supporting this program constrain liberty?

Aside from compulsory taxation, to what degree and in what ways
are the liberties of benefit recipients constrained?

To what degree and in what ways is the liberty of various third-
party providers constrained?

Economic Efficiency

To what degree and in what ways might this program stimulate or
retard propensities to work in the paid labor force?

To what degree and in what ways might this program stimulate or
retard household propensities to save?

To what degree and in what ways might this program influence the
propensity for corporate managers or entrepreneurs to take
risks?

To what degree and in what ways might this program influence the
international competitiveness of American goods and services?

What are the direct monetary costs of the program and who pays
them? Is redistribution horizontal, intergenerational, or vertical?

To what degree does this program target a population with particularly difficult problems? What, if any, disturbing consequences do these problems hold for program operations?

Administrative Complexity

How do the tasks the program requires relate to its administrative
capacities? What is the program's administrative efficiency?

How effectively are limits or harmonization problems managed?

How does the public profile of the program relate to abstract
American preferences for limited and local government?

Conflicts of Interest and Compliance

To what degree and in what ways does the program raise important conflicts of interest among explicitly targeted beneficiaries,
national government officials, and third-party (public or private)
providers?

To what degree and in what ways is the program structured to provide incentives for cooperation with program objectives from
explicitly targeted beneficiaries, national government officials,
and third-party (public or private) providers?

Five

Social Security

As a social insurance program that provides income protection against the hazards of old age, survivorship, and disability, social security represents a limited but generally encouraging model for the investments approach. Medicare, the medical services component of social security, involves both social insurance and other characteristics and is therefore discussed separately, in chapter 7.

Historical Background

The Social Security Act of 1935 marked the first inclusive, long-term effort on the part of the American national government to cope with social hazards.[1] Civil War pensions, for example, were both categorical and short-term. When these pensioners died off, the United States did not, as some progressives had hoped, follow the industrial nations of Western Europe in creating social insurance for the general population.[2] Instead, national government efforts declined, and there was less federal public social provision in the early twentieth century than there had been in the late nineteenth. A few state governments, spurred by the American Association of Labor Legislation and other groups, launched their own programs, but these efforts were slow and piecemeal at best.[3] The principal successes were in workers' compensation programs and, to a lesser degree, unemployment benefits and "widows' pensions."

The depression of the 1930s brought the national government back into the enterprise of helping victims of social hazards. Prior to 1940, however, this help came in the form of emergency programs offering work or public assistance in response to the exceptional difficulties posed by the worldwide economic crisis. The Social Security Act, meager as its initial provisions now seem, was the first effort on the part of the national government to help vulnerable citizens generally and on a continuing basis. The Social Security Board (SSB) portions of the 1935 act involved three programs: unemployment; public assistance for poor elderly and blind citizens (now SSI) as well as some children (now AFDC); and—of least significance at the time—social insurance for the elderly.

Payroll taxes, an equal and modest 1 percent of a $3,000 wage base on both employer and employee, were instituted in 1937; at that time only workers employed in good-sized private industrial and commercial operations were covered. Under the original plan, modest benefits, starting at $10 a month, were to begin in 1942. But in 1939 the initiation of benefits was moved up to 1940, and eligibility was extended to dependents of both retired and deceased covered workers. This had the effect of shifting social security from a reserve to a pay-as-we-go system.[4] Additionally, SSB became part of the newly created Federal Security Agency and no longer routinely reported directly to the president. In 1946 SSB was renamed the Social Security Administration (SSA), and in 1949 the unemployment compensation program was moved to the Department of Labor.

Under a major expansion of social security in 1950, benefits were raised by about 75 percent, coverage was extended to self-employed persons and domestic and farm laborers, and state and local government employees were given the option of participating. In 1953 SSA became part of the new Department of Health, Education, and Welfare (HEW). The expansion of eligibility and increases in benefits, tax rates, and the wage base continued such that by 1954 benefits were about double their pre-1950 level, and the vast majority of the labor force was covered.

After a lengthy struggle, disability coverage was added in 1956. Other changes included the extension of coverage to professional groups and the liberalizing of rules, particularly with respect to disability claims. Administration of public assistance was transferred in 1963 to a newly created bureau within HEW. Health insurance for the elderly (Medicare), the focus of a gargantuan debate, was introduced in 1965; SSI, a public assistance program for

poor, blind, elderly, and disabled citizens and administered by social security, was inaugurated in 1974. Throughout this period, the
tax rate and wage base continued to climb.

The new era of expansion begun in the early 1970s marked a
break with SSA's tradition of careful growth shepherded by the
program's senior executives and a pair of congressional commit-
tees (Ways and Means in the House, and Finance in the Senate).
Some attribute the impetus for growth to the ambitious aspirations
of Robert M. Ball, then the SSA commissioner, and his fellow
executives. But a variety of interest groups and public officials were
also eager to see the program expand. Generous increases in benefits proved to be politically popular, and benefits were raised by 15
percent in 1969, by 10 percent in 1971, by 20 percent in 1972, and
by roughly 10 percent in 1973–74.

Two dramatic changes were introduced in 1972. First, benefits
were to be subject to automatic cost-of-living increases. Some proponents argued that price-indexing was essential to ensuring steady
purchasing power, thus maintaining the relationship between benefits and need. Others viewed the automatic increases as a politically expedient way of rationalizing election-year increases in
benefits.

The second change concerned the economic assumptions to be
used in calculating the program's future stream of revenues. From
the early 1950s the program had calculated its fiscal soundness
through a comparison of future liabilities and income. Under an
assumption that the program would be continued indefinitely, social security, in contrast to private insurance programs, had not at-
tempted to accrue the funds to cover all future liabilities. Rather, it
sought balance through assuring the future revenues to cover these
liabilities. One aspect of the calculation of future revenues involved
the *level wage assumption,* under which future revenues were estimated on the basis of current wage levels. But since wages increased over time, the level wage assumption repeatedly produced
short-term surpluses. This manner of calculation, with its built-in
margin for error, typified the conservative approach of SSA executives during the program's formative years. The dropping of the
level wage assumption in 1972, however, removed this actuarial
cushion.

Unfortunately, these two changes were enacted just as the economy slipped into stagflation. The ensuing double-digit inflation meant hefty annual increases in benefits, while high levels of unemployment meant lower revenues for the program.[5] Short-term deficits occurred and long-term deficits were predicted, based on the falling worker-beneficiary ratio forecast for the early twenty-first century. For the first time since the program's earliest years, serious concerns were voiced about social security's financial solvency.

These difficulties gave rise to a decade-long struggle over funding and benefit practices.[6] Both the Carter and Reagan administrations took modest measures to cut costs and increase revenues. If these measures are maintained, the program will be solvent through the year 2025, but more fundamental changes are likely to be necessary to accommodate the long-term decline in the worker-beneficiary ratio.

Despite current efforts to slow program growth, social security has continued to expand, both in the numbers of labor-force participants and beneficiaries and in absolute and relative costs. In 1986, nearly 38 million Americans (slightly less than 20 percent of the population) received cash transfers from social security, and benefits are now, even by Western European standards, fairly generous. Although opposition to particular operational aspects has been growing, the program remains popular, and many would agree that "the social security system is among the most effective and successful institutions ever developed in the United States."[7] As noted in earlier chapters, much of social security's success and popularity reflects the visions of its creators, who presented their innovative program in terms of cherished American political symbols. More importantly, the success of social security in helping citizens survive old age and disability in a dignified manner has indelibly influenced Americans' attitudes toward the general concept of public social provision.

Distributive Justice

Social security operationalizes a sense of vertical, or work, equity.[8] Recipients have extensive work histories (or, minimally, work histories covering the bulk of their adult lives) and have made regular contributions through payroll taxes.[9] The program posed some horizontal, or support, equity problems for workers who were ineligible because of their age at the time social security was initiated, and a few related problems occasionally arise. However, today roughly nine of every ten workers and retirees participate in the program.[10] The largest single group of workers currently not covered are federal government employees, who have their own pension programs, but under current legislation, they will eventually be brought into social security. For employees of state and local governments, participation in the program is optional but widespread.

Eligibility for social security benefits has been based on a rigorous interpretation of the investments (effort) principle of distributive justice, to use Hochschild's terms.[11] Benefits may be viewed as a reward for regular exertion in the paid labor force (or, minimally, for being a dependent of such a person). The scaling of benefits to wage histories fits Hochschild's criterion of results, although since the early 1970s the overall benefit structure has been redirected toward meeting basic needs.

This firm link to regular participation in the work force has facilitated SSA's argument that recipients have an earned right to their benefits, a point bolstered by the use of carefully selected terms: "contributions," rather than "taxes," for example. The most important rhetorical strategy in distinguishing these earned rights from other forms of social provision has been the concept of individual social security accounts. By calling the records of workers' payroll taxes "accounts," the creators of social security effectively evoked the image of bank accounts, sums of money that workers accumulate through their contributions and that are held in their names by the SSA.[12] And while recipients of means-tested public assistance must exhaust their resources in order to receive benefits, social security recipients simply draw on their personal accounts of prior contributions regardless of current means or need. This concept of earned rights to public income-maintenance benefits rather nicely conforms to American attitudes about human dignity, self-reliance, and self-help, thus clearly distinguishing social security recipients from the "undeserving poor."

Because need is not a criterion for receiving benefits, the program cannot ensure that benefits are used for basic needs rather than for frivolous luxuries. But we have good reasons to assume that most benefits paid out through the mid-1970s were spent on basic needs. For one, professionals and some other high-income workers were not covered by the initial act; physicians, for instance, were not added to the program until 1965. Additionally, because social security was designed to supplement individual initiative with respect to thrift and savings, the proportion of a retiree's former earnings that benefits provide, the replacement rate, is generally low—around 25 percent for high-income recipients, rising to 40 percent for medium incomes, and climbing to 55 percent or so for those with low incomes.[13] Indeed, state means-tested benefits have frequently been more liberal than social security pensions. Even in the early 1980s the minimum annual benefit was only $1,464, and the average monthly pension for a couple was $640.[14] Earned (but not unearned) income greater than a specified amount (currently $7,500) reduces—and once eliminated—benefits.

Since the mid-1970s the system has included increasing numbers of high-income citizens, and benefit levels have risen. But not until 1980 did the percentage of elderly households below the official poverty thresholds fall to levels similar to those among the population at large.[15] To some degree the formula by which benefits are calculated offsets recent trends. While the dollar value of benefits is directly related to recipients' earnings histories, the replacement rate rises as income falls.[16] In contrast, the peculiarities of the indexing system adopted in the early 1970s led for a time to gradually rising replacement rates for everyone.

From the standpoint of an individual the redistribution that social security entails can be described as life-cycle: a covered individual contributes to the system when he or she is working and draws benefits when covered social hazards interrupt or halt employment. In comparison to means-tested programs that characteristically redistribute from more affluent strata to the poor, social security thus cannot be viewed as an attack on traditional property rights or wealth. As we will see, even the moderately progressive replacement rates are offset to some degree by regressive taxation and differences in the contributor-recipient ratios of high- and low-income workers.

Given the increases in benefit levels, the rising proportion of affluent beneficiaries, and the concerns about the program's financial solvency, it is no surprise that social security has in recent years attracted wider critical attention.

Negative Liberty

Involuntary participation was an issue in the legislative wrangling over the 1935 Social Security Act; some analysts and officials preferred a system of voluntary annuities. But since then, involuntary participation has spawned surprisingly little criticism, except from the libertarian position.[17] This counterintuitive development may be an example of Americans' operational or pragmatic views overwhelming more Lockean abstract or ideological views. But social security has also represented an extraordinarily good investment. Recipients have to date received vastly more in benefits than they have contributed in taxes, and benefits have, particularly over the last fifteen years, offered protection against inflation that few private annuities could equal.[18]

Social security taxes a fixed percentage of a given wage base—currently (1988–89) 7.51 percent on $45,000. Employers match the worker's contribution. This tax is minimally not progressive in that it takes an equal proportion of earnings from low- and medium-wage earners within the wage base, and it is regressive in that people who earn beyond the wage base pay a lower overall rate. SSA has argued over the years that the progressivity built into the benefit structure adequately compensates for this tax regressivity, but not all analysts are convinced on this point.[19] One problem with SSA's interpretation is that low-income workers tend to spend a greater period of their lives under this tax structure than do high-income workers, who usually start working later in life. And low-income workers often die younger than do professionals, so the former spend a smaller portion of their lives under the progressive benefit structure.

Social security taxes clearly reduce discretionary income, and for many low-income workers social security taxes exceed their federal income taxes. But aside from the compulsory reduction of discretionary income, the program leaves recipients unconstrained. Because it is a national program, there are no residency restrictions; nor do workers forfeit any contribution credits when they change jobs—a penalty often levied by private retirement pensions.

One of the virtues of direct national government delivery of social programs without third-party intervention is that it obviates
complaints about constraints on the liberty of providers. Whenever private physicians have to alter their customary and preferred
practices in order to deal with Medicare or other public patients,
they can complain that the state constrains their freedom. But social security does not divert providers from their normal tasks to
deal with paperwork or transfer payments. Even in the disability
program, where SSA relies on state-level vocational rehabilitation
agencies, public restrictions on the liberty of private providers are
inconsequential.

Economic Efficiency

Relations between social security and various aspects of economic
efficiency are disputed.[20] With respect to social security's effect on
work incentives for working-aged adults, some economists see a
substitution effect: As taxes reduce the return from work, individuals increasingly prefer leisure. But other economists see an income
effect: Higher tax burdens increase the need to work in order to
take home enough to meet fixed or rising household expenses.[21]
Under the latter assumption, however, off-the-books moonlighting
may seem preferable to labor that is taxed—a phenomenon that
undermines social security's revenue base.[22]

Social security entails some work incentives, but their importance is disputed. The central incentive is that a steady work history will be rewarded by an economically secure retirement.[23] However, a worker armed with "economic man" preferences and good
information would not necessarily produce steadily over a working
life of thirty or forty years on the basis of this incentive alone, since
social security does not require more than ten years of effort for
any category of benefit. Clearly, other incentives—eating in the in-
terim—come into play, and the middle-class character of social security recipients probably reinforces these incentives. By and large
social security beneficiaries believe, in part on the basis of their life
experiences, that effort returns a variety of encouraging results.
Also, in contrast to private or union pensions, social security facilitates labor mobility, easing for instance, the process of mid-career
workers shifting from sunset to sunrise industries.

For recipients, the program provides modest work incentives. For example, the earnings test that defines retirement has risen steadily over the years, and the current $7,500 disregard provides an incentive for productive labor. But overall social security appears to act as a work disincentive for those eligible for retirement or disability.[24] This disincentive is probably stronger for those whose jobs offer few if any intrinsic rewards and for those whose jobs entail hard physical labor. Whether these disincentives are bad is a separate question. During the Great Depression a program that enticed older workers into retirement and made room for unemployed younger workers in the labor force was desirable. As the worker-beneficiary ratio continues to decline, however, these same disincentives may be undesirable. To contain costs, Congress is likely to raise the age at which people become eligible for benefits. But such a move could threaten program work incentives if people, especially low-income workers, cannot reasonably expect to collect benefits for more than a few years.

Some aspects of the survivors and particularly the disability portions of social security have been criticized as sufficiently generous to discourage recipients from working, especially if their options for work are dreary, dirty, or dangerous jobs that offer no rewards other than money. In seeking to protect working-aged adults from episodic social hazards, this argument runs, social security may create "unintended rewards" for experiencing such hazards.

The question of how social security influences the risk-taking decisions of corporate managers or entrepreneurs involves subtle judgments about the relative strength of other factors—such as social security's consequences for work incentives and saving—that are themselves hotly disputed. One smaller issue is, however, clear: social security does increase the cost of doing business. The costs related to handling the paperwork afflict all employers roughly equally, but economists disagree on the effects of the payroll tax. To the degree that this tax—particularly the employers' portion— is considered an added expense necessitated by the program, social security does raise the cost of doing business and thus discourage some risk taking. But to the degree that the payroll tax is considered deferred wages that would go directly to the employee in the program's absence, this deleterious effect disappears. This latter interpretation seems less applicable on the fringes of the labor

market, among small-scale employers or relatively unskilled workers, but even in the mainstream economy social insurance costs
may contribute to incentives to move jobs offshore, particularly to
third-world countries.

Because payroll taxes contribute to the costs of production, one
might also argue that social security hampers the international
competitiveness of American goods and services. But cost is by no
means the sole determinant of competitiveness. BMWs are not
clogging American highways because they are less expensive than
Mercurys or Buicks. More importantly, the people who manufac-
ture BMWs pay higher social insurance costs than do American
producers. Thus it does not seem appropriate to lay any significant
portion of the blame for America's competitiveness problems on
social security taxes.

Although the United States does not spend as large a percentage
of GNP on public social provision as do most other advanced industrial societies, against the consciousness of American political
elites and the population generally, social security commands impressive resources.[25] And there is the temptation to think that
somewhere in the $202 billion that SSA expended in 1987 there
exists waste. In response, SSA has repeatedly boasted that administrative operations consume only 1 to 2 percent of revenues, a low
rate by comparison with most other social programs or private insurance operations. SSA has also reminded the public that, since
no general revenues are used, the costs of the system are borne entirely by the beneficiaries. While this is in a sense true, the pay-as-
we-go funding means that current workers are paying for current
beneficiaries, and in turn they hope to be supported by the next
generation of workers.

During the program's early years, these intergenerational transfers did not attract great attention or create funding difficulties.
The program was largely perceived as facilitating a life-cycle redistribution, with old-age benefits bearing a direct and sensible relationship to a recipient's prior contributions. But once benefits substantially exceed contributions—even when adjusted for interest,
inflation, and greater productivity with higher standards of living—
systematic disparities develop and the intergenerational redistribution cannot easily be recouped.

American social security, like the social insurance systems of many other advanced societies, currently faces this difficulty. To the degree that Americans take their individual claims to benefits on an "I paid for my benefits!" criterion as opposed to a more general good-faith effort approach, their claims are dubious.[26]

In order to reduce these intergenerational transfers to reasonable proportions, several changes regarding program taxes and benefits have already been legislated for introduction later. Further changes seem likely. Overall, the program will probably continue to shift further away from a defined-benefit approach and toward a defined-contribution approach.[27]

Finally, on the criterion of target efficiency, the degree to which benefits are focused on the neediest, social security by design gets generally low marks. Unlike a public assistance program intended to help the impoverished, a system of social insurance serves a socioeconomic cross-section of the public and aims to keep those who confront various episodic hazards from falling into poverty. Thus target efficiency is not among the criteria relevant to the evaluation of social security.

Administrative Complexity

Social security is a federal program that for the most part does not rely on state or local officials. In centralized Baltimore offices, national officials rather quietly carry out an array of complex operations: actuarial calculations, rule development and interpretation, and record keeping. SSA's fairly clear, if not exceptionally simple, instructions do not allow for much decentralized discretion in its field offices. Thus while social security is not a simpler program than the notoriously complex AFDC, its complexities are centralized and hidden, and recipients and the public generally perceive its operations as relatively straightforward. Senior program administrators have also been efficient and effective in choreographing adroit political maneuvers to ensure the program's popular success.[28] Until the early 1970s SSA executives confidently knew what needed to be done to fulfill the program's objectives, had the requisite expertise to plan the necessary tasks, and had the autonomy to execute and monitor their plans.

Since then, program executives have seen the size and complexity of their tasks grow while their autonomy has been eroded by the executive and legislative branches.[29] Given that social security now touches the vast majority of American households, it is not surprising that Congress and the White House have begun to take more interest in the program. In the face of increasing outside intervention in program decisions, even this gifted and devoted program bureaucracy can no longer assure a high degree of administrative efficiency.

Executive and congressional interventions designed to counter funding shortfalls have also focused attention on several distinct limits issues. The first, sometimes referred to as the adequacy-equity dilemma, concerns in part the adequacy of benefits for workers in the lower socioeconomic strata. By design, social security does not single out pockets of exceptional disadvantage and focus its resources on them. Indeed, the program's contributory prerequisites exclude the most disadvantaged, and retirees with histories of low earnings qualify for only modest pensions. At the program's founding, problems of social disadvantage were believed to lay in the bailiwick of short-term public assistance. Public-employment efforts begun during the Great Depression and worldwide economic recovery were expected to ease unemployment, and the addition of survivors benefits to social security would, it was hoped, eventually eliminate the need for public assistance. This view, however, overestimated the national commitment to full employment and overlooked social discrimination, structural unemployment, the inadequacy of the wage structure for household support, and the resulting underclass. Today it seems both necessary and reasonable to ask social insurance to do more than social security now does for the disadvantaged. Early SSA administrators were probably correct that "a program for the poor is a poor program."[30] Precisely because this is so, the disadvantaged must be incorporated into broadly inclusive insurance programs to the maximum degree that the nature of their resource inadequacy problems allows.

The equity aspect of the dilemma emerges at the other end of the socioeconomic spectrum in the practice of granting relatively high benefits to persons with substantial unearned income. Social security currently serves some households that cannot reasonably be seen as experiencing a social hazard. But halting earned benefits in instances in which aging poses no financial threat carries the risk of diluting the firm association social security currently has for Americans with principles of distributive justice of which they generally approve—effort and results.

An independent limits concern stems from the narrowness of the range of social hazards that social security covers. In addition to the deficiencies with respect to the three social hazards that are covered, social security offers no general security against catastrophic illness or against wage disruption due to childbirth and or child-rearing to name two basic gaps in protection.

Because social security focuses almost exclusively on people who are no longer expected to work due to age or disability, until recently the program had not prompted many of the harmonization concerns that frequently arise in discussions of social programs. One of the rationales used to sell social security to a hesitant Congress in the 1930s was the encouraging effect it was anticipated to have on aggregate demand, and there is little reason to suspect that these hopes have gone unfulfilled. Precise effects are difficult to estimate, but most social security benefits are spent rather than saved, so they contribute, minimally, to maintaining demand and employment levels. That these benefits therefore also contribute to inflation did not until recently attract a great deal of attention from economists, with the exception of caveats against the double indexing of the 1972 benefit increases (corrected in 1977). Today, however, the overall size of the program, particularly in conjunction with recent federal budget deficits, casts an increasingly long shadow over federal fiscal policy. In the words of Peter G. Peterson, a former secretary of commerce, "the prospects for social security and for general prosperity are now inseparable."[31]

As noted earlier, social security has had an odd relationship with American concerns for limited and local government. The Roosevelt administration's initial plan for social security was assaulted by Townsendites, among others, as too little, too late for the elderly who faced immediate resource inadequacy problems. At the same time, the Chamber of Commerce and the American Medical Association (AMA) decried the compulsory program as an attack on individual freedom and discretionary income.

In anticipation of these latter concerns, the program's formulators made every effort to distinguish social security from the limited and rather disappointing record of previous American efforts at public social provision. So, for example, the SSB portion of the 1935 Social Security Act did not use the term *social insurance*. Two separate bills, one authorizing the collection of payroll taxes by the Treasury and the other authorizing the appropriation of these revenues by SSB, were based, respectively, on Congress' power to tax and appropriate funds.[32]

Surprisingly, amidst all this hostility, social security prospered. The Great Depression no doubt facilitated the acceptance of the three-rights conception of democracy and the contemporary conception of human dignity, but most appealing was the program's firm basis in the effort-oriented principle of distributive justice. As social security grew to benefit a larger group of people more thoroughly, it increasingly fulfilled its theoretical underpinnings, which in turn themselves became more popular despite American preferences for limited and local government.

Conflicts of Interest and Compliance

Since social security's inception, SSB/SSA program executives have been the public elites most actively involved with social security policymaking. If we examine their initiatives over time, it is hard to argue that they have not been concerned with the objective of helping vulnerable citizens.[33] The disparities between SSA preferences and what we might regard as recipient interests reflect in part matters of timing and emphasis. The cautious, conservative approach adopted by SSB in the early days can be justified by the need to carve out a secure niche for the immature system in a hostile environment. Nonetheless, as Jerry Cates convincingly argues, several preeminent SSB executives were also swayed by their pre–New Deal experiences with the Wisconsin school of social policy.[34] Their idea about the proper way to handle social hazards, which Cates terms "conservative social insurance," led them to limit the initial extent of social security benefits and to later reject various liberalizing alternatives. All in all, program executives were more concerned with safeguarding the philosophy and form of their new program than with addressing the needs of the nation's depression-era elderly.

From the mid-1950s on, as social security officials became less fearful of their opponents, the program's conservative orientation became less obvious, and an effective incremental approach to program development was adopted.[35] But program executives still insisted on extensive and limiting eligibility prerequisites, the supplemental and wage-based character of social security benefits, and financing through regressive taxation. Since program executives were far more involved in initiating policy than were others in the legislative or executive branches,[36] their conceptions prevailed. In the 1950s, however, increases in social security benefits were a relatively common accoutrement of election years, and by the late 1960s political candidates enthusiastically associated themselves with program development. And while Congress exhibited considerable reluctance with respect to initiating disability benefits, once the disability program was in place, members of Congress tended to side with disgruntled disability applicants against SSA. To many beneficiaries' advantage, SSA executives are no longer the independent arbiters of their interests.

Employers represent another affected constituency, with the program dependent on employers' cooperation in completing the paperwork and paying their share of the payroll tax. Collectively, individual small-scale employers can limit the program's reach at the fringes of the labor market. Employers of domestic workers and restaurant help have at times circumvented social security by imposing exchanges of desperation on their employees. Other than that, private third-party providers are involved only marginally (disability determination) in the non-Medicare operations of social security.

In the area of compliance with program objectives, social security offers various incentives. For the working-age population, the program reinforces socially approved behavior, namely working regularly and earning as much as possible in covered employment.[37] The program's capacity for relying on positive reinforcement is bolstered by two exceptional features of retirement as a social hazard. First, it happens to most people and, second, it happens at a fairly predictable time, late in life. A social program aimed at the elderly thus avoids the disincentive problems that plague such programs as unemployment insurance.

Up to now, participant noncompliance with the retirement aspects of social security has come only from small, fairly unrepresentative groups. For instance, some workers would like to opt out of social security, arguing that they could do better financially with a private alternative. Other workers, particularly those in low-income jobs, are troubled by the tax bite and seek work in the un-recorded labor market.

Recipient noncompliance with social security's disability provisions is more problematic. Although the disability program remains a modest portion of social security ($23 billion as opposed to $171 billion in 1986),[38] the number of recipients has grown much more rapidly than was anticipated. It is hard to ignore the possibility that people working in low-paying, dispiriting jobs may abuse the program, and the potential for such abuse cannot be eliminated entirely. During the lengthy struggle to add disability coverage to social security, Roswell B. Perkins, an assistant secretary of HEW, argued forcefully that a safeguard would be provided by having disability determined by state vocational rehabilitation agencies.[39] But the recent growth of disability claims suggests that a revised approach may be needed.

Through it all, SSB and SSA program executives have perceived themselves to be acting in the national interest, and their actions represent a relatively rare example in which statist interpretations fit American politics.[40] In the last fifteen years the executive branch has increasingly sought to slow the proportion of national resources consumed by social security. This effort will necessarily continue. But antagonistic third-parties such as the Chamber of Commerce and the AMA are unlikely to overturn the program. Even if a serious intergenerational struggle develops over social security in the early twenty-first century, the program might be altered but hardly scrapped.

Summary and Implications

Despite recent controversies, against the criteria applied here social security is a strong program that enjoys an exceptionally encouraging set of attributes from the perspective of the American political culture. Some of social security's strengths, however, cannot be transferred to programs directed at other social hazards. As a public pension program for the elderly, social security intrinsically enjoys greater popular support than any other category of public social provision.[41] The program's inclusiveness is clearly one attraction: though not everyone lives to be elderly, most people probably expect and hope to do so, whereas far fewer people expect or minimally hope to experience serious illness, unemployment, disability, or divorce. Additionally, by and large it is not difficult to make the case that elderly recipients have made some contribution to society. Further, the social hazard of retirement is clearly defined by age, although specific eligibility rules (age 62, 65, or 67) may be controversial. Also, the program has a relatively stable beneficiary population, a characteristic that facilitates efficient administration. Recipients die, but rarely do they move off and then back on the rolls.

In contrast, those strengths of social security that arise either from the inherent characteristics of social insurance or from certain politically acceptable design features could be extended to other social hazards. Among these strengths are the focus on distributive justice, the prerequisite of sustained effort, the indexing of benefits to prior wages, and the supplementary character of benefits. The theme of personal accounts, which gives workers a sense of having a personal stake in the program, is preferable to the unemployment insurance system's reliance on employer accounts. Additionally, social security, apart from the taxation it entails, poses few constraints on negative liberty or property. And since social security taxes are regressive, the wealthy cannot on the whole claim that they are paying for benefits accorded to others, even though the benefit formula is progressive. The economic features of the program include some work incentives and some support for aggregate demand and employment. While the cost of the program is high, this cost is in a sense borne by the beneficiaries, although potential intergenerational inequities exist. Finally, because the program targets a fairly representative cross-section of the population, recipients are not stigmatized.

This degree of fit between social security practice and the values of distributive justice, negative liberty, and economic efficiency is insufficient for strict libertarians and free-marketeers. But as social programs go, social security involves less conflict with these values than do some others.

The practical virtues of social security may also provide useful models for other programs. SSA executives have accrued an enviable record of administrative efficiency, and their strong commitment to their vision of what the program should become has contributed importantly to improving American attitudes toward public social provision.

Additionally, social security relies heavily on a structure of incentives that allows for the positive reinforcement of interests people have for acting in productive, responsible ways. It does so by rewarding work and thrift.[42] It enables people to meet some of life's most disturbing hazards in a dignified socially approved way.

Juxtaposed to these strengths are some weaknesses. Social security creates a pattern of distribution that deviates from what the market would produce. The intergenerational transfers occurring now are hardly modest, and whenever a larger generation is followed by a smaller one, the systematic granting of benefits that vastly exceed contributions are apt to produce serious funding difficulties and intergenerational resentment.[43] Imbalances between benefits and contributions also become more troubling as a growing proportion of benefits flow to households for whom retirement does not produce much economic vulnerability or constitute a social hazard.

Another potentially disruptive facet of social security derives from its constraints on individualism and negative liberty. Thus far, however, the program's compulsory character has not been keenly contested. This is a surprise, given the position of negative liberty in American political culture. One explanation may be that social security has represented a good deal financially. And perhaps various features of the program's design offset the provocation that compulsory participation poses for individualism and negative liberty.

With respect to economic efficiency, social security clearly reduces the work incentives of people over sixty-five. In 1935 this disincentive was deemed desirable; today many argue the opposite. As a program financed through payroll deductions, social security contributes to production costs. So in both cost-push and demand-pull senses, the program contributes to inflation. As we have seen, however, we cannot attribute America's lack of competitiveness to social security.

In theory social security may be faulted for violating American preferences for limited and local government, but in practice this clash has not affected the program's popularity. Again, this counterintuitive result most likely reflects the program's design: complex operations are centralized in low-profile, efficiently administered bureaucracies.

Despite social security's track record as a good deal, until recently the retirement benefits have been of questionable adequacy. The introduction of Medicare in 1965 and the cost-indexing of benefits have provided some remedies. But social security's targeting of both social hazards and population remains limited, and the program thus presents some horizontal or support equity problems.

Finally, it is reasonable to expect that current obligations to future beneficiaries in conjunction with the declining ratio of workers to beneficiaries portends increased conflict over social security. When the interests of elected officials, SSA administrators, workers, and beneficiaries differ, the burden is all too likely to be borne by the most vulnerable.

That the preceding list of weaknesses and potential problems has not seriously undermined social security's political popularity and programmatic success suggests that some of social security's strengths eclipse its weaknesses—such as its compulsory character, its size, and its central administration. Part of social security's aura derives from its focus on retirement and is not transferable to other social programs. But social security's three quintessential design features can be applied to other forms of social provision: (1) eligibility rests on doing what society deems appropriate for able-bodied adults—working regularly and building a private contribution to financial security; (2) efforts exerted in the labor force create a clear index by which rights to social insurance benefits are earned; and (3) the program's specific features and language evoke symbols richly laden with traditional American values. Such design features have been crucial to the success and political viability of social security, and they can be adapted and extended to protect Americans against some social hazards now under the aegis of public assistance, as my proposals in chapter 8 will show.

Six

Aid to Families with Dependent Children

AFDC is a public assistance program designed to mitigate some consequences of destitution for a category of the poor. While AFDC is managed pursuant to national guidelines, states have considerable leeway with respect to specifics. This case study emphasizes the common features of program operation.

Historical Background

In the Anglo-American tradition, children in households that cannot support them have long been considered among the "deserving poor" who are thought to merit public support.[1] In the United States the institutions for such support have changed over time. In the nineteenth century widows unable to support their children frequently had to give them up. In the twentieth century, at the prodding of reform groups, several states enacted guidelines for "widows' pensions." Local options were allowed, and the discretion of local administering officials was generally broad. This precedent of state and local control exerted a fateful influence on the organization of the public assistance and unemployment insurance programs established by the Social Security Act of 1935. Both the officials (many of whom were from Wisconsin) who dominated the executive initiatives and numerous state congressional delegations were anxious to shield peculiarities of existing state programs from federal intervention.[2] So, unlike social security, both public assistance and unemployment insurance were constituted as state programs under loose federal guidelines.[3]

From 1935 through 1962 Aid to Dependent Children (ADC), as the program was then known, was managed by the Bureau of Public Assistance under the direction of SSB/SSA. The national government set standards—generally procedural rules—and provided a portion of program funds. In essence ADC made transfer payments, with the titular beneficiaries being children in households whose adults were unable to support them. By and large these households were headed by unmarried, divorced, or widowed women who had few, if any, vocational skills and little experience in the labor market.

SSB officials prefered social insurance to public assistance. They saw the latter as an exceptional response to the Great Depression, and they thought that the need for ADC would gradually wither away. But to officials' consternation, the use of ADC increased in the late 1940s and accelerated in the 1950s. Between 1950 and 1960 the number of children in the program increased from slightly less than 1 million to over 2.5 million; during the 1960s repeated efforts to slow program expansion were met by a nearly identical increase in the number of families served. Although the relative importance of various factors contributing to this growth was disputed, much of the growth during the sixties is attributable to an increase in the proportion of eligible families making use of the program.[4]

SSA officials were severely pressed to account for these trends.[5] The Depression was long over and yet use of ADC was higher than ever. Based on the experience of ADC's predecessors, particularly state-initiated widows' pensions, officials had at first assumed that ADC would serve primarily a population of children whose fathers had died. When survivors' benefits were added to social security in 1939, it seemed reasonable to project that ADC would wither away, given the economy's long-term capacity to provide new jobs and the continuation of public employment efforts. The withering thesis reflects as well the limited scope of earlier local and state-level relief efforts that the federal government was now beginning to coordinate and help fund. These local programs had made relatively little effort to plumb the depths of social disadvantage. Widows' pensions, for example, went almost exclusively to white widows, and even among this group a variety of explicit and tacit restrictions limited claims. SSA's view also reflected naivete with respect to social disadvantage. SSA executives understood episodic social hazards such as aging, disability, illness, and even unemployment, but they were far less aware of the size and problems of the nation's socially disadvantaged underclass. They did not contrue "the poor" as a focus for public policy; their primary concern was keeping the elderly and others with records of regular self-support from joining the poor.

But by the mid-1950s it was clear that divorce and desertion, rather than widowhood, were accounting for the growing numbers of women that ADC served. Some observers argued that ADC in effect encouraged desertion by restricting eligibility to households with no able-bodied adult male—even as the national economy hindered males with relatively modest job skills (thus a high proportion of minority males) from finding steady employment and wages sufficient to support a family. While most ADC recipients were (and still are today) white, the proportion of minority recipients was increasing, and in the large cities they were becoming a highly visible and concentrated group. Through the early 1960s ADC appears to have served to a considerable degree as a substitute for unemployment insurance for these families: as nonwhite male unemployment increased or decreased, so did ADC cases.[6]

The problems of family instability among households on the economic fringes of society were far more complex and intractable than those the program's initiators had foreseen. In 1962 the program was renamed and transferred to a new bureau, roughly the coequal of SSA, within the Department of Health, Education, and Welfare. The new AFDC included a variety of social services— family planning, basic adult education, child-care, vocational rehabilitation, and employment assistance—designed to increase the likelihood of employment among adults in recipient households.[7] After 1962 a series of new programs—AFDC-UP for unemployed fathers, Community Work and Training (CWT), Work Experience Training (WET), and Work Incentive (WIN)—combined AFDC benefits and job training with the ultimate objective of enabling families to become self-supporting. As we will see later in this chapter, these new efforts all foundered on a combination of inadequate labor market opportunities, design features that created weak work incentives, and problems particular to program recipients. Despite these failures, reformers clung to an implicit version of the withering thesis. They persevered in the objective of reducing the AFDC recipient population.

Both the population designated as impoverished by federal guidelines and the population that uses AFDC have fairly high rates of turnover.[8] Thus while poverty and AFDC usage are transitory conditions for many, the pools of persons experiencing poverty and AFDC usage over the span of a decade are quite large, about a quarter of the American population in each case.[9] Furthermore, AFDC serves recipients with two distinctive patterns of use. Most recipient households use the program episodically to cope with a given social hazard—the loss of a job or separation of parents—whose resolution generally leads to leaving the program.[10] For the most part these households have modest resources in the best of times, and their need for public assistance can be prompted by relatively modest hazards. In addition, parents in these households are frequently among the nearly one-third of the American work force to whom unemployment benefits are not extended.

Although public perceptions of widespread persistent use plague AFDC, less than 3 percent of the U.S. population, disproportionately urban and black, persistently use AFDC, and persistent dependence (relying on AFDC for over half of family income) is less than one-half of this level.[11] Over the course of a decade persistent users constitute about one-sixth of AFDC recipients; but at any given point in time persistent users typically constitute a bit over half of the program's beneficiaries, and some of these households depend on public support for lengthy periods of time.

Implicitly recognizing the inadequacy of the withering thesis, the Nixon administration sent a version of a guaranteed-income plan to Congress in 1969.[12] This proposal, known as the Family Assistance Plan (FAP), would have reduced the national government's payments to AFDC recipients in high-benefit states (California, Massachusetts, and New York, for instance) and would have provided help to the working poor who did not qualify for cash-transfer programs.[13] Revisions of this plan were eventually defeated in Congress.

President Carter came into office on a campaign pledge of welfare reform, but his administration proved similarly unable to elicit congressional enthusiasm and support. Carter's proposal, Program for Better Jobs and Income (PBJI), resembled FAP in many respects, although it was more ambitious with regard to employment and coverage (childless couples and single adults were included).[14]

The Reagan administration has been concerned largely with reducing the national government's financial support for AFDC.[15] It has also encouraged states to experiment with various workfare options. From the recipients' perspective, the single most important change has probably been the four-month limitation on allowing beneficiaries to keep the first $30 of earnings and one-third of the remainder. After four months—once limited work-related (including child-care) expenses are deducted—most earnings are offset by reductions in benefits.

In sum, little improvement has been made in the policy or design of public assistance in the last two decades. By and large recipients, program personnel, political leaders, organized interests, and the general public have little good to say about AFDC, but as yet there has been no consensus about how to reform the program. The 1988 legislation that emerged from conflicting ideas in Congress unfortunately deviates only slightly and unimportantly from the practices of the recent past.

Distributive Justice

AFDC has continually run afoul of American conceptions of distributive justice, in part because benefits are based on need and not explicitly linked to responsible, constructive behavior by recipient households and in part because benefits to the target group—needy children—are supplemented by "caretaker" grants to their parents. While the public generally supports the policy of providing for needy children,[16] public attitudes are skeptical at best toward the parents of these children. Most of these parents are not employed full time, and the attention they devote to childrearing no longer elicits the public approval it did a half century ago when predecessor widows' pension programs served predominantly white women. Today, adults who use AFDC are often censured for their inability to provide for their families; frequently they are the subject of racial slurs and accusations of sexual promiscuity as well.

As a public assistance program, AFDC involves the vertical redistribution of resources from better to less well off. At current funding levels (approximately $15 billion a year), the program is a modest attack on taxpayers' property that regularly serves roughly 11 million persons (nearly 5 percent of the population). But while AFDC benefits are not linked to prior effort or current results, neither does the program systematically apply the criterion of need to all Americans. Rather, AFDC responds to the needs of one category of people—poor children primarily in single-parent households—and ignores other equally needy people. The remediation of this horizontal inequity was one aspect of both the Nixon and Carter proposals for guaranteed annual income plans.

The public's response, at both elite and mass levels, to AFDC stresses two distinct themes.[17] Americans believe that legitimate needs should be met by public social provision, but there is a widespread feeling that some proportion of the adults who draw on AFDC do not really need to do so, but lazily choose to do so. Thus AFDC benefits are perceived as inconsistent with human dignity, as indicative of dependence, and as destructive of work incentives and other aspects of economic efficiency.

Questions of distributive justice became particularly vexing in the late 1960s and early 1970s. Prior to 1967, AFDC benefits were, with only occasional erroneous or fraudulent exceptions, so low as to extend to only food, shelter, and clothing. But a series of changes in 1967 allowed recipients to keep (in addition to allowances for work expenses) the first $30 of monthly earnings and one-third of the remainder. In conjunction with relaxed eligibility for Medicaid and food stamps, these changes enabled a small proportion of AFDC recipients, generally residents of urban areas in industrial states, to combine earnings and public program benefits into household incomes bordering on the national median income.[18] Such income levels threatened the otherwise close association between program benefits and basic resources. And as recipients in the higher-income brackets stayed on AFDC, the proportion of program resources going to the neediest families declined.[19] The changes that permitted these aberrations have largely been rescinded by the Reagan administration.

Negative Liberty

From the libertarian perspective, participation in AFDC as a beneficiary is voluntary. Public assistance, in contrast to social insurance, characteristically involves no compulsion in the form of government pressure. The destitute are free to ignore public aid, although the drive to survive may compel many disadvantaged and vulnerable citizens to make use of the program. But this is, from the libertarian perspective, a choice freely made.

Taxpayers involuntarily participate in the program by funding it. Federal tax revenues cover over half of the national cost, with states covering the rest. The amount of taxpayers' discretionary income redirected to AFDC is far less than that allocated to social security, but AFDC transfers involve a higher degree of vertical redistribution.

Historically, AFDC has been associated with a number of constraints on recipient liberty. The legal basis for some of the more notorious of these practices was withdrawn in the late 1960s when the federal courts invalidated residency and "man-in-the-house" rules. Considerable infringement is still possible, although its actual imposition varies widely with region, time, and caseworker.[20] Most states have also dropped the elaborate intrusive investigations of recipient need, and some use a self-report system similar to that used by the Internal Revenue Service for taxes.

At the level of the field office the extraordinary complexity of AFDC holds conflicting implications for the freedom of program providers. On one hand, case workers are free to exercise individual discretion within a set of complex rules that cover a variety of matters, such as the determination of work-related expenses. In practice, heavy caseloads and high turnover lead caseworkers to substitute intuition and discretion for laborious bureaucratic procedures.[21] On the other hand, the diversity of complicated social services provided by AFDC requires service providers, such as the Department of Labor, to conform to overall program guidelines and desiderâtâ.[22]

Economic Efficiency

AFDC executives and welfare reformers have continually struggled over the issue of work incentives for recipients. One overriding work incentive, stronger among some groups than others, is the stigma associated with AFDC status. The complexities of the application process and subsequent eligibility testing also provide some deterrent to program use and thus may serve as a work incentive. As a group, however, AFDC mothers tend to have low levels of education, job skills, and work experience. So even those who are eager to work, as most initially are,[23] have difficulty finding jobs that provide either much job security or income sufficient to support their families. For many, earnings from even full-time employment fall below official poverty levels or, in some cases, below the value of AFDC grants in conjunction with the benefits of other programs—food stamps, Medicaid, and housing—for which AFDC recipients are generally eligible.

Despite these obstacles to household support, adult AFDC recipients generally do work, frequently part-time, using the program episodically when work runs out. Recipients thus do not constitute a perverted culture whose members are unwilling to contribute to the support of their households. Instead they generally do contribute, but their economic position is fragile and highly contingent on periodic changes in family composition and employment status.[24]

This fragile situation is complicated by AFDC's design features. Since 1962 AFDC has experimented with different approaches intended to encourage recipient self-help. But in practice these measures have penalized recipients who are too diligent. For example, until 1967 recipients' earnings, less work-related expenses, were deducted from their program benefits, a practice that "taxed" earnings at about 70 percent. In 1967, in connection with the WIN program, Congress effectively reduced this rate to about 50 percent.[25] Then in 1981 the Reagan administration limited the more generous treatment of earned income to the first four months of a claim. Thus recipients eventually encountered a "notch," a point at which additional earnings cause a drop in total household income because they render the household ineligible for AFDC benefits and programs such as Medicaid and food stamps.[26]

Although the term *work incentives* arises repeatedly in discussions about AFDC, it is fair to say that there is no agreement as to what work incentives or disincentives are associated with the program. Some critics of the program argue that the very distribution of resources to working-aged adults reduces their incentive to work. Other critics cite the high rate of benefit reductions against earnings and the aforementioned notches as the major disincentives.[27] Proponents and detractors of AFDC also disagree on the interpretation of the program's results. For instance, attrition rates in job training programs are high, but some people do achieve independence from AFDC through WIN training and job placement.[28] Yet the attrition rate is commonly interpreted as an index of the failure of work incentives, rather than as a measure of the difficulty of the circumstances faced by recipients.

The various social services introduced in 1962—child-care, basic adult education, family planning, work training—are frequently viewed as work incentives. The delivery of these services, however, has been spotty, largely because funding has been much more limited than the initial program announcements suggested. Additionally, the objectives of services such as basic adult education have never been clearly defined and are sometimes delivered in ways that serve the needs of providers more than those of program recipients. For instance, since the federal government picks up a higher portion of costs associated with social services, state welfare agencies have renamed offices that scrutinize recipients' budgets as budget-counseling services.[29]

Regarding incentives for household savings, AFDC's means test is clearly counterproductive. State regulations vary, but in general means tests restrict program eligibility to households that have virtually no income or saleable assets.[30] Means tests thus mesh poorly with the episodic character of most AFDC usage: families are not eligible for assistance until they have depleted their resources—a small savings account, marketable possessions—a practice that only reinforces a sense of hopelessness with respect to savings. Means tests also make leaving AFDC protection risky, since the recipient will have to fall back into destitution in order to reenter the program.

Guaranteed-income experiments conducted in Seattle and Denver suggest that means tests which ignore assets in determining eligibility may be a more constructive approach to aiding the working poor and encouraging savings.[31] The abolition of means testing would reduce target efficiency but would bring AFDC in line with social security and unemployment insurance, both of which use current earnings as a measure of eligibility. (No one would ever suggest that laid-off workers covered by unemployment insurance sell their homes, cars, and other possessions before applying for benefits.) Since AFDC serves as a substitute for unemployment insurance for a high proportion of workers on the fringes of the economy, parity in the type of eligibility rules does not seem unreasonable.

For businesses and corporations AFDC's consequences for risk-taking are mixed. Because the program is financed from general revenues, rather than payroll taxes, the association between levels of program support and the costs of doing business are small and indirect. The program's deleterious effects on work incentives may hurt recipients but should have little influence on business. The argument that AFDC curtails participation in the labor force by offering a limited and unrepresentative segment of the labor market roughly comparable levels of financial support for rearing children may have considerable face validity for businessmen, but this contention is of dubious empirical accuracy. Nor can AFDC be implicated in debates about the competitiveness of American goods and services in global markets. The taxes that sustain AFDC are paid largely by individuals, not by business enterprises, and they represent less than 0.5 percent of GNP (compared to 5 percent for social security), or about 1.5 percent of the federal budget (compared to 20 percent for social security).

The total costs of AFDC are modest: less than $15 billion to serve about 11 million persons in 1986. Herein lies one of the program's virtues from the standpoint of economic efficiency. It is inexpensive—far less expensive than any program attempting to achieve self-support among AFDC's adult recipients would be.

Slightly more than half of AFDC's costs are covered by the federal government from general revenues. The redistribution of resources is thus strongly vertical: since the incomes of AFDC recipients are low, few of them pay federal income tax, and higher-earning citizens shoulder the bulk of AFDC's costs.

States fund the balance of AFDC expenditures through a variety of taxes that are usually more regressive than the federal income tax. The tax burden that AFDC poses for residents of different states varies sharply. Nearly one-half of the benefits are disbursed in three states (California, New York, and Massachusetts) that provide high benefits, based on high costs of living, to large numbers of recipients.[32] But other states do not share these exceptional fiscal problems.

Overall AFDC is a highly focused program that concentrates on a particular swath of urgent need. Consequently, AFDC has a reputation for target efficiency; that is, AFDC benefits—in contrast to those of social security—go to extremely needy households. Prior to the late 1960s varying interpretations of what constituted a "suitable home" and other restrictions combined to deny aid to many needy families within the ostensible target population.[33] Between 1967 and 1981 target efficiency was diluted somewhat by more lenient rules covering earnings retention, but only a small proportion of AFDC households were able to take advantage of these rules.[34]

Specific aspects of AFDC's highly focused design, critics claim, exacerbate the plight of destitute households and undermine economic efficiency. One argument of this sort is that by supporting only single-mother households, AFDC encourages family dissolution.[35] Fathers who cannot or who are reluctant to take responsibility for the support of their dependents either leave the household or never become a formal part of it. Empirical evidence for this argument is sparse: one analysis shows that the variation in the level of AFDC benefits across states has no effect on family structure and living arrangements, but other data suggest that the incentive structure to which this feature of AFDC contributes is not overlooked by some of the males associated with AFDC families.[36] Nonetheless, experiments with the negative income tax, particularly the Seattle/Denver work, suggest that programs that aid households regardless of composition may facilitate family dissolution as well, through an independence effect—that is, women who have independent resources are apt to leave a bad marriage.[37]

A second troublesome feature is the wide variation of benefits among states and their subdivisions. Economic efficiency is not well served if poor households migrate from the rural south, where benefits are lowest, to northern and western cities. Any concentration of AFDC-dependent households in cities already facing impressive structural unemployment problems produces a permanent urban underclass. A program of standardized national benefits, in contrast, might encourage poor households to move to areas in which the cost of living is lower and job opportunities are more plentiful. Social security, for instance, has probably facilitated a migration of elderly citizens from the frost to the sunbelt, and the Denver guaranteed-income experiment suggests a similar migration pattern.[38]

In summary, little about AFDC contributes to economic efficiency, but programs that target narrow, highly vulnerable segments of the population are, by nature, not intended to realize economic efficiency. Nevertheless, extending help to the impoverished
and economic efficiency may not be as incompatible as is generally
thought. As we will see, the economic efficiency of a program
aimed at helping the poor can be enhanced, but such improvements exact a price in terms of program budget.

Administrative Complexity

For a national program, AFDC allows an astonishing degree of regional variation,[39] with each state having its own rules for eligibility, subsequent household budgets, and a variety of other matters.
Typically, these rules are extraordinarily complex, and their application requires continual interpretive decisions by state-level and
field-office personnel. The density of substantive field-office decision making, fostered through decentralization, is further complicated by high turnover among recipients and their concurrent use
of other public assistance programs.

AFDC's original objective was to supervise transfer payments,
but the addition of social services components in 1962 presented
more demanding and less well-defined program objectives. So-
called hard services, those clearly related to employment such as
job training and placement, have had relatively modest success,
and providers in other government agencies have complained about
the constraints that serving AFDC recipients places on them. The
so-called softer services—basic adult education—have less clear-
cut objectives and have sometimes become twisted to serve the
needs of state financing rather than those of recipient merging.[40]

Compounding the difficulties posed by complex procedures and
ambitious objectives, AFDC operates in a highly decentralized
fashion. Decentralization opens the door to differences in objectives among the national, state, and local levels as well as among
the various agencies involved at any given level. Additionally, decentralization places a great deal of decision-making responsibility
at the bottom of the organizational pyramid, where a variety of
personnel problems and high rates of employee turnover hamper
administrative efficiency. To reduce some of these complexities, the
guaranteed-income proposals of the 1970s sought to standardize

many rules on a national basis and to return the program's focus from social services to income transfers.

AFDC's most prominent limits issues involve the types and degrees of need covered by the program. To take but one prominent example, fewer than half of the states chose to expand eligibility to households with an unemployed male by instituting AFDC-UP.[41] State-by-state guidelines about what constitutes need reinforce the notion that AFDC is, despite its formal legal standing, a type of gratuity rather than a socioeconomic right.[42] The English poor laws linger on in contemporary AFDC practice.

AFDC's harmonization with other relevant public policy objectives is sharply uneven. Public revenues allocated to AFDC are usually spent quickly, so the program minimally helps to maintain consumer demand and therefore employment. But since most AFDC recipients are not full-time members of the labor force, one could argue that the program removes potential workers from labor-market participation. Unlike social security, AFDC is not considered as an important contributor to inflation.

AFDC's central harmonization problem lies in the insulation of the program from the labor market—an inherent aspect of program design that is highly artificial in a society that places great emphasis on work. Efforts by the Nixon and Carter administrations to reform public assistance by replacing AFDC, rather than by tinkering with the specifics of the existing program, were well intended, but their guaranteed-income proposals were also seriously at odds with American political values about work.

With respect to the values of limited and local government, AFDC offers a mixed but not generally encouraging fit. The program is relatively small, but it looms large in the public's perception. Regional and, less legitimately, case discretion provide some measure of local governance, and there have been several interesting state-level experiments in recent years. But local discretion can just as easily become a tool for institutionalized racism and other disturbing practices.[43]

Conflicts of Interest and Compliance

A program such as AFDC is, by nature, a locus for conflicting interests, the most central of which is that between public officials' desires to restrict spending for "the poor" and the needs of the program's clientele. Throughout AFDC's history, this conflict has taken different forms. At the program's inception the administrative officials at SSB sought to limit public assistance relative to social insurance, and this preference persisted for a number of years. Up through the early 1960s program executives viewed AFDC as a transfer program concerned with maintaining a limited number of households beset by highly exceptional circumstances. This view was gradually superseded by the alternative conception of AFDC as serving a more progressive task. In 1962 increasing costs prompted the Kennedy administration, on the advice of social work professionals in HEW, to add a social services emphasis to AFDC. Representing the social work view about the path to self-reliance, these services were intended to reform recipients in ways consistent with increased self-sufficiency, but they also enhanced the role of social workers, offering them more interesting tasks than handling caseload paperwork.[44]

Successive initiatives by political leaders through WIN in 1967 were driven most immediately, though not exclusively, by a concern with controlling costs. Since the early 1970s a concern with limiting program costs has been joined, and occasionally even eclipsed, by concerns relating to vertical or work equity and permissiveness. Overall, however, interest among political elites in AFDC has been extremely uneven. The relatively small federal expenditures for AFDC and the concentration of costs in a handful of states means that most members of Congress need not pay much attention to the program. Representatives from affected states have often viewed fiscal relief for state government as more of an issue than program reform, and few House members have significant AFDC constituency interests.[45] Nor have AFDC program executives typically exhibited the devotion and adroitness of their social security counterparts.

At the state level, conflicts of interest between public officials and program clientele vary over time. Some states have been relatively generous in extending eligibility and higher benefits; others have adopted practices designed to deter or discriminate against applicants and restrict benefit levels. The primary federal sanction for achieving state-level adherence to those aspects of the program covered by federal guidelines—the withdrawing of federal funds—

has not proved effective. A few states have been so bold as to call the federal government's bluff in such matters.

The incentives for compliance and cooperation among beneficiaries, federal officials, and third-party providers are no less problematic. With respect to the majority of episodic users, AFDC does provide invaluable assistance for bridging social hazards, but the means test, which generally requires program applicants to be indigent before qualifying for services, is clearly counterproductive. Rather than stimulating self-help efforts, the means test creates strong cross-pressures between self-sufficiency and dependence among persons whose views about their economic futures are understandably uncertain. Once a household qualifies for the program, these conflicting pressures continue, as increased earnings are penalized by reduced benefits. Episodic users work their way toward renewed self-sufficiency in spite of, rather than because of, the program.

For the less numerous persistent users of AFDC, the bonds of habit and dependency have thus far proved intractable. Whether such bonds can be broken humanely—without disruption, suffering, and controversy—is a troubling question.

Three factors mitigate against persistent users' achieving independence from AFDC. First, these are people who have limited or undeveloped capacities with respect to the existing labor market; they are caring for young children and have little in the way of job skills and experience. Second, in addition to information and transportation problems that complicate the matching of recipients and jobs, the existing labor market does not offer enough paid positions capable of sustaining the families that require support. Third, against this structural inadequacy, AFDC offers an enticing form of economic security, one that in extreme cases invites recipient abuse. But while New York City, for example, has been troubled by systematic patterns of abuse, the vast majority of these abuses concern extremely small sums of money. (The popular myth of AFDC recipients driving Cadillacs is precisely a myth.) Nonetheless, cases of abuse do illustrate how the program's design features encourage certain kinds of counterproductive behavior from recipients.

As a program that deals with a narrow and unrepresentative group of vulnerable and generally disadvantaged citizens with whom upper-middle-class bureaucrats do not readily empathize, AFDC is at a disadvantage compared to programs serving a broad cross-section of the population. Between 1935 and 1962, when AFDC was administered by SSB/SSA, the program executives who were so dedicated to social security exhibited far less enthusiasm for the public assistance program.[46] Even after AFDC became an organizationally coequal division of HEW, program officials did not display the resourcefulness and commitment that characterized their counterparts at social security. The joint national-state character of the program surely impedes administrators' efforts, but the crusade to keep the elderly and the disabled from joining the poor has never been extended to those who are poor.

National elected officials have similarly evaded a strong commitment to AFDC and related public assistance issues. With the exception of Ford, every president since Roosevelt has taken some important initiative with respect to welfare reform, but only Johnson found these programs compelling enough to make persistent efforts on their behalf in the face of congressional opposition. In Congress, as noted earlier, interest in AFDC is sparse and more concerned with formulas for federal cost-sharing than program design or success.

From the perspective of the federal government, state and local officials are third-party providers of various sorts. Characteristically these providers have priorities that differ from those of AFDC's federal program executives. A few states offer aid that exceeds federal guidelines, but other states are reluctant to adhere to the spirit of the law, particularly in the implementation of the social service components. Two key problems have been the use of private contractors whose agendas do not match program objectives and the misappropriation of federal cost-sharing available for social services to finance routine administrative operations.

Summary and Implications

On the whole, AFDC fares much worse than social security on the criteria used in this case study. One must bear in mind, however, that AFDC, confronts tasks that are inherently tougher than the providing of pensions for the elderly, a particularly favored task among social insurance programs.

Despite a poor fit with American notions of distributive justice, AFDC distributes resources that are important, if not essential, to the survival of a shifting recipient population that currently numbers about 11 million people a year, most of them children. The program's effects in reducing starvation, homelessness, and other forms of human misery are laudable, especially given its low cost.

Additional strengths include the noncompulsory nature of participation, minimal effects on economic efficiency, relatively high target efficiency, and—for better or worse—a considerable degree of regional and local discretion.

The list of AFDC's weaknesses is far longer. Because the distribution of benefits is not systematically related to either need or effort and does not require effort-based certifying activities from beneficiaries, the consequent public skepticism about AFDC beneficiaries' true neediness undermines the program's goal of enhancing human dignity. The financing of AFDC poses relatively few constraints on citizens' discretionary income, but the income transfers are highly vertical, and additional constraints are posed on the liberty of recipients and providers. The program's consequences for work, savings, and risk-taking, while uncertain and probably modest, do not look promising.

AFDC also receives low ratings on administrative efficiency. Its artificial insulation of program recipients from the labor market creates notable limits and harmonization problems. The program has not appealed to traditions and symbols respected in American political culture and has not aroused the interest of political elites on matters other than containing costs.

Finally, the program does not well serve the needs of either episodic or persistent users. In particular, efforts to promote greater self-sufficiency among AFDC recipients have foundered on three central issues: program features that create only weak work incentives, inadequate labor market opportunities for recipients, and the personal disadvantages and limitations of recipients.

The reforms initiated in 1962 focused on improving beneficiaries' capacities for using the labor market through job training and placement, related social services, and simple coercion. It is possible that this approach failed because we simply did not try hard or long enough, but the difficulties experienced along this path suggest that we try other avenues.

Nonetheless, today one sees a resurgence of support for the failed approach of the 1962 reforms. In *Beyond Entitlement,* Lawrence Mead, for example, thoughtfully and provocatively argues that the fundamental fault with the American welfare system is not its size but its permissiveness. Programs of public social provision, according to Mead, should require more rigorous effort at self-development and help among beneficiaries than AFDC or public assistance in general currently do. While I agree with this premise, there are two serious flaws in Mead's proposal that we develop intraprogram policing capacities for assuring that beneficiaries are working, studying hard, treating fellow family members reasonably, and avoiding crime.

The first flaw is the impracticality of such a proposal. For one, programs with administrative teeth are hard to develop. Although California's new Greater Avenues for Independence (GAIN) and Massachusetts's Employment and Training Choices (ET) have reputations as more constructive than workfare generally, both programs ultimately rest on the individual recipient's willingness to cooperate.[47] Furthermore, intraprogram policing takes us back along a route we have already traversed and decided, through a series of court decisions, we did not like. And American political values are not likely to be well served by a set of larger, seriously more intrusive state bureaucracies that monitor public assistance.

The second general flaw in Mead's approach is the particular character of its optimism, which seems in part a reincarnation of the withering thesis. Mead does not imagine that all poverty will wither away through coercively imposed work, but he is optimistic that a good deal of it will. Yet to suppose that a considerable measure of poverty rests on personal actions alone is to ignore characteristics of the labor market that limit its universal usefulness in providing a living wage for many workers. Low wages and modest skills combine to keep the working poor hovering barely above poverty, and the slightest misfortune is apt to plunge them into destitution. Many households recover through their own efforts, but the pool of households likely to experience episodic poverty is so large and the persistence of their collective problems so great that eliminating or even dramatically reducing such poverty through work alone seems unlikely. The overall problem is less one of changing the attitudes of a small subculture, although this may be a factor among persistent AFDC users, than of overcoming a variety of structural problems in the labor market that preclude adults from being able to support their families.

Moreover, Mead's optimism seems to ignore the effects of certain demographic trends, including the birth rates for single mothers and the divorce and desertion rates among couples with young children. To take but one example, for poor women the single most frequent escape route from poverty is marriage or remarriage.[48] But marriage and remarriage rates are notably low among single urban black women who have children. One explanation of this trend holds that the limited economic opportunities of urban black men contribute to their reluctance to take on the obligations of a wife and children or stepchildren; black women, seeing little economic relief in such marriages, might be equally reluctant.[49] Another explanation looks to sex ratios. In those urban areas where women greatly outnumber men, men—and not just American black males—tend to be less responsible toward women and children; in areas where sex ratios are more balanced, stable two-parent families predominate.[50]

In contrast to Mead's vision, the AFDC reforms initiated in 1967 (and dismantled in 1981) represent a nascent example of an approach that incorporates a more adequate recognition of the limitations of the existing labor market. These reforms extended to a category of the poor a minimal level of economic support (a guarantee) that could be enhanced by work. Expanding upon this approach, the FAP and PBJI proposals offered both advantages and drawbacks in comparison to AFDC. They covered more people, thus reducing horizontal or support inequities. But they also brought a much larger population into prospective programs that offered their recipients economic support insulated from requirements of working. And the language of guarantees, as developed from WIN through PBJI, contradicted the core American concerns of work and self-sacrifice as essential to human dignity.

During the last quarter-century, then, public assistance programs have tried either to alter the capacities of people ill suited for the existing labor market or to insulate these people from the rigors of that market. In the renewed debate over workfare conservatives have tended to argue that in order to reduce the public assistance rolls we need to put people to work, and liberals have tended to argue that we therefore need to create jobs that will allow people to work. We can, I believe, carve out a position between these views. Most Americans would agree that able-bodied working-aged adults ought to participate in the paid labor force, rather than be insulated from it. For single adults and childless couples, self-support through the labor market is a reasonable expectation. But for households with children, particularly single-parent households, regular full-time work at or near the minimum wage will not cover basic needs or cushion a household from poverty. And in single-parent households regular full-time employment is extremely difficult in the absence of adequate and affordable child-care. For these households, then, it seems appropriate and socially productive to establish a program of public social provision that would both facilitate labor market participation and supplement wages inadequate to support a family.

In chapter 8 I will propose such a program, one that will create a structure of opportunities and incentives far stronger than any that has characterized AFDC to date. Rather than enlarge existing public assistance bureaucracies for the policing of recipients, my measures would facilitate the socially responsible activities we want to encourage and, as necessary, supplement low-income workers' constructive efforts at self-support. But before I lay out my proposal, we need to examine the special problems associated with the delivery of social services. For this purpose, let us turn to a case study of Medicare.

Seven

Medicare

Delivering a service such as medical care is inherently more problematic than distributing income-maintenance checks. But American efforts to develop public medical-care programs have encountered exceptional difficulties, in large part because such initiatives have generally been perceived by physicians and other medical-care providers as infringing on their professional autonomy. Whereas public income maintenance fills a void that intrigues few if any private practitioners, public medical-care policy challenges increasingly powerful private interests. Thus ideological positions concerning the boundary between public and private spheres become pretexts for entrenched private economic interests.

As we shift our attention to indispensable services such as medical care, questions about how recipients are to earn their benefits no longer monopolize our attention because providers' attitudes become a much more prominent issue. Nonetheless, there are two important reasons for including service provision in our analysis of the investments approach. First, by examining a basic service such as medical care we learn something about the limitations of the investments approach with respect to social services in general. Second, we are reminded that severe resource inadequacy problems cannot be resolved by income maintenance alone. Access to medical care is an integral aspect of comprehensive protection against severe social hazards.

Historical Background

In comparison to other advanced industrial societies the United States remains a "laggard" with respect to public medical-care programs.[1] Although the nation's preventive public health measures—water and sewage treatment, garbage collection, and inoculation against selective infectious diseases—are generally sound, public programs involving therapeutic medicine are distinctly more circumscribed in the United States than in comparable industrial societies. Most noticeably, the United States has no public program to assure universal or minimally widespread and comprehensive medical care. In the twentieth century four separate and lengthy efforts to achieve some form of national health insurance in the United States have failed.

The first of these crusades, in the years preceding World War I, was prompted by the American Association for Labor Legislation (AALL) and other progressive groups.[2] AALL leaders saw public health insurance as a natural extension of workers' compensation insurance. Having had some success at the state level on the latter, the AALL began state campaigns for public health insurance programs. The AALL's proposals focused primarily on protecting low-income workers against poverty arising from illness. Provisions included sick pay and some coverage for the costs of medical services. Given the relatively low medical costs at the time, sick pay was as important as the insurance provisions.

The AALL argued strongly for the macroeconomic benefits of its plan: health insurance would improve economic efficiency by reducing various industrial costs—worker absenteeism—associated with existing working conditions. As the Progressive candidate for the presidency in 1912, Theodore Roosevelt put a political twist on this proposition, maintaining that no nation could be strong if its population was highly vulnerable to illness.

But business interests rejected these claims of economic efficiency. The AALL plan was also opposed by organized labor, particularly Samuel Gompers and the American Federation of Labor, primarily because they saw it as preempting the unions from winning medical benefits for their workers and thus undercutting the advantages of union membership. For a time the American Medical Association (AMA) cooperated with AALL, but members increasingly perceived the proposal as threatening.[3] Having thus failed to establish broad-based support, the AALL campaign dissipated during World War I. The war effort distracted attention from public health insurance, and German social programs—from which the AALL proposal borrowed—became the subject of a barrage of intense and highly negative propaganda.

A strikingly different campaign for public health insurance surfaced in the late 1920s. By this time medical care had become much more expensive, and now reformers focused on public health insurance as a vehicle for helping the middle class afford medical care. The Great Depression, however, posed more urgent social issues, and public health insurance did not get much attention from the New Deal until 1938. Physicians and hospitals had not been spared from economic disasters, and some welcomed talk of public health insurance as a means of expanding the demand for medical care. But by the time the Roosevelt administration sent its proposals to Congress in late 1938, Congress had become more conservative and resistant to New Deal efforts. In 1939 a related proposal, sponsored by New York Senator Robert F. Wagner, was also rejected. And again international turmoil and a world war turned everyone's attention away from domestic issues.[4]

The third wave of reform began in 1943 and eventually led to the creation of Medicare in 1965. Unlike its two predecessors, this initiative was increasingly dominated by the federal government and garnered the support of new interest groups, particularly organized labor. These proposals looked to the federal government, rather than state governments, and more nearly embodied the concepts of universal and comprehensive coverage. The Wagner-Murray-Dingell bills, introduced in 1943, were the first such proposals. In 1945 President Truman wrested initiative from the Congress with a broader and in some respects more ambitious plan that called for federal funding of hospital expansion, medical research, and medical education and the expansion of the largely preventive public health program for mothers and children— the Maternal and Child Health Program.[5] The most controversial point was Truman's proposal for a national health insurance scheme that would cover not only social security recipients but citizens generally.

Certainly Truman's proposals had several features that were attractive to medical providers: federal subsidies to enhance the profession's capital—hospitals, research, and education—and to finance demand for medical services. None of Truman's proposals would have affected existing patterns of medical-care delivery; the dominance and autonomy of physicians were to remain intact. Nonetheless, the AMA, the American Hospital Association, and the Chamber of Commerce, among other groups, opposed aspects of the plan with varying degrees of ferocity. The AMA led the battle against a government presence in medical care with an unprecedented lobbying and public relations effort. As the Cold War intensified, opponents of national health insurance tarred the proposal as a socialist ploy.

In the aftermath of this defeat, proponents of national health insurance—officials in the Social Security Administration and a few other executive bureaucracies, specific members of Congress, some presidents, organized labor, and an assortment of liberal funders and intellectuals—generally adopted an incremental approach to achieving a legislative victory.[6] A similar tactic proved effective in bringing disabled workers into the social security system, but the government's entry into the provision of medical care was more troublesome than adding disabled citizens to the social security rolls.[7]

By the mid-1960s, however, the notion of public medical insurance for the elderly—a group generally held to be worthy, medically vulnerable, and of limited material means—had garnered fairly broad-based support. In 1965 innovative compromises within the House Ways and Means Committee resulted in a two-part Medicare program. Under Part A, Hospital Insurance (HI) became a standard social security benefit. An increase in social security taxes was authorized to finance this program. And under Part B, Supplementary Medical Insurance (SMI) for physicians' bills could be purchased by citizens sixty-five and older. This portion was financed in part through monthly premiums paid by beneficiaries and in part through general tax revenues. Finally, the legislative compromise expanded federal support of health care for the poorest Americans (Medicaid).

To reduce opposition from organized medicine, the architects of Medicare chose not to incorporate any provisions affecting the delivery of medical services.[8] Most importantly, no effort was made to alter the prevailing high-technology, therapeutic orientation with its practices of hospital bills based on costs and physicians' fees based on services rendered. Thus, Medicare bolstered the demand for medical care without creating any cost-control mechanisms, and the program exceeded cost projections from the outset. In the face of Medicare's rapidly rising costs, Congress has been unwilling to expand the program. Benefits were extended to disabled social security beneficiaries and end-state renal dialysis patients in 1972, but Medicare has not developed into the program of national health insurance that some of its early proponents had hoped for.

Indeed, the fourth campaign for national health insurance, during the 1970s, suggests that if national health insurance is ever developed, it is unlikely to follow the model of Medicare.[9] For this fourth campaign resurrected a prominent theme of the AALL's pre–World War I crusade: economic efficiency. And in light of the federal budget deficits of the 1980s, any future proposal, even remotely universal and comprehensive in scope, would have to offer greater economic efficiency than Medicare.

From the standpoint of meeting the medical-care needs of the elderly, Medicare represents a distinct improvement over the conditions that prevailed prior to its enactment. However, Medicare's accommodation of existing practices in the medical-care professions limits both its effectiveness in assuring appropriate, efficient medical care and its value as a model for any expanded program of national health insurance.

Distributive Justice

In part Medicare represents an attempt to use public means to redistribute medical care in accordance with the criterion of effort rather than by the market criterion of ability to pay. HI benefits go largely to elderly people who have earned them by working for extended periods of time in jobs covered by the social security program.[10] Medicare's attempt to distribute benefits in accordance with effort is imperfect, however, in two respects. First, it excludes those elderly people who have exerted sustained effort—in or outside the paid labor force—but not in jobs covered by social security. Second, with few exceptions, it excludes people who have exerted sustained effort in jobs covered by social security but who are under age sixty-five. Thus effort is not the sole criterion. Medicare relies as well on ascription—age—as a principle of distributive justice.

Certainly, the elderly are particularly vulnerable to health problems, and they characteristically have both limited incomes and limited access to employer-sponsored private group medical insurance. But other citizens are equally in need of medical coverage. By using ascription as a criterion for distributive justice, Medicare is by design unable to produce results consistent with the criteria of effort or need.

Even among elderly beneficiaries, Medicare coverage has its limits and is far from comprehensive.[11] Beneficiaries pay a deductible and coinsurance that increases with the length of a hospital stay. SMI involves premiums, coinsurance, and limits on reimbursement for specific services. Outpatient prescriptions and nursing-home care are not covered at all. So while Medicare, particularly with the recent adoption of catastrophic-cost protection, does limit a hospitalized patient's financial responsibility for acute care, it all but neglects a common medical need of the elderly: custodial care for chronic ailments.[12]

This focus was adopted by Medicare's designers to avoid antagonizing physicians and hospitals. But the emphasis on acute services has also provoked a debate about the relation between medical care and basic goods. In the sense that a wide variety of medical procedures, applied in varying contexts, may save lives, these procedures are as basic as food and water. Yet the dramatic developments in medical technology over the last several decades pose ethical and economic challenges to the simple equation of medical care with basic goods. The ethical question is whether the use of extraordinary life-maintenance techniques prolongs the suffering of patients and their families and constitutes an unnatural or unethical manipulation of life.[13] The economic question is what proportion of its resources can or should a society allocate to expensive life-maintenance technology. The opportunity costs of systematically applying a variety of expensive treatments to lengthen minimally the lives of terminally ill patients are high.[14] Indeed, data on cross-national medical expenditures show that these costs rise rapidly with increases in per capita gross national product—a pattern exemplified by luxury goods rather than by necessities such as food and shelter.[15]

Our final consideration regarding distributive justice concerns vertical redistribution. The program's beneficiaries are primarily elderly people representing the middle ranges of the socioeconomic spectrum. Medicare does involve significant intergenerational transfers, but vertical redistribution from rich to poor is not prominent. But when we consider the market value of Medicare services, we confront a novel form of vertical redistribution. Payments for the medical services provided by Medicare flow to physicians, other medical professionals, and investors in health-care companies. This upward flow makes it difficult to construe Medicare as an attack on property.

Negative Liberty

The HI component of Medicare is financed, like social security, by payroll taxes on prospective beneficiaries. So while recipients have in a sense earned their benefits, their contributions are also compulsory. SMI is paid for in part by voluntary premiums from current recipients, and thus involves no constraint. Subsidies from general tax revenues slightly constrain the liberty of all federal taxpayers in order to extend benefits to recipients who elect SMI.

Apart from the taxes associated with the program, recipients are left unconstrained by Medicare. Medicare beneficiaries generally have as much freedom as privately insured patients in matters such as choice of physician and accepting care.

With respect to medical-care providers, only modest constraints have been introduced by Medicare. In order to facilitate provider cooperation, Medicare's architects explicitly rejected any proposals to intrude upon the organization of medical care. For a while, medical-care providers were important beneficiaries of the new legislation: Demand for medical care expanded slightly, but prices rose rapidly.[16] Alarmed at the cost, the Nixon administration tried to introduce cost controls and other regulatory devices, and made efforts to stimulate the creation and use of health maintenance organizations (HMOs), which provide comprehensive care for a fixed annual fee.

But provider interests managed to hold the line against these efforts. The medical-care profession has retained the economic benefits bestowed by Medicare without surrendering its autonomy.

The greatest threats in this regard have been the limitations on hospital charges for various diagnostically related groups (DRGs), imposed in 1983, and the Reagan administration's effort since 1984 to encourage physicians to accept Medicare payment limits.[17] But provider groups may have left their flank unguarded. While they were watching the government, medical care, buttressed by public financing, has grown immensely profitable, and private corporations are moving in to share the proceeds.[18]

Economic Efficiency

Medicare has reinforced a variety of inefficiencies that characterized the medical-care market into which it was introduced. Among these inefficiencies are: a focus on therapeutic as opposed to preventive medicine, a reliance on expensive medical technologies, hospital charges based on costs, the prevalence of solo and small-scale fee-for-service practices among physicians, the litigious environment of contemporary American medicine, and third-party insurers who insulate both medical-care providers and many of their patients from the most direct, troubling consequences of spiraling medical-care costs. Some of these tendencies are interdependent; fee-for-service practice, for example, lends itself to a therapeutic approach.

This lengthy list of features contributing to economic inefficiency, however, cannot be blamed on Medicare or public policy. Rather these inefficiencies derive from the practices of the private market that the program was designed to leave unchanged. Before examining the provider-related problems for economic efficiency, let us quickly survey the recipient-related economic issues.

Since it serves a population that is already retired or disabled, Medicare has limited effects on labor-market participation. Recipients' rates of use for particular medical services increased somewhat following the introduction of Medicare, but not dramatically. Since use of medical services is not limited simply by economic concerns, public sponsorship of medical insurance seems unlikely to stimulate use any more than private medical insurance available to well-organized workers.[19]

By providing partial payment for highly specified services tailored to a recipient's immediate needs, rather than income that can be freely used, Medicare would appear to have little affect on savings incentives. It is unrealistic to imagine that people fail to save because Medicare will cover a portion of the medical expenses they might subsequently experience. Nor could most people ever save enough to cope with the costs of extensive medical care.

Like any social insurance program funded in part by payroll taxes, Medicare may retard corporate or entrepreneurial risk-taking. But since Medicare costs employers less than one-third of the income-maintenance components of social security, its effects on the competitiveness of American goods and services in the global market are minimal.

In 1967 Medicare benefits cost $4 billion; by 1986 benefits had increased more than fifteenfold, to $76 billion.[20] Serving about 36 million persons in 1986, Medicare consumed approximately 7.5 percent of the federal budget (compared to 20 percent for social security and 1.5 percent for AFDC) and just under 2 percent of GNP (compared to 5 percent for social security and less than 0.5 percent for AFDC). More than two-thirds of Medicare expenditures were for HI, nearly all of that for inpatient hospital care. Of the slightly less than one-third devoted to SMI most was spent on physicians' fees.

The dramatic growth in Medicare expenditures—outrunning inflation generally— is attributable to many factors, but increases in hospital and physicians' fees account for the bulk of it.[21] Shortfalls in Medicare's trust fund are not far down the road,[22] and the United States is already spending a greater proportion of GNP on medical services than many advanced industrial societies that provide national health insurance.

Medicare involves several forms of redistribution. From the perspective of individual recipients, HI is an example of life-cycle redistribution, but current practices also involve intergenerational transfers that probably cannot be recouped. Since the incidence of poverty among the elderly has now fallen to the level prevailing among the population generally, the vertical redistribution effected by federal subsidies for SMI is probably less than that entailed by AFDC. But since social security payroll taxes are more regressive than the federal income tax, SMI may contribute somewhat more to vertical redistribution.

As mentioned earlier, Medicare's economic inefficiency reflects the program's relatively good fit with a sector of the private economy riddled by inefficient practices. This is an unusual predicament in a culture that tends to saddle public programs with charges of inefficiency. Even more unusual have been the efforts of the federal government to stimulate greater market efficiency in the private medical sector. Until recently, in contrast, private insurers have done little in this regard.

Federal initiatives to promote economic efficiency in the private medical sector have been of two types: measures to regulate and efforts to encourage price competition. To date, regulation has predominated. With respect to providers, the Nixon administration applied price controls as part of a more general scheme of economic intervention. His administration also developed Professional Standards Review Organizations (PSROs), which are primarily attentive to hospitalization statistics, and Health Systems Agencies (HSAs), which focus on capital investment decisions. President Carter was unable to secure legislation that would have limited hospital price increases, but the Reagan administration did enforce limits on the federal government's liabilities for Medicare hospitalization and has made modest moves in a similar vein with respect to physicians. These efforts have all helped somewhat to control costs, but the price of medical care has continued to outpace inflation.[23] Sterner regulatory procedures (bargaining, explicit rationing, and centralized planning) are apt to be required.

As part of its overall effort to control costs, the federal government has also repeatedly raised Medicare premiums and deductibles, and it has kept allowable fees for various services from rising as rapidly as physicians' charges. As a result, Medicare recipients' out-of-pocket expenses have increased, and some analysts recommend increased patient copayments as a cost-control device.[24] While copayments do reduce federal expenditures, they will not reduce the nation's aggregate health-care bill unless they deter use of services. But there is not much evidence that suggests elderly citizens flock to physicians unnecessarily by contemporary standards. The most prominent increase in services has been in the area of short-term hospital stays, a service attributable more to physicians' choices than to patients' actions.[25] So copayments appear to be less effective at reducing unnecessary services than at shifting costs to patients.

The limited success of federal regulatory efforts has prompted some analysts and policymakers to suggest that restructuring the medical-care market for better price competition is the strategy most likely to achieve greater economic efficiency. Throughout most of the 1970s, policymakers looked hopefully at group practices, such as HMOs, that provide medical care for a fixed annual fee, thus placing a premium on preventive and ambulatory care. This internal incentive structure seems an encouraging mechanism for cost containment.[26] Indeed, the most successful and widely known HMOs—Kaiser Permanente, for instance—have kept costs and cost increases well below those of conventional hospitals and fee-for-service practices.[27] In some metropolitan areas competition among HMOs and between HMOs and conventional medical-care delivery practices has slowed the growth of medical-care costs.[28]

Despite the interest of federal government leaders and other elites, only modest restructuring has occurred. Many private insurance carriers have integrated specific changes into their operations, but the federal government's repeated efforts to stimulate the development of HMOs have had little success. HMOs are complex, relatively fragile organizations that face difficult circumstances in the current medical-care market,[29] and some efforts to stimulate new HMOs have constrained existing ones.

Competition and cost-conscious incentives have also led to new problems. Cutting costs by cutting care and self-dealing group practices are abuses every bit as disconcerting as price increases.[30] Regulation is apt to be necessary under any system of delivering medical services, not just Medicare.[31] For example, the activities of PSROs in isolating underuse and overuse of hospitalization can be as important in detecting shortcuts in care by HMOs as in detecting cost padding by fee-for-service practitioners.

Today, reformers insist that some sort of restructuring is necessary to improve the economic efficiency of the medical-care market. And almost all analysts interested in reform agree that the only actor with both a sufficiently strong incentive and the necessary organizational capacity is the federal government. Providers have no economic incentive, at least in the short run. Some members of the public have the incentive, but no organization. Insurance companies also have some incentive, but until recently have found it easier to pass along increased costs to their customers. For the moment, Medicare is not large enough to provide sufficient leverage for a general restructuring,[32] but some future national health insurance program might.

Administrative Complexity

In part Medicare's complexity is dictated by its mandate. Medical and health services require extensive cooperation from both patients and providers. While Medicare is associated with improvements in health among the elderly,[33] both patients and providers routinely follow counterproductive practices. Some patients persist in unhealthy habits (smoking, excessive drinking, and poor nutrition). Others cannot escape from environmental dangers at home or at work. Meanwhile, providers practice the episodic acute care for which they have been trained in expensive well-equipped institutions. Most show little interest in either preventive care or in less intensive forms of treatment for the nonacute chronic illnesses that tend to afflict the elderly.[34]

If we use provision of medical care rather than health as the appropriate objective of Medicare, the inherent requirements for cooperation are still high, but they do appear to fall within the capacities of many providers and patients. Medicare and other federal medical-care initiatives have improved the availability, accessibility, and affordability of medical care.[35]

Beyond requiring complex cooperation from providers and patients, Medicare requires a fairly complex bureaucracy to handle patients' claims and other aspects of program administration. The complicated rules for coverage, copayments, deductibles, and allowable fees place heavy demands on the Social Security Administration (SSA). Medicare recipients are reimbursed for only a portion of their costs, while covered amounts are paid directly to providers. HI claims are processed either by a recognized intermediary—frequently by Blue Cross—or directly by SSA, while SMI claims are handled by intermediaries. (In contrast, public programs that provide direct services, such as the British National Health Service, are generally less complex to administer but have other characteristics—direct employment of the majority of physicians—unlikely to ever be adopted in the United States.) Despite these complexities, SSA administers Medicare in a fashion that

compares reasonably well with the efficiency of many private insurance operations.[36] Medicare does enjoy some advantages—
large-scale and easy marketing—that help in this regard.

As was the case with AFDC, some of the most troubling questions about Medicare involve limits and harmonization issues. The
first limits issue concerns eligibility. The HI component of Medicare is essentially a program for elderly social security recipients.
In 1972 elderly non–social security recipients were allowed to enroll, but they must pay the full actuarial cost for coverage. Only
fifteen thousand of the roughly one million elderly in this group
have chosen to enroll,[37] with cost the prohibitive factor. A portion
of the elderly not covered by Medicare are eligible for Medicaid,
and Medicaid has "spend-down" provisions for people who are
medically needy but not otherwise recipients of public assistance.
But Medicaid, a form of public assistance, is available only to
people who have almost no assets.

SMI has from the start been available at the same subsidized
rate to all persons sixty-five years of age or older. Over 300,000
non–social security recipients are currently enrolled as well as
over 95 percent of the HI beneficiaries.

Medicare's categorical focus on the elderly, of course, excludes
the participation of working-aged adults and their dependents, of
whom as many as one-third have either no medical insurance coverage or inadequate coverage.[38] Since the late 1970s the issue of
cost control has so dominated discussions of public medical-care
policy that questions of access have largely been ignored.

Concerns about the costs of Medicare are exacerbated by several harmonization issues. First, Medicare has contributed to the
demand for medical services. While rising demand has generally
sustained employment in this sector of the economy, it has no
doubt contributed to extremely high levels of inflation in this sector as well. Second, policymakers have developed growing misgiv-
ings about the activities of recipients and providers. Access to
medical care is only one aspect of health care. Healthy personal
habits—diet, exercise, defensive driving—and preventive health
care are far more cost-effective ways to promote health.[39]

Finally, public respect, even reverence, for the medical profession has declined somewhat in the last decade. The industrial character of medical care in America has disillusioned the public and

policymakers alike. By the late 1970s expansion of Medicare was precluded as much by a reluctance among members of Congress to funnel more money into this segment of the economy as by the resistance of physicians and other medical-care providers.

Medicare's public image—cost issues aside—has been generally good. Even concerns about costs have increasingly been directed at providers rather than at the appropriateness of helping vulnerable elderly citizens defray medical expenses. One explanation for the near absence of controversy is that Medicare's public profile is relatively low. Functioning in a manner similar to a private insurance carrier, Medicare has required no dramatic changes in practice for most recipients or providers. While Medicare does not respect Americans' preference for limited and local government, it is not an intrusive manifestation of government. Additionally, most people think about Medicare in tandem with social security and their good will toward the latter rubs off on the former.

Conflicts of Interest and Compliance

Medicare was created to ease the financial concerns of the elderly with respect to medical care. On this score, the program may count several successes. Despite limitations in coverage and increases in recipients' copayments, the proportion of recipients' incomes devoted to medical expenditures has generally declined,[40] even as the dollar amounts the elderly spend on medical care have increased. And Medicare patients generally pay an extremely modest portion of the extraordinary costs of extensive care. Further, fears that recipients would overwhelm the medical-care system have proved unfounded. We have seen no dramatic surge in the use of medical services by Medicare recipients. Compliance with program objectives by recipients has simply not been an issue.

In contrast, the conflicts between public officials and medical-care providers continue, even though public officials have tried to ensure both profits and relative autonomy to providers. The government has won the struggle over "first principles"—the entry of the state into financing medical care.[41] But providers remain ambivalent: Medicare is clearly at odds with principles that organized medicine has not abandoned, yet Medicare has bestowed considerable short-term financial rewards on practitioners. Medicare's limitations on public provision of medical services have turned out to be a mixed blessing in this regard. By enrolling a relatively high-risk population that private carriers were not interested in insuring at affordable rates, Medicare has raised the demand for services and contributed to a situation that has supported larger incomes and profits for medical-care providers. But it has also cracked open the door to public regulation of providers.

For public officials, the primary concern has been the cost of Medicare. Since the early 1970s officials have named rapid cost increases as the major problem afflicting contemporary American medical care.[42] In their efforts to reduce the rate of cost increases, federal officials have increasingly pitted themselves against the interests of both Medicare's targeted beneficiaries and medical-care providers.

Finally, the decline in the "sovereignty" of physicians at the hands of corporate enterprise may hold a silver lining for advocates of national health insurance.[43] The more obvious the industrial character of medical care, the less persuasive is the industry's claim to special status. Many service industries—certainly the most basic services—are regulated. If corporate managers continue to displace doctors from control of the medical-care industry, medicine's claims for exceptional treatment will lose credibility.

Summary and Implications

Given the lengthy period of organized medicine's resistance to any sort of public provision for medical care, one hears surprisingly little debate today about whether the elderly need the help Medicare provides or whether it is morally appropriate for the state to provide such help. Instead, the debates focus on costs and cost-benefits. Perhaps even more surprisingly, the culprits with respect to cost are generally held to be private providers and their lack of cost consciousness.

In part Medicare's relatively good image derives from its kinship and similarities to social security. Among social hazards, aging has a special character: its near certainty and fixed position in the life cycle, the widespread perceptions of the elderly as worthy citizens, and the stability of its beneficiary population. And Medicare shares some of social security's popular design features—individual accounts of earned rights, most prominently.

Among Medicare's specific strengths is its criterion of effort, which imparts consistency between the program and American conceptions of distributive justice in the economic domain. And Americans, more so than citizens of most other advanced industrial societies, view medical care as part of the economic domain.[44] As we have seen, Medicare's infringement on negative liberty is modest; its administration is as efficient as that of its private counterparts; and recipient abuse is not a problem. The program targets a population that has particularly extensive medical-care needs and exceptionally limited capacity for meeting these needs, and has carved out an important area of complementary interests in limiting the financial obligations of program recipients for episodes of acute care.

Medicare also exhibits several important weaknesses. In terms of distributive justice, its egalitarian principles of need and effort mesh poorly with the differentiating criterion of ascription by age. Large numbers of people who need assistance and who have exerted effort in the paid labor market are excluded from Medicare. Even within the ranks of the elderly, Medicare's coverage is incomplete and fails to emphasize basic goods. The program's bias toward episodic acute care covers extraordinarily expensive treatments while needs for the most mundane sorts of care go wanting. This bias also promotes economic inefficiencies that were present in the private sector before Medicare was established. Finally, although Medicare's infringements on providers' professional autonomy are modest, it has perhaps contributed to the profession's concern with economic rather than health matters.

From the central focus of the investments approach—justifying the extension of socioeconomic rights to those confronting social hazards—little about Medicare is disconcerting. Medicare recipients earn their benefits and do not abuse their access to medical care. However, Medicare cannot simply be thrown open to serve all those who need medical care and have no private insurance. The two primary obstacles to extending Medicare into national health insurance are the opposition of medical-care providers and the aggregate cost of such a program. But since other advanced industrial nations do provide universal health coverage, perhaps these obstacles are not insurmountable.

To elicit the cooperation of medical-care providers, any program for the public provision of medical care must address providers' two principal concerns: profitability and professional control. If we look at the experiences of other nations in creating systems of public medical-care provision, we find no prevailing model for compromises on these issues. But the brief history of Medicare suggests the kind of compromise most likely to work in the United States: Maintain the lucrativeness of providing medical services in return for greater public policy control over the goals and means of medical care. Indeed, since the late 1920s proponents of national health insurance have tried to persuade provider groups that this compromise is in the national interest. Providers resisted this direction forcefully and successfully for a long time, but with Medicare's passage they lost a crucial battle in this struggle. In the aftermath of Medicare's enactment it became easier for providers to accept the payoffs of the program than to continue their earlier resistance. Corporate inroads in the medical-care fields have also been based on this pattern.

To make this compromise explicit and to expedite its implementation, the federal government should create a national bargaining council whose members would represent the federal government, providers, and perhaps other relevant constituencies. This council's central task would be to hammer out a series of guidelines that would assure profitability for providers in exchange for providers' cooperation on the goals and means of medical care. These guidelines should draw on existing institutions and practices. For example, private insurance companies should not be displaced; rather the federal government should expand, coordinate, and perhaps subsidize the efforts of these companies in a national drive to extend at least minimal insurance coverage to more Americans. This insurance could be similar in many respects to Medicare, but would specify affordable out-of-pocket annual maximum liabilities for households in different income ranges.

In return for these financial considerations, providers would be asked to increasingly resolve issues pertaining to the goals and means of medical care collectively with their public official counterparts on the council. These agreements, which would be subject to periodic renegotiation, would specify the sorts of care national health insurance would cover, how that care would be delivered, and the responsibilities of providers and patients. Such agreements might also limit the responsibilities of public policy in prolonging the lives of the terminally ill, or include custodial care for chronic conditions, or make public financial help for certain health problems contingent on patient cooperation in giving up health-threatening personal habits.

The details of such agreements are less important than the initiation of a collaborative process between public officials and providers. In the absence of such a process, no one should expect any broad initiatives in the area of national health insurance.

Eight

The Investments Approach

The investments approach to American public social provision is based on the five general principles introduced in chapter 2 and developed in subsequent chapters: reciprocity, supplementing efforts at self-help, inclusivity, social insurance, and social merging. Before detailing specific proposals to realize socioeconomic rights, I want to briefly review these principles.

Reciprocity is the foundation of the investments approach: Those who make constructive contributions to society may reasonably expect nurturing assistance from society with respect to basic needs when social hazards afflict their lives. The moral substance of this norm would probably not be questioned by most Americans. Popular reactions even to AFDC bespeak a willingness to help those who are really in need.[1] However, applications of this principle are bound to create controversy and conflicts with important tenets of American political culture. To minimize such disharmony, I have narrowly defined constructive contributions as participation in the paid labor force; dependents of participants are also included. To recognize concurrent as well as prior participation, satisfactory performance in a training program is also deemed evidence of constructive contribution to the social product.

In developing the specifics of the basic level of support earned by citizens in exchange for their constructive contributions, I have tried to steer between the opposing reefs of classical liberalism and class-conflict theories. The contemporary libertarian interpretation of liberalism is hesitant about using large-scale public programs to provide nurturing assistance when hazards befall citizens and resists the notion that these public benefits are rights.[2] But most Americans are willing to relax classical liberalism and re-mediate some of the social hazards of contemporary advanced society.[3] Mainstream political opinion recognizes the distressing limitations of both the labor market and community in a purely individualistic society.

Proponents of class-conflict theories, of course, will challenge the rationale of making social program benefits generally con-tingent on participation in the paid labor market, which they view as an instrument of exploitation. I have sympathy for this view. To be sure, there is little free consent on the labor side of the labor-management nexus.[4] Nonetheless, this perspective will not be po-litically influential in America in the foreseeable future. Accord-ingly, it is only by partaking of certain socially approved activities that those on the fringes of society can hope to merge with the socioeconomic mainstream, thus achieving societal membership and earning personal dignity. And despite the inequities of the la-bor market, most Americans want the membership status and per-sonal dignity that come from constructively taking part in society as others do.[5] The investments approach would replace the stig-matizing aspects of public assistance with opportunities for digni-fied social merging.

My second principle is that social programs be designed as sup-plements to citizens' self-help efforts. Accordingly, benefits should be formulated to augment—rather than replace or discourage—a recipient's income. Two distinct implications follow from this principle. First, benefits should generally provide less than com-plete support. Recipients of income-maintenance benefits should be required to augment those benefits in order to live comfortably and should pay a share of the costs of medical services. Second, although benefits are earned, social programs should not be ex-pected to readily supplement the incomes of well-to-do households that cannot reasonably be portrayed as suffering from a social haz-ard. A minority, but nevertheless a significant number, of social security households now pose problems in this regard. If retire-ment represents a period of luxurious leisure rather than a social hazard, the case for applying social program benefits is increas-ingly untenable. Rather than reducing or eliminating earned bene-fits through means or income tests, however, I recommend taxing benefits in order to limit the public support that goes to wealthy households.

Inclusivity means that assistance in times of hazard will be accessible for all citizens who meet two criteria. First, the individual must have experienced a covered social hazard: disabling illness or injury; childbirth and child-rearing; aging; family dissolution due to death, divorce, or desertion; and unemployment. Second, the individual must have either made or be making the required contribution with respect to the labor force. In other words, a relevant need of assistance buttressed by the willingness to engage in constructive activity are the sole requirements to be certified. Broad measures of eligibility will make social programs useful to a wide portion of the population over time. Wide usage and the certification of recipients ought to prompt stronger support for these programs from the public and from powerful political figures.

These three principles—reciprocity, supplementation, and inclusivity—point us toward social insurance as a vehicle for resolving many resource inadequacy problems. The concept of social insurance, as we have seen, fits fairly well with American political culture, and the example of social security has set a successful precedent for social insurance using personal accounts. Thus my proposals rely heavily on social insurance programs.

Some resource inadequacy problems, however, do not lend themselves to programs requiring prior contributions. In these instances, social merging programs can extend the social insurance concept to allow for concurrent rather than prior efforts. Social merging programs that demand an effort-based quid pro quo rather than providing means-based public assistance also fit fairly well with American political culture. Their undeniable disadvantage is that they would inevitably force many people to accept undesirable jobs, thereby contributing to the exploitation of the economically weak by the economically powerful. But the advantages of this approach are nonetheless compelling: the effort requirement would allow recipients to maintain their dignity and societal membership; the provision of benefits to supplement recipients' self-help efforts would create incentives for recipients to act in socially approved ways; and the public perception that benefits were not handouts but earned assistance would reduce political attacks on welfare.

The heart of the investments approach resides in these principles, not in the specific proposals outlined in this chapter. Although the following proposals are indicative of my preferences for realizing socioeconomic rights, implementation of the investments approach could take many alternative forms.

Social Insurance

My central suggestion here is to expand the social hazard coverage of the social security program to provide short-term income-maintenance benefits in the event of disabling illness and injury, childbirth, absence of the primary household breadwinner due to desertion or divorce, and unemployment. In order to fund these new benefits with minimal increases in payroll taxes, I offer three proposals to reduce social security outlays for retirement benefits.

Retirement. The current income-maintenance provisions for retirees and their surviving spouses are adequate. My proposals are directed at controlling the cost of these benefits.

First, I propose selectively raising retirement ages so that people in relatively sedentary jobs will retire later than people in jobs that are physically demanding. The range for eligibility to receive full social security benefits might extend from sixty-two to seventy. Such a system of scaled retirement ages would offset to some degree the bias of the current system in favor of white-collar workers, who begin work later in life and generally live longer. As a safeguard, career tracks could be defined such that people could not qualify for early retirement by shifting occupations late in life.

Second, I propose linking benefit levels to increases in the consumer price index after retirement, rather than the current system of continuous benefit indexing during future beneficiaries' working years. This change would have the practical effect of making social security less like a defined-benefit plan and more like a defined-contribution plan.[6] Increases in initial benefit levels for succeeding cohorts of retirees would be left to the discretion of the political process. As they do now, benefit cash values would vary directly with earnings, and replacement rates would vary inversely with earnings.

Third, I propose taxing a progressively larger portion of retirees' benefits as household income rises. For example, a portion of benefits would become taxable when a household's total income reaches one-half of the national median income. The portion of benefits subject to tax would increase with income, and all benefits would be taxable for households at or above the median income. Such an approach would assure benefits for those who have paid into the social security system but also reduce the net cost of public social provision for households with relatively comfortable incomes.[7] This approach also reflects the basic purpose of social insurance, to mitigate social hazards. If little hazard appears, only minimal insurance needs to be applied.

Other proposals might be made to address such issues as the equitable treatment of couples as opposed to single persons, but these are beyond the scope of my intentions here.

Disability. The social security system now provides income-maintenance benefits for qualified workers who suffer a long-term total disability. I propose extending this program to cover short-term disability due to illness or injury. This coverage would supplant the income-maintenance aspects of workers' compensation and would extend protection to non–job-related illness or injury. Benefit levels would be determined under formulas similar to those now used by social security as amended by my proposals above.

With respect to long-term disability, I propose that we reexamine the concept of total disability, particularly for younger workers. It seems reasonable to retrain younger workers for whatever occupations their disabilities allow and to assist them with job placement.[8]

Childbirth. I propose providing women workers with income-maintenance benefits for a brief period (say, three months) before or after childbirth. Restrictions could be placed on the number of times (twice?) a woman could use these benefits. Again, benefit levels would be linked to earnings histories.

Survivorship. Social security now provides survivorship benefits for dependents of qualified workers. These benefits seem appropriate for retirement-aged surviving spouses, but I propose restricting survivorship benefits for working-aged adults. Working-aged spouses would be allowed to collect benefits for no more than, say, five years, and children could collect benefits until age eighteen (age twenty-two for full-time students). These provisions would restore college benefits for children but require that spouses adjust to their new circumstances within a fixed period.

Desertion and Divorce. I propose that working-aged adults and children separated from their family's primary breadwinner by divorce or desertion receive short-term (perhaps one month) income-maintenance benefits at levels comparable to other social insurance coverage. (Longer-term provision is discussed in the following section on social merging.) As with childbirth benefits, eligibility could be restricted to two or three times in an individual's life.

Unemployment. I propose that short-term (perhaps one month) unemployment insurance benefits be offered through social security. (Again, long-term provision is discussed in the following section on social merging.) Limits on eligibility could be set at once every two or three years. This proposal would replace the current system of unemployment insurance.

Administrative safeguards. Some safeguards will be needed to prevent workers who have achieved initial eligibility for extended benefits from abusing the system by creating a series of illnesses, injuries, childbirths, family dissolutions, or unemployment episodes to avoid the workplace. One such set of safeguards includes my proposed limits on the duration of benefits and the number of times a worker could collect certain benefits.

In addition, a blanket rule could restrict the overall use of benefits to a specified portion of a person's working life (from the end of his or her formal education to retirement). This proportion could be expressed on a sliding scale, with younger workers eligible to receive benefits for a fairly high proportion (say, 30 percent) of their working life thus far, and older workers limited to a much lower percentage (say, 5 percent) over a roughly forty-year working life. This scale would accommodate the high incidence of legitimate hazards appearing early in life, while clearly implying that sustained periods of participation in the labor force are required to earn benefits.

Costs. I have suggested several ways to cut the current costs of social security benefits for retirement, long-term disability, and survivorship as well as outlays for current workers' compensation and unemployment provisions. Though no one can accurately predict the results, I suspect that these savings will be more than offset by the costs of my proposals to extend social security coverage to short-term disability, childbirth, and household dissolution.

Should it be necessary to further increase revenues, my preference is for a progressive social security tax on all wages. The rate for a worker's first $10,000 of annual income could be held at the current rate (7.51 percent) or even reduced a bit, with slightly higher rates for each tier of income, defined in increments of $10,000. In conjunction with the progressive taxation of social security benefits, this proposal would require ever closer coordination between the Social Security Administration and the Internal Revenue Service.

Social Merging

The heart of my proposals to facilitate social merging lies in expanding the incentives, opportunities, and capacities for self-support for those persons near or beyond the fringes of the labor market. Complementary measures are intended to enhance the capacity of the existing labor market to provide these people with full-time employment.

Incentives. In order to increase the incentives for self-support and decrease the "unintended rewards" that our current system sometimes provides for not working, I propose limiting public assistance to Supplementary Security Income (SSI) and including only persons with certifiable total physical or psychological disabilities and elderly persons not covered by social security. We should be fairly hard-nosed about admitting people to this program, but those who do meet the criteria should also be entitled to more intensive therapeutic and custodial care than is now typically available. Such care might be entrusted to private charities that accepted federal guidelines, perhaps with some public funding assistance.

Rather than terminating much of current public assistance in one motion, we could gradually phase out assistance to various categories of recipients, beginning with those who have the surest prospects for success in social merging programs.

Opportunities. First, to assist unemployed working-aged adults in increasing their opportunities for self-support, we can reinvigorate our system of public employment services so that they serve more adequately as labor exchanges.

Second, to facilitate parents in entering the labor force and contributing to the support of their households, I recommend establishing a social insurance program of universal supplementary child allowances. In contrast to the social insurance programs mentioned in the preceding sections, these allowances would be sharply income-variable and would involve substantial vertical redistribution. Since this is the least conventional of my proposals, I will describe it in greater detail.

Let us consider a program that would provide income-variable supplementary benefits for up to three children per household. This program would cover all American households, including the vast majority of the children now served by AFDC, without subsidizing undesirably high birthrates. Households with annual pretax incomes up to that resulting from full-time work at the minimum wage (currently about $6,700) would be eligible for the full benefits; there would be no work disincentive for these low-income families. Benefit levels would be sharply staged so there would be minimal incentives for new births. And benefits would be taxed as income, further reducing the income-variable benefits for middle- and upper-income families.

Full benefits would be set at $175 a month for the first child, $125 a month for the second child, and $75 a month for the third child—for a maximum of $375 a month, or $4,500 a year. Thus a household with wages equal to those derived from full-time employment at the minimum wage and three children would have a total pretax income of $11,200 ($6,700 + $4,500), placing it at approximately the current federal poverty level for households of this size.

Households with income above the level provided by full-time employment at the minimum wage would see their benefits reduced dollar-for-dollar down to a universal minimum benefit of $75 a month for three children ($35 for the first, $25 for the second, and $15 for the third).[9] This scaling would keep benefits extremely modest for middle- and upper-income families, although it might reduce incentives for low-income families to increase wages modestly. But these graduated levels of benefits would concentrate public social provision on households with the greatest need for child allowance supplements; that is, this program would have high target efficiency.

This program would be financed by a progressive payroll deduction on all wage earners. In addition to involving a substantial degree of vertical redistribution, this program presents an unusual case of life-cycle redistribution, since child-rearing characteristically comes fairly early in adulthood.

It is possible that the benefit levels I have suggested would allow some rural households to subsist with little or no labor-market participation or would encourage families to migrate to rural regions.[10] Should these consequences become problematic, benefits could be adjusted to discourage such activities, although moderate levels of migration might well be preferable to current inner-city conditions.

There are other means of striving to assure minimum levels of support to children. Indexing the minimum wage to the consumer price index and enforcing child-support court orders to noncustodial parents are frequently discussed. While neither of these options would contradict the general principles of the investments approach, neither would as efficiently and thoroughly accomplish the ends served by the child allowance system I have described. Indexing the minimum wage is not likely to concentrate resources such that single parents with limited skills can support more than one child. Increasing the rigor of child-support payments, as Wisconsin and other states are doing, will not facilitate household support for children whose noncustodial parent is unidentified, incommunicado, unemployed, or destitute. Thus I see these two options less as alternatives to child allowances than as sensible additional measures serving related, but distinct objectives.

My third concern regarding opportunities is that we cannot reasonably insist that parents, particularly single parents, work full time unless affordable child-care is available to them. Here, we have several alternatives in addition to commercial child-care centers: subsidies to employers who create child-care facilities in their workplaces, public child-care extended through the public school system, and reimbursements to parents for the costs of paying relatives or neighbors to look after children. The crucial point is that, while child-care raises the costs of social merging, many parents—especially single parents—cannot contribute to the support of their households in the absence of some provision for child-care. Whatever specific measures we adopt, we must make child-care available at subsidized rates for low-income families.

Collectively, the proposals in this section are designed to enhance individual opportunities by: (1) improving information about work opportunities, (2) supplementing the financial returns of work on the fringes of the labor market for households with children, and (3) facilitating employment through the provision of adequate, affordable child-care.

Capacities. My recommendations here comprise measures intended to improve unemployed and underemployed workers' capacities for greater labor market participation. First, we need public work programs for young unskilled workers. Such programs could take many forms, including the model of the Civilian Conservation Corps (CCC). These would not be expensive or extensive training programs designed to teach sophisticated skills, but rather programs intended to instill basic work habits (attendance, punctuality) and to provide participants with an employment history.[11] In effect, these programs would certify participants as good bets for subsequent employment and training by private employers. Small-scale work programs would be particularly appropriate in remote areas; in that context programs would be minimally disruptive of local economies.

Second, we should offer sophisticated training, retraining, or education programs to adults with satisfactory records of employment (say, encouraging work histories of at least five years) who face sudden labor market problems—such as layoffs in declining industries—and to parents (generally mothers) in households that experience changes in membership that compel them to enter the labor market. Giving individuals in these two categories opportunities to upgrade their labor market capacities is a social investment more than likely to return its costs, as participants' subsequent income tax payments are apt to exceed training expenditures. Among all high-unemployment groups, for example, single-parent homemakers have been the most successful in taking advantage of training opportunities to move on into full-time employment.[12]

By satisfactory progress in these training programs, participants would also earn temporary income-maintenance support, in effect a scholarship to subsidize their vocational education. The amount of this support would equal that provided for unemployment or family dissolution under social insurance.

Complementary measures. To further expand the demand for unskilled, semiskilled, and entry-level workers, the federal govern-

ment could create more low- and midlevel positions as well as provide subsidies for state and local governments that wish to do the
same. These efforts would help to replace the decent-paying jobs
lost in manufacturing and thus increase the capacity of the labor
market to provide positions capable of supporting households,
particularly for the residents of central cities.

Demand could also be enhanced by offering employers in the
private sector tax incentives for creating new low- and midrange
positions. For example, a sharp tax break could be available to
employers who increased their payrolls by a small percentage. This
percentage would deliberately be relatively small to minimize dis-
placement and training problems.

Implications for Housing and Education

Although housing policy and education are not an integral part of
my analyses and proposals, the investments approach holds several important implications for public services in these areas. Chief
among these is the principle that the public provision of basic
goods and services needs to be tailored as closely as possible to the
peculiarities of our nation's political culture. In many other advanced industrial nations, for instance, direct public provision of
housing units is widely practiced and accepted. But in the United
States such programs are generally aspects of public assistance
and, with the exception of projects categorically limited to the
elderly, residents often feel stigmatized.

Housing subsidies. Consistent with current trends in American
policy,[13] approaches that help recipients of public assistance participate in the regular housing market are desirable. This preference is not so strong as to mandate massive and abrupt changes in
housing policy. And in specific urban areas, and perhaps other
locales, expanded direct provision of accessible public housing
units remains essential.[14] But overall I would suggest that housing
is best regarded as an aspect of income maintenance and that we
continue to reduce the direct public provision of housing units, as
feasible.

The use of housing vouchers, rather than cash payments, is an
option that has achieved some support in recent years.[15] Vouchers
involve more complicated administrative services than cash, but

they may be more politically acceptable to citizens who raise suspicions about how public program recipients use their benefits. Vouchers are compatible with an approach to housing as an income-maintenance matter as long as the vouchers are legal tender for housing, and recipients are allowed some flexibility with respect to rents. For instance, households eligible for income-maintenance payments under social merging programs might be given a housing voucher worth one-half of their monthly cash benefits. Thus benefits for housing would amount to one-third of the income-maintenance total. Recipients could choose whatever housing they preferred, paying higher rent or home payments out of their pocket. This feature would be particularly helpful for families who do not want to move or sell their homes during a short-term disruption of income. And we ought also to continue giving recipients cash rebates for rents that do not consume a stipulated portion of their income-maintenance benefits.

Education. My analyses and proposals also hold interesting implications and opportunities for expanding the public school system. First, the system could be expanded to provide more vocational education for adults. Such programs would facilitate my proposal to offer training for experienced workers and would also create good jobs in the public sector.

Second, as mentioned in my discussion of child-care, one mechanism for providing affordable child-care would be to extend the public school system to include preschool programs for younger children.[16] This suggestion would also serve to create new jobs in the public sector.

Together these two programs would also link people's lives more thoroughly to the public school system. And public support for the schools might increase as schools expanded their service capacity and became a focus for family and community services.

Finally, the principle of using social policy to reinforce desirable activity could be applied to stem the tide of parents' transferring their children from public to private schools. A particularly troubling aspect of this trend is that many parents who have opted out of the public school system are precisely the concerned activists who, had they stayed, would have expressed their dissatisfactions to teachers and school administrators, and thereby would have instigated changes and improvements.[17] One way to encourage parents to keep their children in the public schools would be to give students who attend public schools some degree of preferential treatment with respect to public financial aid for postsecondary education.

Medical Care

Some crucial aspects of the provision of medical care—gaining the requisite cooperation from physicians and other medical-care providers—lie outside the primary focus—socioeconomic rights of citizens—of the investments approach. Unfortunately in light of this, other aspects of medical-care provision—assuring people financial access to medical care—remain integral concerns of the investments approach. It would be much simpler to follow the libertarians by limiting ourselves to an income-maintenance system;[18] however, such an approach will not assure citizens protection from common social hazards. The need for medical care is highly intermittent for most people, but the costs—once care is needed— are frequently quite high. These features make it infeasible to cover the provision of medical care through income-maintenance means. Instead, health insurance that assures access to care at manageable cost—the technique adopted by the contemporary American upper middle class—is the appropriate tool.

The process of assuring access to medical care in such a fashion need not entail confronting the providers of medical services with intolerable changes. What I have in mind is a system similar in some respects to the decentralized, quasi-public national health insurance of the Federal Republic of Germany. This system should have the following general features. With respect to depth of coverage we need to develop a reasonably comprehensive national minimum. In most areas of provision this minimum could be similar to the current Medicare. But we should place some feasible, income-graduated maxima on out-of-pocket annual expenditures (for incomes below $10,000, $500; for incomes between $10,000 and $20,000, $1,000; and so on). With respect to breadth of coverage, this program should represent an integral aspect of employment. The carriers themselves would be the existing private insurance companies. And coverage would be extended throughout the working population by public subsidy for certain groups of employers and employees. Households with children, even those with no employed adult, would be served through the deduction of the relevant insurance premiums from the universal child allowances. These broad features leave the practice of medicine relatively unchanged for most providers. The basic changes are the extension of access to medical care through the requirement that employers offer their employees insurance coverage meeting the minimum criteria and the use of public subsidies to help pay for coverage.

With this brief overview behind us, let us look with greater care at the specifics. My guess is that developing this sort of coverage requires as a prerequisite the establishment of a national bargaining council, as discussed at the end of chapter 7. This council, operating within general guidelines such as those outlined in the previous paragraph, would create an initial version of the specific rules about prices and limits. Existing providers could expect to continue their activities as relatively autonomous units as well as to receive their customary incomes. Public officials in return would gain assurances about future cost increases. I would anticipate that limitations on provider practices would initially be fairly modest and would grow with time, experience, and the gradually broadening recognition that the providers of medical care in America form an industry, and that, as is the case for other important service industries, some degree of public regulation is necessary.

The most important aspects of the initial measures involve extending access to medical care to working-aged Americans and their dependents. The basic mechanism here involves a program of subsidies to low-income employees, and as necessary to small-scale employers, that allows employees to join a system of compulsory medical-care insurance meeting minimum national criteria. The employees of small-scale employers might, for instance, be consolidated into several groups for which risks are shared by private carriers with federal subsidies.[19] Employers could be required to offer a choice of plans varying in coverage, expense, and manner of care—HMO or traditional fee-for-service. And a variety of cost-control features should characterize minimum coverage as is increasingly the case for existing private group insurance. The central objective of this coverage would be to place feasible upper limits on the annual out-of-pocket medical expenses of families in varying income ranges. Conventional practices with respect to deductibles and coinsurance would not be excluded—only limited—by this goal. Whether coverage would extend to all known treatments would have to be debated in the bargaining council. These aspects as well as other facets of coverage limitations would be subject to change and, as with other rights' limits issues, would represent public decisions about cultural conventions.

Households with children would be covered under this program, regardless of the employment status of their adults, by virtue of an automatic system of deducting the relevant insurance premiums from the child allowances. This practice is consistent with the conception developed in chapter 2, that children are not responsible for their predicaments and should have support extended to them on the basis of need. Collectively, these two proposals would cover employed households and households with children. Unemployed single adults and childless couples should be able to join this insurance scheme at subsidized rates similar to those available for employed persons. These high-risk individuals could be spread across insurance carriers so as to minimize the problems of specific companies.

Individuals for whom an episodic social hazard did not mean an end to employment would be covered by the system described above. Those whose hazards spelled an end to employment—retirement or long-term total disability—would be picked up by the Medicare program. This program would also serve those enrolled and making satisfactory progress in job training programs. People whose disabilities placed them in the residual SSI program would also come under Medicare, but hopefully under expanded provisions that allowed appropriate human-intensive care.

Existing Medicare provisions can generally stand. But I do propose some changes that would bring Medicare into line with my other medical-care proposals. First, I propose an out-of-pocket ceiling for covered care similar to that for the households of working-aged adults. Second, we should extend limited coverage of low-intensity care for chronic conditions. Third, I propose cutting back the degree to which public programs support prolonging the lives of terminally ill patients.

Realizing these provisions would assuredly add to the proportion of GNP that is funneled into the medical-care sector of the economy, and it would add as well to the costs of public programs directed at medical-care problems. For these reasons it is crucial that the provisions follow the efforts described in chapter 7 to create cost-control structures by both public regulation and market means. I suspect that no one could predict with any accuracy the cost increases that these proposals would involve, but I will identify major components. Extending minimum national medical-care insurance coverage to working-aged adults and their dependents will involve the largest single cost increase. I have suggested a way of placing limits on these increases by explicitly raising the possibility of placing some new, expensive, and exotic treatments beyond the limits of this minimum coverage. Coverage for these treatments should be available for those who want and can pay for it, but it need not be included in the initial basic minimum public coverage. Within Medicare, expenses would rise as a consequence of realizing these proposals, primarily due to the addition of new beneficiaries—participants in job training programs and SSI beneficiaries. The three recommendations that I made with respect to the existing Medicare provisions offset one another. Adding annual out-of-pocket payment ceilings and limited low-intensity care for chronic conditions would both increase expenses, but these increases would be largely offset if substantial cuts were made in the use of Medicare to prolong the lives of the terminally ill. The overall increases in public medical-care expenses that these proposals entail would add to the case for building progressive tiers into social insurance payroll tax deductions.

The Investments Approach and American Values

Anyone can, of course, trot out a series of social policy measures that sound encouraging to sympathetic ears. That is, however, not the point of the foregoing. Rather these proposals not only address a broad range of the social hazards prominent in contemporary America, but they do so in a fashion consistent with the five general principles discussed at the outset of this chapter. These principles are, in turn, consistent with important values of the American political culture. I will argue the case for these claims by applying the questions used in the case studies of chapters 5−7 to these proposals. Since my proposals cover a broader gamut than any of the individual programs examined earlier, I will only sketch out the highlights, both encouraging and discouraging.

Distributive Justice

As important as any characteristic that this package of proposals offers is a set of criteria for the distribution of benefits that is more rigorous than either contemporary public assistance or some aspects of American social insurance. The dominant distributive criterion realized through these proposals is the exertion of effort in the paid labor market. Benefits are earned through prior or concurrent contributions of effort, which are recorded in individual accounts. The investments approach thus affords vulnerable citizens a dignified means for coping with a variety of social hazards. The distributive criterion of results (vertical equity) characterizes these proposals as well, since benefit levels reflect past earnings, just as current social security benefits do. This effect, however, is diluted by the taxation of benefits paid to middle- and upper-income households. Taxation also reinforces the fairly strong linkage of benefits to the provision of basic resources, a tie established by the supplementary character of the benefit levels. That benefits are intended to supplement recipients' efforts at self-support both precludes total dependency and enhances dignity.

Considered collectively, these proposals involve enough vertical redistribution to represent an assault on property more extensive than that entailed by existing social programs. Both the child allowances and the medical-care proposals, for example, address distinct concerns by redistributing resources toward our most vulnerable and needy populations. But these proposals temper vertical redistribution with the constructive-efforts requirement for working-aged adults; only children and the severely disabled are excused from this rule.

In summary, these proposals do not assure every citizen of support; rather, benefits are a quid pro quo. In this regard, these proposals have more in common with the market than with a system of distributive justice based on need. But whereas the market represents a results-oriented struggle, the survival of the most capable, these proposals operate on the basis of effort. Under the investments approach, market forces are supplemented by a measure of public provision so that people who apply themselves to support their households will have a much better chance of being able to afford basic goods and services.

Negative Liberty

One drawback of relying more heavily on social insurance is that its compulsory character would pervade life more thoroughly. As noted in chapter 5, however, the compulsory nature of social security has not provoked even moderate opposition. Indeed, in chapter 7 we found an example of people jumping at the chance to participate in a voluntary program of publicly subsidized insurance, SMI (Part B of Medicare). We do need to keep in mind, of course, that most social security beneficiaries to date have received far more in benefits than they have paid into the program,[20] and far more than they might have reasonably expected from committing similar amounts to private investments. But, for the programs I am proposing, the ratio between contributions and benefits will be less heavily weighed in favor of benefits, which may create more reluctance about compulsory participation. The breadth of social hazard coverage and its inclusivity regarding potential recipients may, in turn, offset this reluctance to some degree. Apart from compulsory taxation, these proposals do not restrict the liberty of recipients in formal ways.

The private professionals most obviously affected by these proposals are physicians and other providers of medical services. My proposals require that, in return for reasonable income guarantees, these providers will increasingly have to share decision making about the ends and means of medical care with public officials. Like other basic service industries, the medical-care industry will become increasingly regulated.

Additionally, these proposals have disconcerting consequences for social workers. Apart from the scaled-down program for psychological and physiological disability, my proposed programs do not call for caseworkers. The role of caseworkers in the public sector would be reduced to activities in the criminal justice system and medical institutions.

Economic Efficiency

These proposals embody strong work and savings incentives. By and large, contributions in the form of paid labor would be necessary for program eligibility, and benefit levels would be designed to supplement household efforts at self-help. The proposed limitations on the use of individual hazard provisions and the blanket maximum-use provision represent safeguards against abuse and malingering.

The starkness of the work incentives would appear to strengthen the hands of corporate managers and entrepreneurs, although program costs would offset to some degree whatever advantages accrue to managerial risk-takers. The higher payroll taxes would surely increase the cost of doing business in the United States, but they would not raise such costs beyond those now incurred by some of our important international competitors—the Federal Republic of Germany, for instance.

A less sanguine possibility is that these proposals might reinforce either of two disturbing trends in the labor market: the bifurcation of the labor market between highly skilled, well-paid workers and relatively unskilled, minimum-wage workers or the exportation of jobs offshore.

Without doubt, these proposals would cost more than we now spend for social security, Medicare, Medicaid, AFDC, unemployment benefits, workers' compensation, and SSI. One cannot predict how much more. While the social insurance components would dominate expenditures, the greatest proportional cost increases are likely to come in the social merging programs. Relying more heavily on social insurance would shift the costs of public social provision more thoroughly to those who enjoy its benefits; the increased costs of social merging would represent the price of dignity, the price of creating conditions that facilitate dignified self-help.

The heavy reliance on social insurance and the supplementary character of benefits would create a life-cycle redistribution pattern. Substantial vertical redistribution would be injected by the child allowances, the proposals to expand the labor market, and the benefits for adults enrolled in training programs. These elements are essential for social merging, however, and each requires formally or informally some type of quid pro quo from program recipients.

Through their inclusivity these proposals generally avoid the problems associated with focusing public social provision on particularly disadvantaged groups. Even the child allowance program is universal, albeit income variable, thus affording higher target efficiency.

Administrative Complexity

The social insurance proposals would require a substantial escalation of administrative activities within SSA and related bureaucracies. For this reason, the programs should be phased in over time rather than implemented simultaneously.[21] The income-maintenance programs call for precisely those activities we already accomplish fairly well; they would require an increase in the quantity of administrative activities, but not a change in their nature. Other proposals, such as job training and child-care in particular, would require a greater degree of decentralized complexity. In dealing with particular recipient groups, these programs are likely to confront the difficulties identified in chapter 4. But even here we have some encouraging experience in each of these areas,[22] and my proposals are generally tailored to these experiences.

Overall, these proposals attempt to come to grips with the major limits and harmonization issues. With respect to limits, different mechanisms apply to income maintenance and medical care. For the former, the principle of supplementary benefits and the progressive taxation of benefits assure that most benefits will be used to purchase basic material resources and that households with high incomes from other sources will receive only limited benefits.

In the case of medical care the limits problems are more severe. Rapidly expanding technological capabilities and growing uncertainties about the cost-benefits of existing practices create systematic dilemmas about the appropriate limits of medical care, particularly the public provision of care. Social programs cannot resolve these problems, but my proposal for a bargaining council provides a mechanism for focusing national policy discussion of limits issues. More importantly, the bargaining council's initial recommendations and decisions—controversial and inadequate as they might be—could prompt a much-needed ongoing national debate on these issues.

One harmonization benefit of the investments approach lies in the complementary nature of the distinct provisions. The independent programs mesh together to avoid gaps or duplication of coverage and to provide consistent incentives for self-support.

But other harmonization issues may be exacerbated by the investments approach. The cost will create new budgetary difficulties, and the denser public policy environment may provoke unforeseen problems. Additionally, these proposals would stimulate aggregate demand and employment, thereby raising inflationary pressures. Despite selective measures to constrain these pressures—the supplementary character of benefits, the focus on high-unemployment populations, and the regulation of medical costs—these proposals are inflationary.

Overall, however, the investments approach represents a practical realization of the five principles central to American values in the area of socioeconomic rights. As national programs, though, these proposals do not operationalize concepts of limited and local government.

Conflicts of Interest and Compliance

For beneficiaries the investments approach provides broad humane incentives for cooperation in that programs would respect and reinforce the dignity of individual beneficiaries and their membership in society. Inclusivity and reciprocity should also reduce conflicts of interest between public officials and beneficiaries, while enhancing popular perceptions of public social provision. All constituencies would realize that prospective beneficiaries would include a broad cross-section of the American voting population, not just small categories of the particularly disadvantaged, and that through social programs the nation's public policy would be encouraging responsible behavior.

Conflicts of interest between private providers of medical care and public officials over costs and professional autonomy are likely to be aggravated, however. The best that the investments approach offers physicians, hospital administrators, and insurance companies is the tradeoff of fairly lucrative financial returns in exchange for a loss of autonomy with respect to the ends and means of medical care.

While social workers may protest their reduced role in the new programs, these programs would expand opportunities for third-party providers of employment, job training, and child-care services.

Prospects

On balance, the investments approach represents an improvement over existing social programs with respect to core American values. It is reasonable to ask whether this approach will work. Clearly, no set of proposals will meet each and every person's needs. But within the context of American political culture, the programs I have recommended would demonstrably facilitate and supplement socially desirable efforts at self-help.

It is also reasonable to ask whether the investments approach is a neat theory that bears little relation in practice to the day-to-day lives of taxpayers, program beneficiaries, program bureaucrats, or prominent public officials. The investments approach, it might be argued, is just labeling. But in political matters, labeling and perceptions are crucial. And from the standpoint of the personal dignity and societal membership of program recipients, an earned income supplement is far preferable to an imposed workfare assignment or public assistance that is viewed by fellow citizens as a handout.

Compared to current practices in other advanced industrial societies, my proposals may be criticized as being too narrow. The child allowances, for example, assure only poverty-level incomes for parents who work full time. This degree of generosity is not exactly stunning. And American society would probably be the better for it if we could bring ourselves to be more generous, by including, for instance, rearing children and housework among the contributions to the social product that would merit support. However, our political culture would not accept the establishment of the broader programs that many other advanced industrial societies take for granted.

I conclude that we have the moral, political, and economic tools

necessary to reduce social problems through the improvement of
social insurance and the development of social merging programs.
I will now turn to the question as to whether we will choose to use
these tools. Can we expect a set of proposals such as these to be
adopted in the near future?

For several reasons, I think the best we can expect is a slow incremental reform of current policies and procedures. One source of
opposition to the investments approach will come from people
committed to a highly limited state. People for whom market distribution, negative liberty, and the economic efficiency of unadorned
market operations are extremely important will be far less im-
pressed by the proposals offered here than people for whom these
values represent only a portion or a limited conception of "the
good." Further, although the design features of the proposed programs fit important American values, experience has shown us
that compatibility or incompatibility is not a good predictor of the
ease in adopting new social programs. Despite its compatibility
with American values, Medicare faced decades of opposition,
while the notably incompatible AFDC was adopted far earlier.
Value compatibility does appear to have eased problems for Medicare's operation once it was adopted, however.

Yet even if we set aside lingering value conflicts, my proposals
would have to compete with a host of meritorious projects for
scarce public resources. The dollar cost of the investments approach is high, and so, too, therefore is the opportunity cost of implementing it. Successful adoption of the investments approach
would require a fairly broad cross-section of prominent American
public officials—the president and key members of Congress—to
place it high on their priorities and political agendas. But a constellation of factors makes a broad consensus on reform a relatively rare event in American politics. Some of these factors are
cyclical. Samuel P. Huntington describes sixty-year cycles in American politics that involve impressive reform efforts at one juncture,
but he conceives of these reform periods largely in terms of *attacks*
on state power.[23] (For that reason, he does not include the New
Deal—an effort to use state power to solve social problems—
among his reform periods.) Even if Huntington is incorrect about
the duration or motive of reform movements, clearly the mood of
American political elites during the last decade has not been sup-

portive of social program reform in any sense other than cutting costs.[24]

Hugh Heclo detects another historical pattern, identifying four periods in the development of social programs in advanced industrial societies: experimentation (1870s–1920s), consolidation (1930s–1940s), expansion (1950s–1960s), and reformulation (1970s–?).[25] The dates fit Western European history better than American, but the last two phases of this pattern are relevant to recent American experience. The United States expanded social provision sharply in the late 1960s and early 1970s, and it did so in ways that fit poorly with American political culture. As would be expected, these expanded activities—at odds with cherished values—have drawn increasing attention and raised a hue and cry for reformulation. But these dissatisfactions began precisely at a time when the postwar economic boom yielded to the stagflation of the mid-1970s. As a consequence, social programs have had to compete for resources in a more constant-sum economic environment.[26]

Yet another set of obstacles to comprehensive social program reform is posed by the relatively meager capacities American national political institutions have for sorting out diverse claims and forging a coherent national agenda.[27] As social programs have become more prominent in American politics, their development has become a focus for more numerous interest groups, none inclined to compromise.[28] In this light the interlocking character of my various proposals probably represents a political liability. Failing an unexpected cataclysm,[29] such as war or depression, the current political environment is much more likely to allow piecemeal changes rather than a systematic renovation of American social programs.

The relative impotence of American political parties further muddles the characteristically American situation of highly fragmented, competing priorities and agendas among prominent political officials. A determined president joined by key congressional leaders could, for instance, establish the bargaining council that is prerequisite to national medical-care insurance. But the presence of a private insurance system for the upper middle class and well-organized workers siphons off much of the voice that would help prompt such widespread determination among preeminent political officials.[30] And while social programs sometimes draw unexpected benefits from the interaction of competing elites,[31] it is unlikely that the side effects of contention will produce an integrated scheme of proposals.

For all these reasons, the best we can expect is that any new policy increments will follow principles more in accordance with important American values than was characteristic of the changes enacted in the mid-1960s and early 1970s. This forecast may frustrate proponents of public social provision, but it would certainly be preferable to the recent calls among political elites for a general retreat from social programs. The call to retreat is hardly worthy of political theories and practices that profess to place significant value on the individual. Weaknesses in social programs do not discredit the underlying needs that socioeconomic rights address, and we have seen that these rights are crucial to individuals living in an advanced industrial society. In a rush to rectify poorly designed programs, we must be careful not to abdicate our responsibility or abandon our principles about defending individuals. Rather than retreat from the difficult issues of public social provision, we need to make more careful determinations of what forms of defense are appropriate, supported by a clearer vision of the limits of state capacities.

Notes

Introduction

1. Lloyd A. Free and Hadley Cantril, *The Political Beliefs of Americans: A Study of Public Opinion* (New Brunswick, N.J.: Rutgers University Press, 1967), especially pp. 15–40.

2. Joe R. Feagin, *Subordinating the Poor: Welfare and American Beliefs* (Englewood Cliffs, N.J.: Prentice-Hall, 1975), chap. 4.

3. For arguments countering Murray's, see Christopher Jencks, "How Poor Are the Poor?" *New York Review of Books,* May 9, 1985; and Daniel Patrick Moynihan, *Family and Nation* (New York: Harcourt Brace Jovanovich, 1986), chap. 3.

4. Lawrence M. Mead, *Beyond Entitlement: The Social Obligations of Citizenship* (New York: Free Press, 1986).

5. Richard Burn, *The History of the Poor Laws: With Observations* (1764; rpt. Clifton N.J.: A. M. Kelley, 1973), quoted in Daniel P. Moynihan, *The Politics of a Guaranteed Income: The Nixon Administration and the Family Assistance Plan* (New York: Random House, 1973), pp. 159–60.

6. Harold L. Wilensky, *The Welfare State and Equality: Structural and Ideological Roots of Public Expenditures* (Berkeley: University of California Press, 1975). Richard Rose has recently provided a different frame of reference for Wilensky's evidence: in comparison to the most advanced nations of Western Europe, the United States is laggard in these respects, but the United States is much more representative of other Pacific Rim nations. See Rose, "How Exceptional Is American Government?" Studies in Public Policy no. 150, Center for the Study of Public Policy, University of Strathclyde, Glasgow, Scotland, 1985.

7. On the distinctiveness of American political culture and values, see, for example, Norman Furniss and Timothy Tilton, *The Case for the Wel-*

fare State: From Social Security to Social Equality (Bloomington: Indiana University Press, 1977); Anthony King, "Ideas, Institutions, and the Policies of Governments: A Comparative Analysis," *British Journal of Political Science* 3 (July 1973):291–313 and 3 (October 1973):409–23; Samuel P. Huntington, *American Politics: The Promise of Disharmony* (Cambridge: Harvard University Press, 1981). For contrasting views of differences between American and European values, compare Huntington, *American Politics* with Richard M. Coughlin, *Ideology, Public Opinion, and Welfare Policy: Attitudes Toward Taxes and Spending in Industrialized Societies* (Berkeley: Institute of International Studies, University of California, 1980). On the attitudes of American and European elites, see Charles Lockhart, "Values and Policy Conceptions of Health Policy Elites in the United States, the United Kingdom, and the Federal Republic of Germany," *Journal of Health Politics, Policy and Law* 6 (Spring 1981):98–119; Joel D. Aberbach, Robert D. Putnam, and Bert A. Rockman, *Bureaucrats and Politicians in Western Democracies* (Cambridge: Harvard University Press, 1981), chap. 5, especially pp. 122–24.

8. See Theodore Lowi, *The End of Liberalism: The Second Republic in the United States* (New York: Norton, 1979); Grant McConnell, *Private Power and American Democracy* (New York: Knopf, 1960).

9. See Jule M. Sugarman, Gary D. Bass, and Matthew J. Bader, "Human Services in the 1980's—President Reagan's 1983 Proposals, White Paper no. 5: For Citizens and Public Officials" (Washington, D.C.: Human Services Information Center, 1983), pp. 6–7, 9, and 76, and the *Social Security Bulletin* 51 (July 1988). This level of spending for similar purposes is not new in the United States. Roughly similar levels were reached through Civil War pensions in the late nineteenth century; see Theda Skocpol and John Ikenberry, "The Political Formation of the American Welfare State in Historical and Comparative Perspective," *Comparative Social Research* 6 (Greenwich, Conn.: JAI Press, 1983), pp. 87–148, particularly p. 95.

10. Compare with Huntington, *American Politics*, p. 230, and with Carleton B. Chapman and John M. Talmadge, "The Evolution of the Right-to-Health Concept in the United States," in Maurice B. Visscher, ed., *Humanistic Perspectives in Medical Ethics* (Buffalo: Prometheus, 1972), p. 108.

11. On the creation of this public image, see Jerry R. Cates, *Insuring Inequality: Administrative Leadership in Social Security, 1935–54* (Ann Arbor: University of Michigan Press, 1983). Much attention has been devoted to the question of why there is no socialism in the United States; for an early study, see Werner Sombart, *Why Is There No Socialism in the United States?* edited and introduced by C. T. Husbands (1906; rpt.

White Plains, N.Y.: M. E. Sharpe, 1976). In a recent review of the literature Seymour Martin Lipset notes that a growing number of writers believe that socialism, in the form of extensive social programs, has made inroads; see his "Why No Socialism in the United States?" in Seweryn Bialer and Sophia Sluzar, eds., *Radicalism in the Contemporary Age*, vol. 1 of *Sources of Contemporary Radicalism* (Boulder, Colo.: Westview, 1977), pp. 31–149.

12. Compare this general process of tailoring public policy to cultural values with the argument of Iredell Jenkins, *Social Order and the Limits of Law: A Theoretical Essay* (Princeton: Princeton University Press, 1980), chap. 9, especially pp. 122–23, 139, and 154. For a similar example applied to a different cultural setting, see Daniel Levine, "Conservatism and Tradition in Danish Social Welfare Legislation, 1890–1933: A Comparative View," *Comparative Studies in Society and History* 20 (January 1978) 54–69, especially p. 54.

13. See Feagin, *Subordinating the Poor*, chap. 4; Natalie Jaffe, "A Review of Public Opinion Surveys, 1935–1976," in Lester M. Salamon, *Welfare: The Elusive Consensus: Where We Are, How We Got There, and What's Ahead* (New York: Praeger, 1978), pp. 221–28.

14. For a more encouraging view see Tom Campbell, *The Left and Rights: A Conceptual Analysis of the Idea of Socialist Rights* (Boston: Routledge and Kegan Paul, 1983).

15. See T. H. Marshall, "Citizenship and Social Class," in *Sociology at the Crossroads and Other Essays* (London: Heinemann, 1963), pp. 67–127.

16. See David Miller, "Democracy and Social Justice," *British Journal of Political Science* 8 (January 1978): 1–19.

17. Alexander L. George and Richard Smoke, *Deterrence In American Foreign Policy: Theory and Practice* (New York: Columbia University Press, 1974), especially pp. 95–97. These case studies may also be examples of what Harry Eckstein has in mind when he uses the term "plausibility probes"; see his "Case Study and Theory in Political Science," in Fred I. Greenstein and Nelson W. Polsby, eds., *Handbook of Political Science, Volume 7: Strategies of Inquiry* (Reading, Mass.: Addison-Wesley, 1977), pp. 79–137, particularly pp. 108–13.

18. See Lipset, "Why No Socialism?"; Huntington, *American Politics;* Nathan Glazer and Irving Kristol, eds., *The American Commonwealth—1976* (New York: Basic Books, 1976).

19. T. H. Marshall, *Social Policy* (London: Hutchinson, 1967), pp. 177–79.

20. Richard Sennett and Jonathan Cobb, *The Hidden Injuries of Class* (New York: Knopf, 1973).

Chapter 1. Patterns of Resource Inadequacy and American Values

1. See Richard D. Coe, "A Preliminary Empirical Examination of the Dynamics of Welfare Use," in Martha S. Hill, Daniel H. Hill, and James N. Morgan, eds. *Five Thousand American Families—Patterns of Economic Progress, Volume 9: Analyses of the First Twelve Years of the Panel Study on Income Dynamics* (Ann Arbor: Survey Research Center, Institute for Social Research, University of Michigan, 1981), pp. 121–68, especially pp. 159–60; Greg J. Duncan et al., *Years of Poverty, Years of Plenty: The Changing Economic Fortunes of American Workers and Families* (Ann Arbor: Survey Research Center, Institute for Social Research, University of Michigan, 1984), especially chap. 3.

2. This discussion draws on a variety of works; particularly useful are Robert N. Bellah et al., *Habits of the Heart: Individualism and Commitment in American Life* (Berkeley: University of California Press, 1985), especially pp. 253–62; C. B. Macpherson, *Democratic Theory: Essays in Retrieval* (Oxford: Oxford University Press, 1973), chap. 7, especially pp. 145–47; Joseph A. Pechman, Henry J. Aaron, and Michael K. Taussig, *Social Security: Perspectives on Reform* (Washington, D.C.: Brookings, 1968), pp. 28–30; Sidney Ratner, James H. Soltow, and Richard Sylla, *The Evolution of the American Economy: Growth, Welfare, and Decision Making* (New York: Basic Books, 1979).

3. Lester C. Thurow, *The Zero-Sum Society: Distribution and the Possibilities for Economic Change* (New York: Basic Books, 1980), pp. 168–70. See also Richard Parker, *The Myth of the Middle Class: Notes on Affluence and Equality* (New York: Liveright, 1972).

4. William J. Goode, *World Revolution and Family Patterns* (New York: Free Press, 1963), pp. 10–26.

5. Jean Giles-Sims, "Expectations, Behavior, and Sanctions Associated with the Stepparent Role," *Journal of Family Issues* 5 (March 1984): 116–30; Greg J. Duncan and James N. Morgan, "Persistence and Change in Economic Status and the Role of Changing Family Composition," in Hill, Hill, and Morgan, *Five Thousand American Families*, pp. 1–44.

6. See Paul Starr, *The Social Transformation of American Medicine: The Rise of a Sovereign Profession and the Making of a Vast Industry* (New York: Basic Books, 1982), bk. 1, chaps. 1 and 2.

7. Stanley Lebergott, *The American Economy: Income, Wealth, and Want* (Princeton: Princeton University Press, 1976) develops this point at length, pp. 3–20 and 88–107. This view does not take into account Michael Walzer's point that the inability of impoverished people to take part in many customary and important activities effectively denies them

membership in society. See Walzer, *Spheres of Justice: A Defense of Pluralism and Equality* (New York: Basic Books, 1983), pp. 105–8.

8. This account draws on Lee Rainwater, "Persistent and Transitory Poverty: A New Look," Working Paper no. 70, Joint Center for Urban Studies of MIT and Harvard University, June 1981. See also Duncan et al., *Years of Poverty*, and three selections in Hill, Hill, and Morgan, *Five Thousand Families:* Duncan and Morgan, "Persistence and Change in Economic Status"; Coe, "Preliminary Empirical Examination"; and Martha S. Hill, "Some Dynamic Aspects of Poverty," pp. 93–120. Rainwater estimates that 16 percent of American households are persistently poor. The federal government, however, sets the "poverty line" at a lower level of annual income, and by this standard in recent years only about 13 to 15 percent of all Americans live in poverty. See Duncan et al., *Years of Poverty*, chap. 2.

9. See David R. Cameron, "The Expansion of the Public Economy: A Comparative Analysis," *American Political Science Review* 72 (December 1978): 1243–61; David Collier and Richard E. Messick, "Prerequisites Versus Diffusion: Testing Alternative Explanations of Social Security Adoption," *American Political Science Review* 69 (December 1975): 1299–1315; Hugh Heclo, *Modern Social Politics in Britain and Sweden: From Relief to Income Maintenance* (New Haven: Yale University Press, 1974); Arnold J. Heidenheimer, Hugh Heclo, and Carolyn Teich Adams, *Comparative Public Policy: The Politics of Social Choice in Europe and America*, 2d ed. (New York: St. Martin's, 1983); Howard M. Leichter, *A Comparative Approach to Policy Analysis: Health Care Policy in Four Nations* (New York: Cambridge University Press, 1979); Gaston V. Rimlinger, *Welfare Policy and Industrialization in Europe, America, and Russia* (New York: Wiley, 1971); Harold L. Wilensky, *The Welfare State and Equality: Structural and Ideological Roots of Public Expenditures* (Berkeley: University of California Press, 1975), chap. 3.

10. On the history of these ideas, see Henry Rogers Seager, *Social Insurance: A Program of Social Reform* (New York: Macmillan, 1910); Isaac Max Rubinow, *Social Insurance, With Special Reference to American Conditions* (New York: Henry Holt, 1913). On support and resources see G. John Ikenberry and Theda Skocpol, "Expanding Social Benefits: The Role of Social Security," *Political Science Quarterly*, 102 (Fall 1987): 389–416.

11. See, for instance, Benjamin I. Page, *Who Gets What from Government* (Berkeley: University of California Press, 1983), chap. 3.

12. For a more extensive listing of social insurance programs, see Roy H. Grisham, Jr., and Paul D. McConaughy, eds., *Encyclopedia of United States Government Benefits*, 2d ed., (New York: Avon, 1975). For statistics about the scope of social security, see Jule M. Sugarman, Gary D.

Bass, and Matthew J. Bader, "Human Services in the 1980's—President Reagan's 1983 Proposals, White Paper no 5: For Citizens and Public Officials," (Washington, D.C.: Human Services Information Center, 1983); Henry J. Aaron, *Economic Effects of Social Security* (Washington, D.C.: Brookings, 1982), particularly p. 67; Joseph A. Califano, Jr., *Governing America: An Insider's Report from the White House and Cabinet* (New York: Simon and Schuster, 1981), pp. 323–25; Martha Derthick, *Policymaking for Social Security* (Washington, D.C.: Brookings, 1979), p. 3. Data are periodically reported in the *Social Security Bulletin*.

13. Wilensky, *Welfare State*, pp. 65–68; Starr, *Social Transformation of American Medicine*, pp. 286–89.

14. Aaron, *Economic Effects*, p. 78.

15. See Mary Jo Bane, "The Poor in Massachusetts," in Manuel Carbello and Mary Jo Bane, eds., *The State and the Poor in the 1980s* (Boston: Auburn, 1984), pp. 1–13.

16. Again, Grisham and McConaughy, *Encyclopedia of Government Benefits* give a more exhaustive listing.

17. See Sugarman, Bass, and Bader, "Human Services," p. 76; Califano, *Governing America*, pp. 323–24.

18. Lawrence M. Mead, *Beyond Entitlement: The Social Obligations of Citizenship* (New York: Free Press, 1986), pp. 21–25, ably distinguishes various categories of the poor.

19. Edward C. Banfield, *The Unheavenly City Revisited* (Boston: Little, Brown, 1974). The attitudinalist position is also espoused by Lebergott, *The American Economy*.

20. Herbert J. Gans, *The Urban Villages: Group and Class in the Life of Italian Americans* (New York: Free Press, 1962). Or see Michael Rutter and Nicola Madge, *Cycles of Disadvantage: A Review of Research* (London: Heinemann, 1976).

21. In the early 1980s full-time employment (forty hours a week, fifty weeks a year) at the minimum wage provided a gross annual income of $6,700—enough to lift one- and two-person households, but not larger families, above the official poverty line.

22. Leonard Beeghley, *Living Poorly in America* (New York: Praeger, 1983); Duncan et al., *Years of Poverty*, particularly chaps. 2 and 3.

23. On psychological factors, see Richard Sennett and Jonathan Cobb, *The Hidden Injuries of Class* (New York: Knopf, 1973); Ann Swidler, "Culture in Action: Symbols and Strategies," *American Sociological Review* 51 (April 1986): 273–86; Leonard Goodwin, *Do the Poor Want to Work? A Social-Psychological Study of Work Orientations* (Washington, D.C.: Brookings, 1972), and his *Causes and Cures of Welfare: New Evidence on the Social Psychology of the Poor* (Lexington, Mass.: D.C. Heath, 1983). Sociological factors are discussed by Duncan et al., *Years*

of Poverty, chaps. 2 and 3; Duncan and Morgan, "Persistence and Change in Economic Status."

24. Indeed, virtually all federal financial aid (grants, loans, work-study) to college students is allocated by need, depending on both the student's means and estimated expenses. This need-testing procedure is an unusual experience for middle-class parents.

25. Duncan et al., *Years of Poverty,* chap. 3; Coe, "Dynamics of Welfare Use"; Duncan and Morgan, "Persistence and Change in Economic Status."

26. See Henry J. Aaron, *Why Is Welfare So Difficult to Reform?* (Washington, D.C.: Brookings, 1973), chap. 4, and his *On Social Welfare* (Cambridge, Mass.: Abt Books, 1980), chap. 2.

27. See Henry J. Aaron, *Politics and the Professors: The Great Society in Perspective* (Washington, D.C.: Brookings, 1978); Frances Fox Piven and Richard A. Cloward, *Regulating the Poor: The Functions of Public Welfare* (New York: Pantheon, 1971).

28. Hugh Heclo, "Income Maintenance Policy," in Heidenheimer, Heclo, and Adams, *Comparative Public Policy,* p. 214.

29. Shail Jain, *Size Distribution of Income: A Compilation of Data* (Washington, D.C.: World Bank, 1975) shows no marked pattern of exceptional poverty in the United States. But this view is contradicted by OECD, *Studies in Resource Allocation, no. 3: Public Expenditure on Income Maintenance Programmes* (Paris: OECD, 1976), pp. 66–68 and 108–9.

30. Heclo, "Income Maintenance Policy," p. 202.

31. In my view, Mead's suggestions for intensive guidance in *Beyond Entitlement* are much more appropriately limited to people in this third category than applied generally to the impoverished.

32. Samuel P. Huntington, *American Politics: The Promise of Disharmony* (Cambridge: Harvard University Press, 1981) pp. 14 and 22.

33. Donald J. Devine, *The Political Culture of the United States: The Influence of Member Values on Regime Maintenance* (Boston: Little, Brown, 1972).

34. Lloyd A. Free and Hadley Cantril, *The Political Beliefs of Americans: A Study of Public Opinion* (New Brunswick, N.J.: Rutgers University Press, 1967), especially pp. 15–40.

35. See Wilensky, *Welfare State,* pp. 28–49; Richard M. Coughlin, *Ideology, Public Opinion, and Welfare Policy: Attitudes Toward Taxes and Spending in Industrialized Societies* (Berkeley: Institute of International Studies, University of Calfornia, 1980), p. 31.

36. Jennifer L. Hochschild, *What's Fair? American Beliefs About Distributive Justice* (Cambridge: Harvard University Press, 1981), especially chap. 3.

37. On the influence of the elite in shaping policy, see Anthony King, "Ideas, Institutions, and the Policies of Governments: A Comparative Analysis," *British Journal of Political Science* 3 (July 1973): 291–313 and 3 (October 1973): 409–23; David Vogel, "Why Businessmen Distrust Their State: The Political Consciousness of American Corporate Executives," *British Journal of Political Science* 8 (January 1978): 45–78. On the elite's influence on public opinion, see Robert Nisbet, "Public Opinion Versus Popular Opinion," in Nathan Glazer and Irving Kristol, eds., *The American Commonwealth—1976* (New York: Basic Books, 1976), pp. 166–92.

38. For an analysis that concurs with Huntington's core values, see Norman Furniss and Timothy Tilton, *The Case for the Welfare State: From Social Security to Social Equality* (Bloomington: Indiana University Press, 1977), chaps. 7 and 8. On the same point see as well Charles Lockhart, "Values and Policy Conceptions of Health Policy Elites in the United States, the United Kingdom, and the Federal Republic of Germany," *Journal of Health Politics, Policy and Law* 6 (Spring 1981): 98–119. For an analysis that diverges from Huntington's core values, see Joel D. Aberbach, Robert D. Putnam, and Bert A. Rockman, *Bureaucrats and Politicians in Western Democracies* (Cambridge: Harvard University Press, 1981), chap. 5, especially pp. 122–24.

39. Huntington, *American Politics,* p. 230; see also p. 15.

40. Again, compare with Huntington, *American Politics,* p. 113.

41. See Friedrich A. Hayek, *The Mirage of Social Justice,* vol. 2 of *Law, Legislation, and Liberty* (Chicago: University of Chicago Press, 1976); Milton Friedman, *Capitalism and Freedom* (Chicago: University of Chicago Press, 1962).

42. These rights have a long history, albeit not always a continuous one in market societies. See Frances Fox Piven and Richard A. Cloward, *The New Class War: Reagan's Attack on the Welfare State and Its Consequences* (New York: Pantheon, 1982), chaps. 2–4; R. N. Tawney, *Religion and the Rise of Capitalism: A Historical Study* (New York: Harcourt, Brace, 1926).

Chapter 2. Socioeconomic Rights and American Conceptions of Distributive Justice

1. On the history of social programs, see Gaston V. Rimlinger, *Welfare Policy and Industrialization in Europe, America, and Russia* (New York: Wiley, 1971), chap. 4. For an interpretation that grants beneficiary rights a lengthier history, see Iredell Jenkins, *Social Order and the Limits of Law: A Theoretical Essay* (Princeton: Princeton University Press, 1980), pp. 246–67 and 312–23.

2. For Beveridge's proposals, see his *Social Insurance and Allied Ser-*

vices (New York: Macmillan, 1942). On the limits of wartime solidarity, see Paul Adams, *Health of the State* (New York: Praeger, 1982). And on changes in British programs since the war, see Hugh Heclo, *Modern Social Politics in Britain and Sweden: From Relief to Income Maintenance* (New Haven: Yale University Press, 1974), chaps. 3–5.

3. The corporatist democracies are the Netherlands, Belgium, Sweden, Norway, Austria, and the Federal Republic of Germany. See Harold L. Wilensky, "Democratic Corporatism, Consensus, and Social Policy: Reflections on Changing Values and the 'Crisis' of the Welfare State," in OECD, *The Welfare State in Crisis: An Account of the Conference on Social Policies in the 1980s* (Paris: OECD, 1981), pp. 185–95. And compare with Gary Freeman, "France's Social Welfare Policy," in Fredric Bolotin and Jack Desario, eds., *International Public Policy Sourcebook* (Westport, Conn.: Greenwood, forthcoming).

4. Compare with Friedrich A. Hayek, *The Mirage of Social Justice,* vol. 2 of *Law, Legislation, and Liberty* (Chicago: University of Chicago Press, 1976); Milton Friedman, *Capitalism and Freedom* (Chicago: University of Chicago Press, 1962).

5. Joel Feinberg, "The Nature and Value of Rights," in Joel Feinberg and Hyman Gross, eds., *Philosophy of Law,* 2d ed. (Belmont, Calif.: Wadsworth, 1980), p. 278.

6. I am using consciousness in Julian Jaynes's "analog I" sense; see his *The Origins of Consciousness in the Breakdown of the Bicameral Mind* (Boston: Houghton Mifflin, 1976), pp. 59–66.

7. Raymond Plant, Harry Lesser, and Peter Taylor-Gooby, *Political Philosophy and the Welfare State: Essays on the Normative Basis of Welfare Provision* (London: Routledge and Kegan Paul, 1980), p. 36. For a seminal argument on the coequal status of freedom and well-being, see Alan Gewirth, "The Basis and Content of Human Rights," in J. Roland Pennock and John W. Campbell, eds., *Nomos 23: Human Rights* (New York: New York University Press, 1981), pp. 148–57. In a related vein see Larry M. Preston, "Freedom, Markets, and Voluntary Exchange," *American Political Science Review* 78 (December 1984): 959–70.

8. For one formulation of freedom as a prerequisite and a right, see H. L. A. Hart, "Are There Any Natural Rights?" in Anthony Quinton, ed., *Political Philosophy* (Oxford: Oxford University Press, 1967), pp. 53–66. On material needs as a prerequisite and a right, see T. H. Marshall, "Citizenship and Social Class," in *Sociology at the Crossroads and Other Essays* (London: Heinemann, 1963), pp. 67–127. Clearly the importance of such needs was widely recognized by human cultures prior to the arrival of the market society; see Karl Polanyi, *The Great Transformation: The Political and Economic Origins of Our Time* (Boston: Beacon, 1957), especially chap. 4.

9. Susan Moller Okin, "Liberty and Welfare: Some Issues in Human Rights Theory," in Pennock and Chapman, *Nomos 23,* pp. 230–56, especially p. 244.

10. See Charles E. Lindblom, *Politics and Markets: The World's Political-Economic Systems* (New York: Basic Books, 1977), pp. 43–50; C. B. Macpherson, *Democratic Theory: Essays in Retrieval* (Oxford: Oxford University Press, 1973), pp. 143–47, and Macpherson's introduction and conclusion to *Property: Mainstream and Critical Positions* (Toronto: University of Toronto Press, 1978). See also the essays in Adrian Ellis and Krishan Kumar, eds., *Dilemmas of Liberal Democracies: Studies in Fred Hirsch's "Social Limits to Growth"* (London: Tavistock, 1983), particularly Raymond Plant, "Hirsch, Hayek, and Habermas: Dilemmas in Distribution," pp. 45–64, and Krishan Kumar, "Pre-Capitalist and Non-Capitalist Factors in the Development of Capitalism: Fred Hirsch and Joseph Schumpeter," pp. 148–73.

11. Bernard Williams, "The Idea of Equality," in Peter Laslett and W. G. Runciman, eds., *Philosophy, Politics, and Society,* 2d ser. (New York: Barnes and Noble, 1962), particularly pp. 122–23. In this regard, compare Plato's related argument in *The Republic,* bk. 1.

12. Robert Nozick, *Anarchy, State, and Utopia* (New York: Basic Books, 1974), particularly chap. 7.

13. Henry Shue, *Basic Rights: Subsistence, Affluence, and U.S. Foreign Policy* (Princeton: Princeton University Press, 1980), especially pp. 114–19.

14. This distinction follows the divisions of negative and positive liberty made by Isaiah Berlin, "Two Concepts of Liberty," in *Four Essays on Liberty* (Oxford: Oxford University Press, 1969), pp. 118–72; see also pp. xliii–xlvii.

15. These examples draw on Shue's ideas; see his *Basic Rights,* pp. 37–46.

16. This distinction is made by Jenkins, *Social Order,* pp. 246–67.

17. Jan Narveson, "Human Rights: Which, If Any, Are There?" in Pennock and Chapman, *Nomos 23,* pp. 175–97.

18. Sidney Verba, Norman H. Nie, and Jae-on Kim, *Participation and Political Equality: A Seven-Nation Comparison* (New York: Cambridge University Press, 1978).

19. Frances Fox Piven and Richard A. Cloward, *The New Class War: Reagan's Attack on the Welfare State and Its Consequences* (New York: Pantheon, 1982); Polanyi, *Great Transformation,* pp. 225–26.

20. Donald W. Jackson, "'Public Police Thyselves': Deadly Force and the Ethos of British Policing," paper presented at the 1984 annual meeting of the Academy of Criminal Justice Society, Chicago, March 27–31, pp. 10–11.

21. David Miller, "Democracy and Social Justice," *British Journal of Political Science* 8 (January 1978): 1–19.

22. See Miller, "Democracy and Social Justice" for political rights; for a similar approach to socioeconomic rights, see George Gilder, *Wealth and Poverty* (New York: Basic Books, 1981), chaps. 5 and 6.

23. Maurice Cranston, "Are There Any Human Rights?" *Daedalus* 112 (Fall 1981): 12.

24. For an alternative formulation see Lee Rainwater, "Persistent and Transitory Poverty: A New Look," Working Paper no. 70, Joint Center for Urban Studies of MIT and Harvard University, June 1981. On the general principle of delimiting such needs contrast William Leiss, *The Limits to Satisfaction: Essay on the Problem of Needs and Commodities* (Toronto: Toronto University Press, 1976) with Michael Walzer, *Spheres of Justice: A Defense of Pluralism and Equality* (New York: Basic Books, 1983), chap. 3; William A. Galston, *Justice and the Human Good* (Chicago: University of Chicago Press, 1980).

25. As indicated in the previous chapter, this book does not focus on the small minority of working-aged adults who are physiologically or psychologically unable to contribute to the social product; accordingly, I will direct only occasional attention to them.

26. Walzer, *Spheres of Justice,* p. xv.

27. See Jack Donnelly, "Human Rights and Human Dignity: An Analytic Critique of Non-Western Conceptions of Human Rights," *American Political Science Review* 76 (June 1982): 103–16; David Miller, *Social Justice* (Oxford: Oxford University Press, 1976), pp. 257–86 and 317–35.

28. Walzer, *Spheres of Justice,* pp. 3–5 and 13–16, argues that different spheres of social life call for distinct criteria of distributive justice. For instance, Walzer believes that people ought to have equal access to basic material goods, but that markets are appropriate for distributing more rarefied goods such as investment counseling.

29. Compare with Cranston, "Are There Any Human Rights?" p. 13, who suggests that positive rights carry such obligations.

30. Harold L. Wilensky, *The Welfare State and Equality: Structural and Ideological Roots of Public Expenditures* (Berkeley: University of California Press, 1975), pp. 87–96; Benjamin I. Page, *Who Gets What from Government* (Berkeley: University of California Press, 1983), especially chaps. 3 and 6.

31. For a disturbing view of these problems, see Carolyn Weaver, *The Crisis in Social Security: Economic and Political Origins* (Durham, N.C.: Duke University Press, 1982).

32. President's Commission on Income Maintenance Programs [Heineman Commission] *Poverty Amid Plenty: The American Para-*

dox—Background Papers (Washington, D.C.: U.S. Government Printing Office, 1969), p. 166.

33. Ronald Dworkin, *Taking Rights Seriously* (Cambridge: Harvard University Press, 1977), pp. 90–94.

34. Jennifer L. Hochschild, *What's Fair? American Beliefs About Distributive Justice* (Cambridge: Harvard University Press, 1981), p. 280. See also pp. 183–86, on conflicts between political and economic norms; pp. 254–57, on the interweaving of egalitarian and classical liberal concepts; pp. 279–81, on poverty as a structural problem.

35. Contrast Joel D. Aberbach, Robert D. Putnam, and Bert A. Rockman, *Bureaucrats and Politicians in Western Democracies* (Cambridge: Harvard University Press, 1981), especially chap. 3, with two narrower studies: David Vogel, "Why Businessmen Distrust Their State: The Political Consciousness of American Corporate Executives," *British Journal of Political Science* 8 (January 1978): 45–78; Charles Lockhart, "Values and Policy Conceptions of Health Policy Elites in the United States, the United Kingdom, and the Federal Republic of Germany," *Journal of Health Politics, Policy and Law* 6 (Spring 1981): 98–119.

36. On egalitarian beliefs among public-sector elites, see Aberbach, Putnam, and Rockman, *Bureaucrats and Politicians*, chap. 5. On the limited utility of addressing egalitarian arguments to elites, see Sidney Verba and Gary R. Orren, *Equality in America: The View From the Top* (Cambridge: Harvard University Press, 1985).

37. A common term to apply to this latter preference is *maximin;* see Douglas Rae et al., *Equalities* (Cambridge: Harvard University Press, 1981), chap. 6. But this technical term denotes the uplifting of the minimum, a concern distinct from typical American concerns for simply having a minimum. See Verba and Orren, *Equality in America,* chap. 4.

38. Ken Auletta, *The Underclass* (New York: Random House, 1982).

39. See Page, *Who Gets What;* Peter Townsend, *Poverty in the United Kingdom: A Survey of Household Resources and Standards of Living* (Berkeley: University of California Press, 1979); Jennifer G. Schirmer, *The Limits of Reform: Women, Capital, and Welfare* (Cambridge, Mass.: Schenkman, 1982).

40. On these points see Macpherson's arguments in *Democratic Theory,* pp. 145–47, and *Property,* pp. 1–13 and 199–207. See also Ellis and Kumar, *Dilemmas of Liberal Democracies;* Lindblom, *Politics and Markets,* pp. 43–50.

41. See Joel Feinberg, *Doing and Deserving: Essays in the Theory of Responsibility* (Princeton: Princeton University Press, 1970).

42. See Nozick, *Anarchy, State, and Utopia,* pp. 224–27; Hayek, *Mirage of Social Justice.*

43. For a pithy rebuttal of this view, see Macpherson, *Democratic Theory,* pp. 145–47; Preston, "Freedom, Markets and Voluntary Exchange."

44. Heclo, *Modern Social Politics,* pp. 1–10.

45. For more detail on this point see Winifred Bell, *Aid to Dependent Children* (New York: Columbia University Press, 1965), p. 182.

46. Hochschild, *What's Fair?* p. 75.

47. Polanyi, *Great Transformation,* pp. 79–88.

Chapter 3. Implications for Prominent American Values

1. See Milton Friedman, *Capitalism and Freedom,* (Chicago: University of Chicago Press, 1962); Friedrich A. Hayek, *The Mirage of Social Justice,* vol. 2 of *Law, Legislation, and Liberty* (Chicago: University of Chicago Press, 1976), respectively. For a contrasting view of the American political tradition see, for example, J. G. A. Pocock, *The Machiavellian Moment: Florentine Political Thought and the Atlantic Republican Tradition* (Princeton: Princeton University Press, 1975).

2. See Henry J. Aaron, *Politics and the Professors: The Great Society in Perspective* (Washington, D.C.: Brookings, 1978); Sar A. Levitan and Gregory K. Wurzburg, *Evaluating Federal Social Programs: An Uncertain Art* (Kalamazoo, Mich.: W. E. Upjohn Institute for Employment Research, 1979); Charles Murray, *Losing Ground: American Social Policy, 1950–1970* (New York: Basic Books, 1984), especially pt. 1.

3. Isaiah Berlin, "Two Concepts of Liberty," in *Four Essays on Liberty* (Oxford: Oxford University Press, 1969), pp. 118–72, and also pp. xxxvii–lxiii. C. B. Macpherson, *Democratic Theory: Essays in Retrieval* (Oxford: Oxford University Press, 1973), chap. 5, particularly pp. 108–19.

4. See Robert Sugden, "Hard Luck Stories: The Problem of the Uninsured in a Laissez-Faire Society," *Journal of Social Policy* 11 (April 1982): 201–16.

5. For a general discussion of individualism in America see Robert N. Bellah et al., *Habits of the Heart: Individualism and Commitment in American Life* (Berkeley: University of California Press, 1985).

6. See Stephen M. Davidson and Theodore R. Marmor, *The Costs of Living Longer: National Health Insurance and the Elderly* (Lexington, Mass.: D.C. Heath, 1980), p. 13. SMI is financed by participant premiums and supplemented by general revenues. All citizens sixty-five or over, not just social security recipients, may enroll at the same subsidized rates.

7. Paul Starr, *The Social Transformation of American Medicine: The*

Rise of a Sovereign Profession and the Making of a Vast Industry (New York: Basic Books, 1982), pp. 286–89; and Arthur J. Altmeyer, *The Formative Years of Social Security* (Madison: University of Wisconsin Press, 1966), pp. 185–86, 196, and 248–49.

8. Friedman, *Capitalism and Freedom*, pp. 187–89.

9. Benjamin I. Page, *Who Gets What from Government* (Berkeley: University of California Press, 1983), chap. 6. Recent reductions in the number of tax brackets may be expected to reduce the progressiveness of the federal income tax, previously the major contributor to progressivity in the overall American tax structure.

10. See Robert E. Goodin, "Freedom and the Welfare State: Theoretical Foundations," *Journal of Social Policy* 11 (April 1982): 156–67; Gaston V. Rimlinger, "Capitalism and Human Rights," *Daedalus* 112 (Fall 1983): 174–79; Henry Shue, *Basic Rights: Subsistence, Affluence, and U.S. Foreign Policy* (Princeton: Princeton University Press, 1980), particularly his priority principle, pp. 114–19.

11. Christa Altenstetter, "Health Policy Making and Administration in West Germany and the United States," Sage Professional Papers in Administrative and Policy Studies, 3 (Beverly Hills, Calif.: Sage, 1974).

12. Lawrence M. Mead, *Beyond Entitlement: The Social Objectives of Citizenship* (New York: Free Press, 1986), recommends reinitiating much more ambitious limitations on recipients. For examples of such practices, see Frances Fox Piven and Richard A. Cloward, *Regulating the Poor: The Functions of Public Welfare* (New York: Pantheon, 1971); Joan Huggins, "Public Welfare: The Road to Freedom?" *Journal of Social Policy* 11 (April 1982): 177–99, especially pp. 191–92; and Jennifer G. Schirmer, *The Limits of Reform: Women, Capital, and Welfare* (Cambridge, Mass.: Schenkman, 1982), pp. 144–45.

13. On social programs, contrast the negativism of Robert Nozick, *Anarchy, State, and Utopia* (New York: Basic Books, 1974) with the more open views of Hayek, *Mirage of Social Justice;* Milton Friedman and Rose Friedman, *Free to Choose: A Personal Statement* (New York: Avon, 1979). That libertarianism is not a mainstream position in America is illustrated by Lloyd A. Free and Hadley Cantril, *The Political Beliefs of Americans: A Study of Public Opinion* (New Brunswick, N.J.: Rutgers University Press, 1967).

14. Many writers have used other terms that are roughly synonymous with this definition. David G. Green, "Freedom or Paternalistic Collectivism?" *Journal of Social Policy* 11 (April 1982): 239–44, following Dewey, uses "effective power"; see also Ralph Barton Perry, "Liberty in a Democratic State," in Ruth Nanda Anshen, ed. *Freedom: Its Meaning* (New York: Harcourt, Brace, 1940), pp. 265–77. Peter Jones, "Freedom

and the Distribution of Resources," *Journal of Social Policy* 11 (April 1982): 217–38, opts for "ability" or "opportunity." Jones's stance is partially consistent with Robert M. McIver, "The Meaning of Liberty and Its Perversions," in Anshen, *Freedom*, pp. 278–87, although McIver is concerned to distinguish liberty from welfare and the tyranny associated with one aspect of what Berlin calls positive liberty. Abraham H. Maslow, *Motivation and Personality*, 2d ed. (New York: Harper and Row, 1970), pp. 35–47, uses "self-actualization" in a sense of developing human potential. Before introducing the term *developmental liberty* (*Democratic Theory*, chap. 5), Macpherson uses the term *power* in a nearly synonymous way.

15. Contrast Nozick, *Anarchy, State, and Utopia*, chap.7, with Shue, *Basic Rights*, pp. 114–19.

16. Macpherson notes that in discussions of liberty, equality, and justice one concept frequently "swallows" another, *Democratic Theory*, pp. 81–82.

17. Charles Lockhart, "Values and Policy Conceptions of Health Policy Elites in the United States, the United Kingdom, and the Federal Republic of Germany," *Journal of Health Policy, Politics and Law* 6 (Spring 1981): 100–103.

18. Martin Feldstein, "Social Insurance," in Colin D. Campbell, *Income Redistribution* (Washington, D.C.: AEI, 1977), pp. 71–97.

19. Norman Furniss and Timothy Tilton, *The Case for the Welfare State: From Social Security to Social Equality* (Bloomington: Indiana University Press, 1978), chap. 3.

20. Lester C. Thurow, "Equity, Efficiency, Social Justice, and Redistribution," in OECD, *The Welfare State in Crisis: An Account of the Conference on Social Policies in the 1980s* (Paris: OECD, 1981), pp. 137–50. Harold L. Wilensky, "Democratic Corporatism, Consensus, and Social Policy: Reflections on Changing Values and the 'Crisis' of the Welfare State," in OECD, *Welfare State in Crisis*, pp. 185–95, particularly pp. 190–91. See also Robert Kuttner, *The Economic Illusion: False Choices Between Prosperity and Social Justice* (Boston: Houghton Mifflin, 1984).

21. See Sheldon Danziger, Robert Haveman, and Robert Plotnick, "How Income Transfer Programs Affect Work, Savings, and Income Distribution: A Critical Review," *Journal of Economic Literature* 19 (September 1981): 975–1028, particularly pp. 995–99.

22. Henry J. Aaron, *Economic Effects of Social Security* (Washington, D.C.: Brookings, 1982), pp. 31–34 and 53–66.

23. For commentary on the results of early experiments see David Kershaw and Jerilyn Fair, *The New Jersey Income Maintenance Experi-*

ment (New York: Academic Press, 1977); Peter Rossi and Katherine C. Lyall, *Reforming Public Welfare: A Critique of the Negative Income Tax Experiment* (New York: Russell Sage Foundation, 1976); Joseph A. Pechman and P. Michael Timpane, eds. *Work Incentives and Income Guarantees: The New Jersey Negative Income Tax Experiment* (Washington, D.C.: Brookings, 1975); the symposium in *Journal of Human Resources* 9 (Spring–Fall 1974). See also Walter Williams, "The Continuing Struggle for a Negative Income Tax: A Review Article," *Journal of Human Resources* 10 (Fall 1975): 427–44. On later experiments see the symposia in *Journal of Human Resources* 14 (Fall 1979), on the Gary experiment; and 15 (Fall 1980), on the Seattle and Denver experiments. On the latter, see also Philip K. Robins et al., eds., *A Guaranteed Annual Income: Evidence from a Social Experiment* (New York: Academic Press, 1980).

24. See Lester C. Thurow, *The Zero-Sum Society: Distribution and the Possibilities for Economic Change* (New York: Basic Books, 1980), p. 86; John E. Schwarz, *America's Hidden Success: A Reassessment of Twenty Years of Public Policy* (New York: Norton, 1983); and Danziger, Haveman, and Plotnick, "Income Transfer Programs," pp. 995–99.

25. Compare with Leonard Goodwin, *Do the Poor Want to Work? A Social-Psychological Study of Work Orientations* (Washington, D.C.: Brookings, 1972), and Goodwin, *Causes and Cures of Welfare: New Evidence on the Social-Psychology of the Poor* (Lexington, Mass.: D.C. Heath, 1983).

26. See Karl Polanyi, *The Great Transformation: The Political and Economic Origins of Our Time* (Boston: Beacon, 1957), pp. 114–15.

27. Wilensky, "Democratic Corporatism"; Aaron, *Economic Effects of Social Security,* pp. 31–34 and 53–66.

28. See Murray, *Losing Ground,* pp. 47–48; Danziger, Haveman, and Plotnick, "Income Transfer Programs."

29. See Murray, *Losing Ground,* p. 212, on "the law of unintended rewards."

30. Feldstein, "Social Insurance." For an explanation of the shift to a pay-as-we-go form, see Martha Derthick, *Policymaking for Social Security* (Washington, D.C.: Brookings, 1979), pp. 142–44 and 232–37; Jill S. Quadagno, "Welfare Capitalism and the Social Security Act of 1935," *American Sociological Review* 49 (October 1984): 632–47, particularly p. 644.

31. Arthur M. Okun, *Equality and Efficiency: The Big Tradeoff* (Washington, D.C.: Brookings, 1975), p. 98.

32. Aaron, *Economic Effects of Social Security,* pp. 29–31; Danziger, Haveman, and Plotnick, "Income Transfer Programs," pp. 1005–06.

33. See the related argument in James Tobin, "Considerations Regarding Taxation and Equality," in Campbell, *Income Redistribution*, pp. 129–30.

34. David Vogel, "Why Businessmen Distrust Their State: The Political Consciousness of American Corporate Executives," *British Journal of Political Science* 8 (January 1978): 45–78.

35. See Quadagno, "Welfare Capitalism," p. 638.

36. Compare with Gary P. Freeman, "Social Security in One Country? Foreign Economic Policies and Domestic Social Programs," paper presented at the 1983 annual meeting of the American Political Science Association, Chicago, September 1–4.

37. As, for example, in James S. Fishkin, *Justice, Equal Opportunity, and the Family* (New Haven: Yale University Press, 1983), and Okun, *Equality and Efficiency*, respectively.

38. See Douglas Rae et al., *Equalities* (Cambridge: Harvard University Press, 1981), chap. 6; Jennifer L. Hochschild, *What's Fair? American Beliefs About Distributive Justice* (Cambridge: Harvard University Press, 1981), chap. 6; Sidney Verba and Gary R. Orren, *Equality in America: The View From the Top* (Cambridge: Harvard University Press, 1985), chap. 4.

39. Michael Walzer, *Spheres of Justice: A Defense of Pluralism and Equality* (New York: Basic Books, 1983), pp. 3–5 and 13–16.

40. See Stanley Lebergott, *The American Economy: Income, Wealth, and Want* (Princeton: Princeton University Press, 1976), particularly chap. 1; Michael B. Katz, *In the Shadow of the Poorhouse: A Social History of Welfare in America* (New York: Basic Books, 1986).

41. I am using what Rae et al., *Equalities*, p. 81, call a means-regarding conception of equality of opportunity rather than a prospect-regarding conception. That is, rather than assuring equal prospects for success, as a lottery might, this conception legitimizes—through performance-related criteria—unequal success.

42. Fishkin, *Justice*, chaps. 3 and 4.

43. Christopher Jencks et al., *Inequality: A Reassessment of the Effects of Family and Schooling in America* (New York: Basic Books, 1972); Christopher Jencks et al., *Who Gets Ahead?: The Determinants of Economic Success in America* (New York: Basic Books, 1979), especially chap. 3; Robert Coles, *Children in Crisis*, vol. 2, *Migrants, Sharecroppers, and Mountaineers* (Boston: Little, Brown, 1971).

44. See Robert A. Dahl and Edward R. Tufte, *Size and Democracy* (Stanford: Stanford University Press, 1973); David Miller, "Democracy and Social Justice," *British Journal of Political Science* 8 (January 1978): 1–19; T. H. Marshall, "Citizenship and Social Class," in *Sociol-*

ogy at the Crossroads and Other Essays (London: Heinemann, 1963), pp. 67–127.

45. Joseph A. Schumpeter, *Capitalism, Socialism, and Democracy*, 3d ed. (New York: Harper, 1950).

46. Sidney Verba, Norman H. Nie, and Jae-on Kim, *Participation and Political Equality: A Seven-Nation Comparison* (New York: Cambridge University Press, 1978).

47. Scholars differ on the importance of various political arenas and resources and thus in their evaluation of which groups are most influential. See, for example, the pluralist interpretation of David B. Truman, *The Governmental Process: Political Interests and Public Opinion* (New York: Knopf, 1951); and particularly as developed by Robert A. Dahl, *Who Governs? Democracy in an American City* (New Haven: Yale University Press, 1961). For revisions of the pluralist interpretation, see Grant McConnell, *Private Power and American Democracy* (New York: Knopf, 1960); Theodore Lowi, *The End of Liberalism: The Second Republic in the United States* (New York: Norton, 1979). C. Wright Mills, *The Power Elite* (Oxford: Oxford University Press, 1956) offers the elitist perspective; for contemporary Marxist insights, see Ralph Miliband, *The State in Capitalist Society* (New York: Basic Books, 1969); Nico Poulantzas, *Political Power and Social Classes*, trans. Timothy O'Hagan (Atlantic Highlands, N.J.: Humanities Press, 1975). The corporatist view is exemplified by Philippe C. Schmitter, "Modes of Interest Intermediation and Models of Societal Change in Western Europe," *Comparative Political Studies* 10 (April 1977): 7–38. A state-centered conception is advanced by Eric Nordlinger, *On the Autonomy of the Democratic State* (Cambridge: Harvard University Press, 1981).

48. See Brian Berry, *The Liberal Theory of Justice: A Critical Examination of the Principle Doctrines in "A Theory of Justice" by John Rawls* (Oxford: Oxford University Press, 1973), pp. 56–57.

49. Robert Michels, *Political Parties: A Sociological Study of the Oligarchical Tendencies of Modern Democracy*, trans. Eden Paul and Cedar Paul (Glencoe, Ill.: Free Press, 1949).

50. Jan Narveson, "Human Rights: Which, If Any, Are There?" in J. Roland Pennock and John W. Chapman, eds., *Nomos 23: Human Rights* (New York: New York University Press, 1981), p. 177.

51. Frances Fox Piven and Richard A. Cloward, *The New Class War: Reagan's Attack on the Welfare State and Its Consequences* (New York: Pantheon, 1982), chaps. 2–4.

52. Emphasis follows C. B. Macpherson, "Justice and Human Rights," Texas Christian University, Fort Worth, Texas, November 16, 1982. See also his "Economic Penetration of Political Theory," *Journal of the History of Ideas* 39 (January–March 1978): 101–8.

53. Charles A. Beard, *An Economic Interpretation of the Constitution of the United States* (1913; rpt. New York: Free Press, 1965), p. 324.

54. John H. Brittain, *Inheritance and the Inequality of Material Wealth* (Washington, D.C.: Brookings, 1978).

55. C. B. Macpherson, "Human Rights as Property Rights," *Dissent* 24 (January 1977): 72–77.

56. See Aaron Wildavsky, *Speaking Truth to Power: The Art and Craft of Policy Analysis* (Boston: Little, Brown, 1979), pp. 174–77.

57. On British feelings about the NHS, see Lockhart, "Values and Policy Conceptions," p. 101. On Sweden, see Furniss and Tilton, *Case for the Welfare State*, chap. 4.

58. For one example of this theme see Bellah et al., *Habits of the Heart*.

59. Joel Feinberg, "The Nature and Value of Rights," in Joel Feinberg and Hyman Gross, eds., *Philosophy of Law*, 2d ed. (Belmont, Calif.: Wadsworth, 1980), pp. 270–82, especially p. 278. See also Jack Donnelly, "Human Rights and Human Dignity: An Analytic Critique of Non-Western Conceptions of Human Rights," *American Political Science Review* 76 (June 1982): 303–16; David Miller, *Social Justice* (Oxford: Oxford University Press, 1976), pp. 257–72.

60. Henry Rogers Seager, *Social Insurance: A Program of Social Reform* (New York: Macmillan, 1910); Isaac Max Rubinow, *Social Insurance, With Special Reference to American Conditions* (New York: Henry Holt, 1913); Roy Lubove, *The Stuggle for Social Security, 1900–1935* (Cambridge: Harvard University Press, 1968).

61. Jerry R. Cates, *Insuring Inequality: Administrative Leadership in Social Security, 1935–54* (Ann Arbor: University of Michigan Press, 1983), especially chap. 5.

Chapter 4. Practical Problems: Complexity and Compliance

1. Private initiatives are frequently influenced by public policy; see, for example, Edward J. Harpham, "Private Pensions in Crisis: The Case for Radical Reform," Faculty Working Paper no. 8507, Center for Policy Studies, University of Texas at Dallas, January 1984. Henry Shue, *Basic Rights: Subsistence, Affluence, and U.S. Foreign Policy* (Princeton: Princeton University Press, 1975), pp. 37–46, shows considerable ingenuity in reducing the practical complexities of extending socioeconomic rights in developing nations, and I drew on his examples in chapter 2. But his arguments cannot directly be applied to advanced industrial societies.

2. On the difficulties of complex action in American public programs, see Aaron Wildavsky, *Speaking Truth to Power: The Art and Craft of Policy Analysis* (Boston: Little, Brown, 1979), pp. 41–61. For an exten-

sion of his reservations see E. E. Savas, *Privatizing the Public Sector: How to Shrink Government* (Chatam House, N.J.: Chatam House, 1982). For examples of similar problems in the private sector, see John Kenneth Galbraith, *The Affluent Society* (Boston: Houghton Mifflin, 1958), pp. 315–17.

3. David Miller, *Social Justice* (Oxford: Oxford University Press, 1976), pp. 136–43.

4. See Ivan D. Illich, *Medical Nemesis: The Expropriation of Health* (New York: Bantam, 1977).

5. William Leiss, *The Limits of Satisfaction: An Essay on the Problem of Needs and Commodities* (Toronto: University of Toronto Press, 1976), pp. 27–28, 63–67, 92–93.

6. Richard M. Coughlin, *Ideology, Public Opinion, and Welfare Policy: Attitudes Toward Taxes and Spending in Industrialized Societies* (Berkeley: Institute of International Studies, University of California, 1980).

7. See Michael Walzer, *Spheres of Justice: A Defense of Pluralism and Equality* (New York: Basic Books, 1983), pp. 105–8; Miller, *Social Justice*, pp. 136–43; and Lee Rainwater, *What Money Buys: Inequality and the Social Meaning of Income* (New York: Basic Books, 1974).

8. T. H. Marshall, *Social Policy* (London: Hutchinson, 1965), pp. 177–79.

9. See, for example, Gary Freeman, "Presidents, Pensions, and Fiscal Policy," in James P. Pfiffner, ed., *The President and Economic Policy* (Philadelphia: Institute for the Study of Human Issues, 1986), pp. 135–59.

10. Samuel P. Huntington, *American Politics: The Promise of Disharmony* (Cambridge: Harvard University Press, 1981), p. 22.

11. See Friedrich A. Hayek, *The Mirage of Social Justice*, vol. 2 of *Law, Legislation, and Liberty* (Chicago: University of Chicago Press, 1976); Milton Friedman and Rose Friedman, *Free to Choose: A Personal Statement* (New York: Avon, 1979). Hayek finds it reasonable that we choose to mitigate such suffering in this way, but he denies that it is just to do so or that these public programs can be appropriately construed as rights. Not all libertarians accept these measures as appropriate; see Robert Nozick, *Anarchy, State, and Utopia* (New York: Basic Books, 1974), particularly chap. 7.

12. Compare with Daniel Bell, "The End of American Exceptionalism," in Nathan Glazer and Irving Kristol, eds., *The American Commonwealth—1976* (New York: Basic Books, 1976), particularly pp. 207–9. Resistance to this trend is particularly obvious in the area of public education. See Jennifer L. Hochschild, *The New American Dilemma: Liberal Democracy and School Desegregation* (New Haven: Yale University Press, 1984).

13. See G. John Ikenberry and Theda Skocpol, "Expanding Social Benefits: The Role of Social Security," *Political Science Quarterly* 102 (Fall 1987): 389–416; Jill S. Quadagno, "Welfare Capitalism and the Social Security Act of 1935," *American Sociological Review* 49 (October 1984): 632–47, especially pp. 636–38 and 642–44.

14. This point is developed extensively by Kathi V. Friedman, *Legitimation of Social Rights and the Western Welfare State: A Weberian Perspective* (Chapel Hill: University of North Carolina Press, 1981).

15. See Joel F. Handler, *Reforming the Poor: Welfare Policy, Federalism, and Morality* (New York: Basic Books, 1972), pp. 34 and 130–31.

16. Quadagno, "Welfare Capitalism," p. 640. See also Edward R. Tufte, *Political Control of the Economy* (Princeton: Princeton University Press, 1978).

17. Jan Narveson, "Human Rights, Which, If Any, Are There?" in J. Roland Pennock and John W. Chapman, editors, *Nomos 23: Human Rights* (New York: New York University Press, 1981), p. 177.

18. Theda Skocpol and G. John Ikenberry, "The Political Formation of the American Welfare State in Historical and Comparative Perspective," *Comparative Social Research* 6 (Greenwich, Conn.: JAI Press, 1983), p. 90. For variations on this idea in different contexts, see Ann Shola Orloff and Theda Skocpol, "Why Not Equal Protection? Explaining the Politics of Public Social Welfare in Britain and the United States, 1880s–1920s," paper presented at the 1983 annual meeting of the American Sociological Association, Detroit, September 2, pp. 60–69; Peter Flora and Arnold J. Heidenheimer, eds., *The Development of Welfare States in Europe and America* (New Brunswick, N.J.: Transaction Books, 1981); Gaston V. Rimlinger, *Welfare Policy and Industrialization in Europe, America, and Russia* (New York: Wiley, 1971), especially chap. 4; Howard M. Leichter, *A Comparative Approach to Policy Analysis: Health Care Policy in Four Nations* (New York: Cambridge University Press, 1979), especially chap. 5; Paul Adams, *Health of the State* (New York: Praeger, 1982); Hugh Heclo, *Modern Social Politics in Britain and Sweden: From Relief to Income Maintenance* (New Haven: Yale University Press, 1974), particularly chap. 6; Charles Lockhart, "Explaining Social Policy Differences Among Advanced Industrial Societies," *Comparative Politics* 16 (April 1984): 335–50; Tufte, *Political Control;* and Frances Fox Piven and Richard A. Cloward, *Regulating the Poor: The Functions of Public Welfare* (New York: Pantheon, 1971).

19. Heclo, *Modern Social Politics,* pp. 288–93, offers doubts about the efficacy of social-program platforms in electoral competition; see as well Harold L. Wilensky et al., *Comparative Social Policy: Theories, Methods, Findings* (Berkeley: Institute of International Studics, University of California, 1985), p. 33. Tufte, *Political Control,* discusses the per-

ceptions of elites, and Piven and Cloward, *Regulating the Poor,* analyze the American situation.

20. Rimlinger, *Welfare Policy and Industrialization,* chap. 4.

21. Piven and Cloward, *Regulating the Poor.*

22. On medical-care providers, see Theodore R. Marmor, *The Politics of Medicare* (Chicago: Aldine, 1970), pp. 67, 86, and 122–23. On housing programs, see Joseph A. Califano, Jr., *Governing America: An Insider's Report from the White House and the Cabinet* (New York: Simon and Schuster, 1981), p. 331. On education, see E. A. Kelly, "Defederalization of Education," in Anthony Champagne and Edward J. Harpham, eds., *The Attack on the Welfare State* (Prospect Heights, Ill.: Waveland, 1984), pp. 165–76.

23. For background on the generalizations that follow, see Lawrence M. Mead, *Beyond Entitlement: The Social Obligations of Citizenship* (New York: Free Press, 1986); Peter Townsend, *Poverty in the United Kingdom: A Survey of Household Resources and Standards of Living* (Berkeley: University of California Press, 1979); and Jennifer G. Schirmer, *The Limits of Reform: Women, Capital, and Welfare* (Cambridge, Mass.: Schenkman, 1982).

24. See Richard D. Coe, "A Preliminary Empirical Examination of the Dynamics of Welfare Use," in Martha S. Hill, Daniel H. Hill, and James N. Morgan, eds., *Five Thousand American Families—Patterns of Economic Progress, Volume 9: Analyses of the First Twelve Years of the Panel on Income Dynamics* (Ann Arbor: Survey Research Center, Institute for Social Research, University of Michigan, 1981), p. 132; Ken Auletta, *The Underclass* (New York: Random House, 1982). Winfred Bell, *Aid to Dependent Children* (New York: Columbia University Press, 1965), p. 113, suggests that AFDC may be an exception to this generalization.

25. Gabriel A. Almond and Sidney Verba, *The Civic Culture: Political Attitudes and Democracy in Five Nations* (Boston: Little, Brown, 1963). See also Handler, *Reforming the Poor,* pp. 34–38; Leonard Beeghley, *Living Poorly in America* (New York: Praeger, 1983), chaps. 4 and 6.

26. See, for example, Richard Sennett and Jonathan Cobb, *The Hidden Injuries of Class* (New York: Knopf, 1973), p. 83.

27. See Bell, *Aid to Dependent Children,* p. 182; Townsend, *Poverty in the United Kingdom;* Wilensky, *Welfare State,* pp. 95–96; Beeghley, *Living Poorly;* and Mead, *Beyond Entitlement.*

28. On this point compare Wildavsky, *Speaking Truth to Power,* pp. 41–61, with Diana B. Dutton, "Explaining the Low Use of Health Services by the Poor: Costs, Attitudes, or Delivery Systems," *American Sociological Review* 43 (June 1978): 348–68.

29. Charles Murray, *Losing Ground: American Social Policy, 1950–*

1980 (New York: Basic Books, 1984), p. 212. Similarly, some West German conservatives protested that increases in medical-care and sick-pay benefits for blue-collar workers would encourage malingering; see William Safran, *Veto-Group Politics: The Case of Health Insurance Reform in West Germany* (San Francisco: Chandler, 1967). These claims were not borne out; see Christa Altenstetter, "Health Policy Making and Administration in West Germany and the United States," Sage Professional Papers in Administrative and Policy Studies, 3 (Beverly Hills, Calif.: Sage, 1974).

30. These generalizations draw on background provided by Lester M. Salamon, "Rethinking Public Management: Third-Party Government and the Changing Forms of Government Action," *Public Policy* 29 (Summer 1981): 255–75; Lester M. Salamon, *Welfare: The Elusive Consensus—Where We Are, How We Got There, and What's Ahead* (New York: Praeger, 1978), especially chap. 4; Gordon Chase, "Implementing a Human Service Program: How Hard Will It Be?" *Public Policy* 27 (Fall 1979): 385–435.

31. Hochschild, *New American Dilemma,* shows, for example, that in the case of school desegregation sharp policy changes backed by active leadership were more apt to succeed than incremental efforts.

32. Coughlin, however, finds that citizens in many advanced societies have lower regard for recipients of unemployment benefits or family allowances, regardless of program design features, than for elderly pensioners; see *Ideology, Public Opinion, and Welfare Policy,* p. 118.

33. See Robert E. Goodin, "Freedom and the Welfare State: Theoretical Foundations," *Journal of Social Policy* 11 (April 1982): 149–76, particularly pp. 156–57; Joan Huggins, "Public Welfare: The Road to Freedom?" *Journal of Social Policy* 11 (April 1982): 177–99, especially pp. 191–92; and Schirmer, *Limits of Reform,* pp. 144–45.

34. On the former point see Greg J. Duncan and James N. Morgan, "Persistence and Change in Economic Status and the Role of Changing Family Composition," in Hill, Hill, and Morgan, *Five Thousand Families,* pp. 1–44; Handler, *Reforming the Poor;* Bell, *Aid to Dependent Children,* particularly pp. 61 and 194–95. On the latter see Sar A. Levitan, Martin Rein, and David Marwick, *Work and Welfare Go Together* (Baltimore: Johns Hopkins University Press, 1972); Murray, *Losing Ground.*

Introduction to Case Studies

1. Compare with Alexander L. George and Richard Smoke, *Deterrence in American Foreign Policy: Theory and Practice* (New York: Columbia University Press, 1974), especially pp. 95–97.

Chapter 5. Social Security

1. This account draws largely but not exclusively on the following sources. The "classics" on social security include: Arthur Altmeyer, *The Formative Years of Social Security* (Madison: University of Wisconsin Press, 1968); Martha Derthick, *Policymaking for Social Security* (Washington, D.C.: Brookings, 1979); and Joseph A. Pechman, Henry J. Aaron, and Michael Taussig, *Social Security: Perspectives for Reform* (Washington, D.C.: Brookings, 1968).

Excellent recent general accounts include: Henry J. Aaron, *Economic Effects of Social Security* (Washington, D.C.: Brookings, 1982); Jerry R. Cates, *Insuring Inequality: Administrat've Leadership in Social Security, 1935–54* (Ann Arbor: University of Michigan Press, 1983); Anthony Champagne and Edward J. Harpham, eds., *The Attack on the Welfare State* (Prospect Heights, Ill.: Waveland, 1984); and Paul Light, *Artful Work: The Politics of Social Security Reform* (New York: Random House, 1985).

More specialized recent accounts include: Henry J. Aaron, *On Social Welfare* (Cambridge, Mass.: Abt Books, 1980); Joseph A. Califano, Jr., *Governing America: An Insider's Report from the White House and the Cabinet* (New York: Simon and Schuster, 1981); Colin Campbell, ed., *Income Redistribution* (Washington, D.C.: American Enterprise Institute for Public Policy Research, 1977); G. John Ikenberry and Theda Skocpol, "Expanding Social Benefits: The Role of Social Security," *Political Science Quarterly* 102 (Fall 1987): 389–416; Ann Shola Orloff and Theda Skocpol, "Why Not Equal Protection? Explaining the Politics of Public Social Welfare in Britain and the United States, 1880s–1920s," paper presented at the 1983 annual meeting of the American Sociological Association, Detroit, September 2; Jill S. Quadagno, "Welfare Capitalism and the Social Security Act of 1935," *American Sociological Review* 49 (October 1984):632–47; and Theda Skocpol and G. John Ikenberry, "The Political Formation of the American Welfare State in Historical and Comparative Perspective," *Comparative Social Research* 6 (Greenwich, Conn.: JAI Press, 1983), pp. 86–148.

Older but still useful works include: Norman Furniss and Timothy Tilton, *The Case for the Welfare State: From Social Security to Social Equality* (Bloomington: Indiana University Press, 1977), chaps. 7 and 8; and Roy Lubove, *The Struggle for Social Security, 1900–1935* Cambridge: Harvard University Press, 1968).

Accounts by participants include: Robert M. Ball, "The American System of Social Security," *Journal of Commerce* 20 (June 15, 1964):17;

J. Douglas Brown, "The American Philosophy of Social Insurance," *The Social Service Review* 30 (March 1956):1–8; Paul H. Douglas, *Social Security in the United States: An Analysis and Appraisal of the Federal Social Security Act* (New York: McGraw-Hill, 1936); and Edwin E. Witte, *The Development of the Social Security Act* (Madison: University of Wisconsin Press, 1962).

2. On the progressives' stance, see Henry Rogers Seager, *Social Insurance: A Program of Social Reform* (New York: Macmillan, 1910). For an explanation of why the U.S. did not institute the progressives' agenda see Skocpol and Ikenberry, "Political Formation."

3. See Lubove, *Struggle for Social Security*.

4. On the reasons for this shift see Altmeyer, *Formative Years*, p. 38; Cates, *Insuring Inequality*, pp. 40–44; and Quadagno, "Welfare Capitalism," p. 644.

5. Actually, the number of people employed also rose across this period, but wages—and thus social security taxes—did not keep up with inflation—and thus inflation-adjusted social security benefits. See John E. Schwarz, *America's Hidden Success: A Reassessment of Public Policy from Kennedy to Reagan*, rev. ed. (New York: Norton, 1988), chap. 3.

6. For an extensive account, see Edward J. Harpham, "Fiscal Crisis and the Politics of Social Security Reform," in Champagne and Harpham, *Attack on the Welfare State*, pp. 9–35; Derthick, *Policymaking*, pp. 392–408; Light, *Artful Work*, pt. 4; and Gary Freeman, "Presidents, Pensions, and Fiscal Policy," in James P. Pfiffner, ed., *The President and Economic Policy* (Philadelphia: Institute for the Study of Human Issues, 1986), pp. 135–59.

7. Pechman, Aaron, and Taussig, *Social Security*, p. 1, and see as well, p. 227: "The history of social security is one of success." On opposition to social security, see Cates, *Insuring Inequality;* Carolyn Weaver, *The Crisis in Social Security: Economic and Political Origins* (Durham, N.C.: Duke University Press, 1982). All in all, however, Derthick's comment still stands: "There is not the slightest evidence that the American people would like to do away with the program" (*Policymaking*, p. 3). See also Light, *Artful Work*, chap. 6 and p. 195.

8. For a discussion of these terms see Lester M. Salamon, *Welfare: The Elusive Consensus—Where We Are, How We Got There, and What's Ahead* (New York: Praeger, 1978), pp. 42–48 and 104.

9. A few exceptions exist: A 1966 amendment extended flat-rate pensions to otherwise ineligible people who turned seventy-two prior to 1968 regardless of their work histories; see Cates, *Insuring Inequality*, p. 85. As to contributions, some economists view the employer's contribu-

tion as an indirect employee contribution in the form of deferred wages.

10. See Salamon, *Welfare,* pp. 42–48 and 104; and Aaron, *Social Welfare,* chap. 1.

11. Jennifer L. Hochschild, *What's Fair? American Beliefs About Distributive Justice* (Cambridge: Harvard University Press, 1981), chap. 3.

12. See Light, *Artful Work,* pp. 61 and 64.

13. Derthick, *Policymaking,* p. 408. Cates *(Insuring Inequality,* p. 150) suggests that Altmeyer, SSB chairman and first SSA commissioner, thought 80 percent represented the upper limit of replacement rates even for people working at the minimum wage.

14. For related statistics see Light, *Artful Work,* p. 91.

15. Aaron, *Economic Effects,* p. 69.

16. Derthick, *Policymaking,* chap. 13, especially pp. 275 and 392–408.

17. Robert Nozick, *Anarchy, State, and Utopia* (New York: Basic Books, 1974), pt. 2; Milton Friedman, *Capitalism and Freedom* (Chicago: University of Chicago Press, 1962), pp. 187–89.

18. Aaron, *Economic Effects,* p. 7.

19. See Cates, *Insuring Inequality,* pp. 5–10. Nor does raising the wage base reduce regressiveness, since the higher wages of covered workers are translated into higher benefits. To avoid this problem, the Carter administration tried in 1976 to raise the wage base for employers' contributions above that for employees' contributions, but this proposal was voted down in Congress; see Derthick, *Policymaking,* p. 408.

20. See Sheldon Danziger, Robert Haveman, and Robert Plotnick, "How Income Transfer Programs Affect Work, Savings, and Income Distribution: A Critical Review," *Journal of Economic Literature* 19 (September 1981): 975–1028; Aaron, *Economic Effects,* pp. 29–31; Robert Kuttner, *The Economic Illusion: False Choices Between Prosperity and Social Justice* (Boston: Houghton Mifflin, 1984); Arthur M. Okun, *Equality and Efficiency: The Big Tradeoff* (Washington, D.C.: Brookings, 1975); Martin Feldstein, "Social Insurance," in Campbell, *Income Redistribution,* pp. 71–97.

21. See the evidence cited by Stanley Masters and Irwin Garfinkel, *Estimating the Labor Supply Effects of Income-Maintenance Alternatives* (New York: Academic Press, 1977), p. 76.

22. This theme is developed in Richard Rose and Guy Peters, *Can Government Go Bankrupt?* (New York: Basic Books, 1978).

23. Harold L. Wilensky, "Democratic Corporatism, Consensus, and Social Policy: Reflections on Changing Values and the 'Crisis' of the Welfare State," in OECD, *The Welfare State in Crisis: An Account of the Conference on Social Policy in the 1980s* (Paris: OECD, 1981), pp. 185–95.

24. Aaron, *Economic Effects,* pp. 31–34; Charles Murray, *Losing Ground: American Social Policy, 1950–1980* (New York: Basic Books, 1984), pp. 59–61.

25. The U.S. spends about 21 percent of GDP on public social provision, compared to an average of 26 percent for the twenty-four nations that belong to the Organization for Economic Cooperation and Development (OECD); see Hugh Heclo, "Income Maintenance Policy," in Arnold J. Heidenheimer, Hugh Heclo, and Carolyn Teich Adams, *Comparative Public Policy: The Politics of Social Choice in Europe and America,* 2d ed. (New York: St. Martin's 1983), pp. 200–236, especially 202 and 204; Richard Rose, "How Exceptional Is American Government?" Studies in Public Policy no. 150, Centre for the Study of Public Policy, University of Strathclyde, Glasgow, Scotland, 1985, p. 14.

26. See Weaver, *Crisis in Social Security.* However, Light, *Artful Work,* pp. 66–68, finds that social class accounts for more impressive attitudinal differences with respect to social security than does age.

27. Edward J. Harpham, "Private Pensions in Crisis: The Case for Radical Reform," Faculty Working Paper no. 8507, Center for Policy Studies, University of Texas at Dallas, January 1984; Martin Rein and Lee Rainwater, "From Welfare State to Welfare Society: Some Unresolved Issues in Assessment," Working Paper no. 69, Joint Center for Urban Studies of MIT and Harvard University, May 1981. On issues relating to parity for couples and surviving women, see Aaron, *Social Welfare,* chap. 1. See as well Robert J. Meyers, "Do Young People Get Their Money's Worth from Social Security?" (New York: Study Group on Social Security, 1985).

28. See Derthick, *Policymaking,* chap. 15.

29. See Charles Lockhart, "Institutional Innovation and Cultural Change: The Case of American Social Security," paper presented at the 1985 annual meeting of the American Political Science Association, New Orleans, August 31; Gary Freeman, "Voters, Bureaucrats, and the State: On the Autonomy of Social Security Policymaking," in Richard F. Tomasson and Nelson Puglach, eds., *Social Security: The First Half-Century* (Albuquerque: University of New Mexico Press, forthcoming).

30. Derthick, *Policymaking,* p. 217.

31. Peter G. Peterson, "Social Security: The Coming Crash," *New York Review of Books,* December 2, 1982, p. 35.

32. Cates, *Insuring Inequality,* pp. 31–38.

33. In this regard, Weaver, *Crisis in Social Security,* hits the mark more closely than does Cates, *Insuring Inequality.*

34. See Cates, *Insuring Inequality,* pp. 15, 23–25, and chap. 3.

35. Derthick, *Policymaking,* chap. 15.

36. For exceptions to this generalization, see Altmeyer, *Formative Years*, pp. 248–49.

37. In this regard see also Wilensky, "Democratic Corporatism."

38. Jule M. Sugarman, Gary D. Bass, and Matthew J. Bader, "Human Services in the 1980s—President Reagan's 1983 Proposals, White Paper no. 5: For Citizens and Public Officials" (Washington, D.C.: Human Services Information Center, 1983), pp. 22 and 76; *Social Security Bulletin* 51 (July 1988).

39. See Derthick, *Policymaking*, chap. 15.

40. Freeman, "Voters, Bureaucrats, and the State."

41. This preference holds in a number of industrial nations and appears unrelated to specific design features of particular programs; see Richard M. Coughlin, *Ideology, Public Opinion, and Welfare Policy: Attitudes Toward Taxes and Spending in Industrialized Societies* (Berkeley: Institute of International Studies, University of California, 1980), pp. 117–20.

42. For a characterization of social security as a deterrent to savings, see Martin Feldstein, "Social Security, Induced Retirement, and Aggregate Capital Accumulation," *Journal of Political Economy* 82 (September–October 1974): 905–26. Feldstein, however, seems unrealistic in assuming that the average social security pension is so generous as to discourage Americans from saving for their retirement.

43. Contrast Herman B. Leonard, *Checks Unbalanced: The Quiet Side of Public Spending* (New York: Basic Books, 1986), especially chap. 2, with Robert Eisner, *How Real Is the Federal Deficit?* (New York: Free Press, 1986).

Chapter 6. Aid to Families with Dependent Children

1. This account draws largely but not exclusively on the following sources. Recent general accounts of public assistance include: Henry J. Aaron, *Politics and the Professors: The Great Society in Perspective* (Washington, D.C.: Brookings, 1978); Jerry R. Cates, *Insuring Inequality: Administrative Leadership in Social Security, 1935–54* (Ann Arbor: University of Michigan Press, 1983); Anthony Champagne and Edward J. Harpham, eds., *The Attack on the Welfare State* (Prospect Heights, Ill.: Waveland, 1984); Tom Joe and Cheryl Rogers, *By the Few, For the Few: The Reagan Welfare Legacy* (Lexington, Mass.: Lexington Books, 1985); Lawrence M. Mead, *Beyond Entitlement: The Social Obligations of Citizenship* (New York: Free Press, 1986); and Lester M. Salamon, *Welfare: The Elusive Consensus—Where We Are, How We Got There, and What's Ahead* (New York: Praeger, 1978).

Recent and more specific accounts include: Henry J. Aaron, *On Social Welfare* (Cambridge, Mass.: Abt Books, 1980); Winifred Bell and Dennis M. Bushe, *Neglecting the Many, Helping the Few: The Impact of the 1967 AFDC Work Incentives* (New York: Center for Studies in Income Maintenance Policy, New York University School of Social Work, 1975); Joseph A. Califano, Jr., *Governing America: An Insider's Report from the Cabinet and the White House* (New York: Simon and Schuster, 1981); Colin Campbell, ed., *Income Redistribution* (Washington, D.C.: American Enterprise Institute for Public Policy Research, 1977); Martha Derthick, *Uncontrollable Spending for Social Service Grants* (Washington, D.C.: Brookings, 1975); Irwin Garfinkel, ed., *Income-Tested Transfer Programs: The Case For and Against* (New York: Academic Press, 1982); G. John Ikenberry and Theda Skocpol, "Expanding Social Benefits: The Role of Social Security," *Political Science Quarterly* 102 (Fall 1987):389–416; Theda Skocpol and G. John Ikenberry, "The Political Formation of the American Welfare State in Historical and Comparative Perspective," *Comparative Social Research* 6 (Greenwich, Conn.: JAI Press, 1983), pp. 86–148; and the series of articles on the urban underclass edited by William Julius Wilson in *Society* 21 (November–December 1983):34–86.

Older but still useful general accounts include: Henry J. Aaron, *Why Is Welfare So Hard to Reform?* (Washington, D.C.: Brookings, 1973); Vincent J. Burke and Vee Burke, *Nixon's Good Deed: Welfare Reform* (New York: Columbia University Press, 1974); Norman Furniss and Timothy Tilton, *The Case for the Welfare State: From Social Security to Social Equality* (Bloomington: Indiana University Press, 1977), chaps. 7 and 8; Joel F. Handler, *Reforming the Poor: Welfare Policy, Federalism and Morality* (New York: Basic Books, 1972); Roy Lubove, *The Struggle for Social Security, 1900–1935* (Cambridge: Harvard University Press, 1968); and Daniel P. Moynihan, *The Politics of a Guaranteed Income: The Nixon Administration and the Family Assistance Plan* (New York: Random House, 1973).

Works on relations between public social provision and the labor market include: Leonard Beeghley, *Living Poorly in America* (New York: Praeger, 1983); Eli Ginsberg, ed., *Employing the Unemployed* (New York: Basic Books, 1980); Helen Ginsburg, *Full Employment and Public Policy: The United States and Sweden* (Lexington, Mass.: D.C. Heath, 1983); Sar A. Levitan and Richard S. Belous, *More Than Subsistence: Minimum Wages for the Working Poor* (Baltimore: Johns Hopkins University Press, 1979); Sar A. Levitan, Martin Rein, and David Marwick, *Work and Welfare Go Together* (Baltimore: Johns Hopkins University Press, 1972); Stanley Masters and Irwin Garfinkel, *Estimating the Labor Supply Effects of Income-Maintenance Alternatives* (New York: Academic Press, 1977); Philip K. Robins et al., eds., *A Guaranteed Annual Income: Evidence from a Social Experiment* (New York: Academic Press, 1980); and Harold L. Wilensky, "Nothing Fails Like Success: The Evaluation-Research Industry and Labor Market Policy," reprint no. 464, Institute of Industrial Relations, University of California, Berkeley, 1985.

2. Ikenberry and Skocpol, "Patronage Democracy"; Salamon, *Welfare*, p. 79.

3. Since 1972 (implemented in 1974) public assistance for the elderly, blind, and disabled has been centralized through a national program, Supplementary Security Income (SSI).

4. See Salamon, *Welfare*, pp. 23 and 83; Levitan, Rein, and Marwick, *Work and Welfare*, pp. 8–18.

5. See Bell and Bushe, *Neglecting the Many*, p. 22; and James T. Patterson, *America's Struggle Against Poverty, 1900–1980* (Cambridge: Harvard University Press, 1981).

6. This relationship may be an example of the "ecological fallacy" since we cannot be certain that the households from which the unemployed came were the same ones seeking ADC assistance. See Moynihan, *Politics of Guaranteed Income.*

7. See Derthick, *Uncontrollable Spending.*

8. Greg J. Duncan et al., *Years of Poverty, Years of Plenty: The Changing Economic Fortunes of American Workers and Families* (Ann Arbor: Survey Research Center, Institute for Social Research, University of Michigan, 1984), chaps. 2 and 3, especially pp. 40–42, 46–51, and 77–79. Other researchers argue that Duncan overestimates turnover. They find that a significant portion of those falling into poverty experience multiyear "spells" of impoverishment. See Mary Jo Bane, "The Poor in Massachusetts," in Manuel Carbello and Mary Jo Bane, eds., *The State and the Poor in the 1980s* (Boston: Auburn House, 1984), pp. 1–13.

9. See Duncan et al., *Years of Poverty*, pp. 40–42 and 74–78. Federal poverty guidelines are strict. Many Americans would consider themselves impoverished if they had to live within several thousand dollars of these guidelines. So many more than 25 percent of the population face near poverty. Also, Duncan's estimates of poverty, (pp. 38–40) are lower than those of the census, perhaps because his longitudinal panel-study procedure was bound to underrepresent the most unstable households.

10. See Duncan et al., *Years of Poverty*, chaps. 2 and 3. See also two essays in Martha S. Hill, Daniel N. Hill, and James N. Morgan, eds., *Five Thousand American Families—Patterns of Economic Progress, Volume 9: Analyses of the First Twelve Years of the Panel Study on Income Dynamics* (Ann Arbor: Survey Research Center, Institute for Social Research, University of Michigan, 1981): Richard D. Coe, "A Preliminary

Empirical Examination of the Dynamics of Welfare Use," pp. 121–68; and Greg J. Duncan and James N. Morgan, "Persistence and Change in Economic Status and the Role of Changing Family Composition," pp. 1–44.

11. Duncan et al., *Years of Poverty*, pp. 74–80.

12. See particularly Moynihan, *Politics of Guaranteed Income;* Burke and Burke, *Nixon's Good Deed.*

13. The working poor may avail themselves of in-kind programs, particularly food stamps, Medicaid, and, in some urban settings, housing. Expenditures for the first two programs grew faster than for AFDC in the 1970s.

14. See Califano, *Governing America,* chap. 8; and Harvey D. Shapiro, "Welfare Reform Revisited—President Jimmy Carter's Program for Better Jobs and Income" in Salamon, *Welfare,* pp. 173–218.

15. Jule M. Sugarman, Gary D. Bass, and Matthew J. Bader, "Human Services in the 1980s—President Reagan's 1983 Proposals, White Paper no. 5: For Citizens and Public Officials" (Washington, D.C.: Human Services Information Center, 1983), p. 76.

16. Children of AFDC families sometimes feel stigmatized, but little public censure is directed at them. See Lee Rainwater, "Stigma in Income-Tested Programs," in Garfinkel, *Income-Tested Transfer Programs,* pp. 19–46; Peggy Thoits and Michael T. Hannan, "Income and Psychological Distress," in Robins, et al., *Guaranteed Annual Income,* pp. 183–205; Natalie Jaffe, "A Review of Public Opinion Surveys, 1935–76" in Salamon, *Welfare,* pp. 221–28.

17. See Patterson, *America's Struggle,* pp. 109–10 and 173–75; Martin Anderson, *Welfare: The Political Economy of Welfare Reform in the United States* (Stanford, Calif.: Hoover Institution, 1978), chap. 3.

18. Bell and Bushe, *Neglecting the Many,* pp. 45–46; Moynihan, *Politics of Guaranteed Income,* pp. 104–6; Burke and Burke, *Nixon's Good Deed,* pp. 163 and 205.

19. In the 1970s growth in in-kind and service public assistance constituted a greater portion of the "welfare crisis" than did AFDC. Bell and Bushe, *Neglecting the Many,* pp. 45–46 and 51.

20. See Handler, *Reforming the Poor,* pp. 34 and 130–31.

21. Handler, *Reforming the Poor,* pp. 43 and 51–54; and Joe and Rogers, *By the Few.*

22. See Levitan, Rein, and Marwick, *Work and Welfare,* pp. 26–35.

23. Evidence that AFDC mothers want to work is plentiful; see, for example, Leonard Goodwin, *Causes and Cures of Welfare: New Evidence on the Social Psychology of the Poor* (Lexington, Mass.: D.C. Heath, 1983), especially pp. 147–48.

24. Duncan et al., *Years of Poverty,* chap. 3; Coe, "Dynamics of Wel-

fare Use"; and Duncan and Morgan, "Persistence and Change in Economic Status."

25. Bell and Bushe, *Neglecting the Many,* pp. 8 and 25.

26. Aaron, *Why Is Welfare So Hard to Reform?*

27. For a detailed discussion of these problems see Mead, *Beyond Entitlement;* Aaron, *Why Is Welfare So Hard to Reform?;* Moynihan, *Politics of a Guaranteed Income,* pp. 464–81 and 506–8.

28. Goodwin, *Causes and Cures,* pp. 147–48; Levitan, Rein, and Marwick, *Work and Welfare,* p. 100.

29. As Derthick relates, the open-ended commitment of the federal government to pay 75 percent—as opposed to the usual 50 percent of these social services expenses, as well as the vague character of some of the services and their objectives led some states into innovative efforts to use AFDC to fund a variety of state agencies by "purchasing" the services of these agencies with federal funds; see *Uncontrollable Spending.* See also, Handler, *Reforming the Poor,* pp. 88–93.

30. Homes, some furnishings, and automobiles up to certain maximum values are usually exempt from these restrictions, but these exemptions are largely irrelevant to most AFDC recipients.

31. Randall J. Pozdena and Terry R. Johnson, "Demand for Assets," in Robins et al., *Guaranteed Annual Income,* pp. 281–90.

32. See the remarks of Barber S. Conable in "Round Table Discussion on Welfare Reform," in Campbell, *Income Redistribution,* p. 247; Levitan, Rein, and Marwick, *Work and Welfare,* p. 17; and Burke and Burke, *Nixon's Good Deed,* p. 172.

33. Winifred Bell, *Aid to Dependent Children* (New York: Columbia University Press, 1965), pp. 174–75.

34. See Bell and Bushe, *Neglecting the Many,* pp. 45–46 and 51.

35. See, for instance, Charles Murray, *Losing Ground: American Social Policy, 1950–1980* (New York: Basic Books, 1983), chap. 8.

36. On the relation between benefits and family structure, see David T. Ellwood and Mary Jo Bane, "The Impact of AFDC on Family Structure and Living Arrangements," mimeo, Kennedy School of Government, Harvard University, March 1984. On the tendencies of AFDC fathers, see Marcia Guttentag and Paul F. Secord, *Too Many Women? The Sex Ratio Question* (Beverly Hills, Calif.: Sage, 1983), chap. 8.

37. These opposing effects are discussed by Lyle P. Groenveld, Nancy Brandon Tuma, and Michael T. Hannan, "Marital Dissolution and Remarriage," in Robins et al., *Guaranteed Annual Income,* pp. 163–81.

38. See Michael C. Keeley, "Migration," in Robins et al., *Guaranteed Annual Income,* pp. 241–62.

39. Moynihan, *Politics of a Guaranteed Income,* p. 407; and Handler, *Reforming the Poor,* pp. 43, 117–18, and 130–31.

40. Derthick, *Uncontrollable Spending,* chap. 7, suggests that funds for these services increasingly went to pay for budgets of state agencies that provided little in the way of services specifically tailored to the merging needs of AFDC recipients.

41. By the mid-1970s AFDC-UP usage had stabilized at slightly less than 10 percent of AFDC households.

42. Kathi V. Friedman, *Legitimation of Social Rights and the Western Welfare State: A Weberian Perspective* (Chapel Hill: University of North Carolina Press, 1981).

43. Handler, *Reforming the Poor,* pp. 130–31.

44. Handler, *Reforming the Poor,* p. 3 and chap. 4; Moynihan, *Politics of a Guaranteed Income,* p. 495.

45. Burke and Burke, *Nixon's Good Deed,* p. 172; on related points see Moynihan, *Politics of a Guaranteed Income,* pp. 174, 215, 412–14, and 552.

46. Cates, *Insuring Inequality,* particularly chap. 5.

47. See, for example, Mickey Kaus, "The Work Ethic State," *New Republic,* July 7, 1986, pp. 22–33, especially pp. 28–30.

48. Duncan et al., *Years of Poverty,* p. 58.

49. For sympathetic views on these problems, see Herbert J. Gans, "The Negro Family: Reflections on the Moynihan Report" in Lee Rainwater and William Yancey, eds., *The Moynihan Report and the Politics of Controversy* (Cambridge: MIT Press, 1967), pp. 445–57; William Julius Wilson, *The Truly Disadvantaged: The Inner City, the Underclass, and Public Policy* (Chicago: University of Chicago Press, 1987). Far less sympathetic is George Gilder, *Wealth and Poverty* (New York: Basic Books, 1981).

50. See Guttentag and Secord, *Too Many Women?* chap. 8.

Chapter 7. Medicare

1. The term is Harold L. Wilensky's; see his *The Welfare State and Equality: Structural and Ideological Roots of Public Expenditures* (Berkeley: University of California Press, 1975).

This account draws largely but not exclusively on the following sources. Recent general accounts of public policy with respect to medical care include: Lawrence D. Brown, *Politics and Health Care Organization: HMOs as Federal Policy* (Washington, D.C.: Brookings, 1983); Karen Davis, *National Health Insurance: Benefits, Costs, and Consequences* (Washington, D.C.: Brookings, 1975); Alain Enthoven, *Health Plan: The Only Practical Solution to the Soaring Cost of Medical Care* (Menlo Park, Calif.: Addison-Wesley, 1980); and Paul Starr, *The Social Transfor-*

mation of American Medicine: The Rise of a Sovereign Profession and the Making of a Vast Industry (New York: Basic Books, 1982).

Recent but more specific accounts include: Henry J. Aaron and William B. Schwartz, *The Painful Prescription: Rationing Hospital Care* (Washington, D.C.: Brookings, 1984); Martha Derthick, *Policymaking for Social Security* (Washington, D.C.: Brookings, 1983) chaps. 15 and 16; Paul T. Menzel, *Medical Costs, Moral Choices: A Philosophy of Health Care Economics in America* (New Haven: Yale University Press, 1983); and Ann Shola Orloff and Theda Skocpol, "Why Not Equal Protection? Explaining the Politics of Public Social Welfare in Britain and the United States, 1880s–1920s," paper presented at the 1983 annual meeting of the American Sociological Association, Detroit, September 2.

Older but still useful general accounts include: Daniel S. Hirschfield, *The Lost Reform: The Campaign for Compulsory Health Insurance in the United States from 1932 to 1943* (Cambridge: Harvard University Press, 1970); Roy Lubove, *The Struggle for Social Security, 1900–1935* (Cambridge: Harvard University Press, 1968); and Theodore R. Marmor, *The Politics of Medicare* (Chicago: Aldine, 1973).

On the consequences of Medicare see Henry R. Brehm and Rodney M. Coe, *Medical Care for the Aged: From Social Problem to Federal Program* (New York: Praeger, 1980); and Stephen Davidson and Theodore R. Marmor, *The Cost of Living Longer: National Health Insurance for the Elderly* (Lexington, Mass.: D.C. Heath, 1980). On the consequences of Medicaid see Karen Davis and Cathy Schoen, *Health and the War on Poverty: A Ten-Year Appraisal* (Washington, D.C.: Brookings, 1978), chaps. 1, 2, 4, 6, and 7.

For statistics on Medicare see Congressional Budget Office, *Changing the Structure of Medical Benefits: Issues and Options* (Washington, D.C.: Congressional Budget Office, 1983); and selected issues of the *Social Security Bulletin.*

2. *Crusade* is an appropriate term in light of Samuel Huntington's description of this period as one of "creedal passion"; see his *American Politics: The Promise of Disharmony* (Cambridge: Harvard University Press, 1981).

3. See Carleton B. Chapman and John M. Talmadge, "The Evolution of the Right-to-Health Concept in the United States," in Maurice B. Visscher, ed., *Humanistic Perspectives in Medical Ethics* (Buffalo, N.Y.: Prometheus, 1972), pp. 72–134, especially pp. 94–103.

4. Hirschfield, *Lost Reform,* passim.

5. See Davis and Schoen, *Health and the War on Poverty,* chap. 5.

6. Marmor, *Politics of Medicare,* pp. 14–16.

7. Marmor, *Politics of Medicare,* pp. 25 and 53. On the extension of

social security to disabled workers, see Derthick, *Policymaking,* chap. 15.

8. Brown, *Politics and Health Care,* pp. 195–96.

9. For a comparison of various proposals see Davis, *National Health Insurance,* chap. 5; and Davidson and Marmor, *Cost of Living Longer,* chap. 5.

10. Other beneficiaries include railroad retirement recipients, persons receiving social security disability payments, and some kidney dialysis patients. For most of these persons the criterion of effort is still applicable.

11. For details of coverage see Brehm and Coe, *Medical Care for the Aged,* pp. 59–63; or Davidson and Marmor, *Cost of Living Longer,* pp. 35–40.

12. Brehm and Coe, *Medical Care for the Aged,* pp. 41–42.

13. See Ivan D. Illich, *Medical Nemesis: The Expropriation of Health Care* (New York: Bantam, 1977).

14. Guido Calabresi and Philip Bobbit, *Tragic Choices* (New York: Norton, 1978); Menzel, *Medical Costs, Moral Choices,* p. 138.

15. Menzel, *Medical Costs, Moral Choices,* p. 82.

16. Marmor, *Politics of Medicare,* pp. 67, 86, and 122–23.

17. M. Kenneth Bowler, "Changing Politics of Federal Health Insurance Programs," *PS* 20 (Spring 1987):202–11.

18. Starr, *Social Transformation,* bk. 2, chap. 5.

19. Starr, *Social Transformation,* p. 311 and bk. 2, chap. 5.

20. Davis and Schoen, *Health and the War on Poverty,* p. 97; Congressional Budget Office, *Changing the Structure of Medical Benefits,* pp. 11–12; *Social Security Bulletin* 51 (July 1988).

21. See Enthoven, *Health Plan,* pp. 16–32; and Davis and Schoen, *Health and the War on Poverty,* p. 97.

22. John Holahan and John L. Palmer, "Medicare's Fiscal Problems" (Washington, D.C.: Changing Domestic Priorities Project, Urban Institute, 1987).

23. See Enthoven, *Health Plan,* pp. 27–28 and 105–6; and Bowler, "Changing Politics of Health Insurance."

24. Enthoven, *Health Plan,* pp. 32–36.

25. See Brehm and Coe, *Medical Care for the Aged,* pp. 68–77; and Menzel, *Medical Costs, Moral Choices,* pp. 120 and 138.

26. Brown, *Politics and Health Care,* pp. 206–8; but see as well pp. 462–64.

27. Enthoven, *Health Plan,* pp. 82–89.

28. Enthoven, *Health Plan,* pp. 84–88; and Brown, *Politics and Health Care,* pp. 377–82.

29. Brown, *Politics and Health Care.*

30. See Brown, *Politics and Health Care,* pp. 234 and 360.

31. On the need for regulation under competitive and current market conditions, see Brown, *Politics and Health Care*, pp. 228, 234, and 360; Enthoven, *Health Plan*, pp. 78–82.

32. Brown, *Politics and Health Care*, p. 527; and Davis and Schoen, *Health and the War on Poverty*, pp. 212–13; and Davidson and Marmor, *Cost of Living Longer*, chap. 5.

33. Davis and Schoen, *Health and the War on Poverty*, p. 92.

34. Brehm and Coe, *Medical Care for the Aged*, pp. 63–64 and 95.

35. These terms as well as *accountability* and *acceptability*—Medicare doing better on the latter—come from Brehm and Coe, *Medical Care for the Aged*, p. 130.

36. Davis, *National Health Insurance*, p. 73.

37. Davidson and Marmor, *Cost of Living Longer*, p. 12.

38. "President Carter's National Health Plan Legislation: Detailed Fact Sheet" (Washington, D.C.: Department of Health, Education, and Welfare, June 12, 1979).

39. But see Louise B. Russell, *Is Prevention Better Than Cure?* (Washington, D.C.: Brookings, 1986).

40. Brehm and Coe, *Medical Care for the Aged*, pp. 79–81.

41. Marmor, *Politics of Medicare*, p. 25.

42. See particularly, Enthoven, *Health Plan*, pp. 105–6.

43. Starr, *Social Transformation*, bk. 2, chap. 5, discusses this decline but has a glum view of it.

44. Charles Lockhart, "Values and Policy Conceptions of Health Policy Elites in the United States, the United Kingdom, and the Federal Republic of Germany," *Journal of Health Politics, Policy and Law* 6 (Spring 1981):98–119, particularly pp. 103–5.

Chapter 8. The Investments Approach

1. Natalie Jaffe, "A Review of Public Opinion Surveys, 1937–76," in Lester M. Salamon, *Welfare: The Elusive Consensus—Where We Are, How We Got There, and What's Ahead* (New York: Praeger, 1978), pp. 221–28. See also the support for this theme in Martin Anderson, *Welfare: The Political Economy of Welfare Reform in the United States* (Stanford, Calif.: Hoover Institution, 1978), chap. 3; James T. Patterson, *America's Struggle Against Poverty, 1900–1980* (Cambridge: Harvard University Press, 1981).

2. See, for example, Friedrich A. Hayek, *The Mirage of Social Justice*, vol. 2 of *Law, Legislation, and Liberty* (Chicago: University of Chicago Press, 1976).

3. See Lloyd A. Free and Hadley Cantril, *The Political Beliefs of*

Americans: A Study of Public Opinion (New Brunswick, N.J.: Rutgers University Press, 1967).

4. C. B. Mcpherson, *Democratic Theory: Essays in Retrieval* (Oxford: Oxford University Press, 1973), chap. 7; or Larry M. Preston, "Freedom, Markets, and Voluntary Exchange," *American Political Science Review* 78 (December 1984):959–70.

5. Leonard Goodwin, *Causes and Cures of Welfare: New Evidence on the Social Psychology of the Poor* (Lexington, Mass.: D.C. Heath, 1983); and Leonard Beeghley, *Living Poor in America* (New York: Praeger, 1983), particularly chaps. 4 and 6.

6. See Edward J. Harpham, "Fiscal Crisis and the Politics of Social Security," in Anthony Champagne and Edward J. Harpham, eds., *The Attack on the Welfare State* (Prospect Heights, Ill.: Waveland, 1984), pp. 9–35; Paul Light, *Artful Work: The Politics of Social Security Reform* (New York: Random House, 1985), chap. 8.

7. Private contributions to well-being in social hazards, particularly for retirement, are growing; see Martin Rein and Lee Rainwater, "From Welfare State to Welfare Society: Some Unresolved Issues in Assessment," Working Paper no. 69, Joint Center for Urban Studies of MIT and Harvard University, May 1981.

8. Compare with Bernadyne Weatherford, "The Disability Insurance Program: An Administrative Attack on the Welfare State," in Champagne and Harpham, *Attack on the Welfare State,* pp. 37–60, especially pp. 43–49.

9. This practice would create an annual income plateau for earnings from $6,700 up to as much as $10,300: $4,500 (maximum annual benefit) – $900 (minimum annual benefit) = $3,600 (plateau range), and $6,700 + $3,600 = $10,300 or the upper limit of the plateau. The plateau would be narrower for households with two children ($2,880, or from $6,700 to $9,580) and one child ($1,680, or from $6,700 to $8,380). And these narrower plateaus might provide some disincentives for new births.

10. This tendency is suggested by Michael C. Keeley, "Migration," in Philip K. Robins et al., eds., *A Guaranteed Annual Income: Evidence From a Social Experiment* (New York: Academic Press, 1980), pp. 241–62.

11. A far broader set of encouraging consequences is suggested in Harold L. Wilensky, "Nothing Fails Like Success: The Evaluation-Research Industry and Labor Market Policy," Reprint no. 464, Institute of Industrial Relations, University of California, Berkeley, 1985.

12. See Judy Gueron, "The Supported Work Experiment," in Eli Ginzberg, ed., *Employing the Unemployed* (New York: Basic Books,

1980), pp. 73–93; and James Q. Wilson, *Thinking About Crime,* rev. ed. (New York: Basic Books, 1983).

13. For a short statement on these trends, see Nathan H. Schwartz, "Reagan's Housing Policies," in Champagne and Harpham, *Attack on the Welfare State,* pp. 149–64, particularly pp. 160–61.

14. David A. Snow, Susan G. Baker, Leon Anderson, and Michael Martin, "The Myth of Pervasive Mental Illness Among the Homeless," *Social Problems* 33 (June 1986):407–23.

15. See Mark Bendick, Jr., "Vouchers Versus Income Versus Service," *Journal of Social Policy* 11 (July 1982):365–77.

16. Placing children from disadvantaged households in preschool programs may have some important long-term benefits for their educational and occupational success; see Lawrence J. Schwienhart and Jeffrey L. Koshel, "Policy Options for Preschool Programs," in *High Scope Early Childhood Policy Papers* (Ypsilanti, Mich.: High Scope Educational Research Foundation, 1986).

17. Albert O. Hirschman, *Exit, Voice, and Loyalty: Responses to Decline in Firms, Organizations, and States* (Cambridge: Harvard University Press, 1970).

18. Milton and Rose Friedman, *Free to Choose: A Personal Statement* (New York: Avon, 1979), especially pp. 110–15.

19. See Alain Enthoven, *Health Plan: The Only Practical Solution to the Soaring Cost of Medical Care* (Menlo Park, Calif.: Addison-Wesley, 1979), pp. 121–23.

20. See Light, *Artful Work,* chap. 8.

21. On this point see Light, *Artful Work,* p. 104.

22. See Wilensky, "Nothing Fails Like Success"; Patterson, *America's Struggle,* chap. 4; Gueron, "Supported Work Experiment"; and Wilson, *Thinking About Crime.*

23. Samuel P. Huntington, *American Politics: The Promise of Disharmony* (Cambridge: Harvard University Press, 1981), especially chap. 4.

24. The electorate does not seem to share this mood. See Seymour Martin Lipset, "Beyond 1984: The Anomalies of American Politics," *PS* 19 (Spring 1986):222–36.

25. Hugh Heclo, "Toward a New Welfare State," in Peter Flora and Arnold J. Heidenheimer, eds., *The Development of Welfare States in Europe and America* (New Brunswick, N.J.: Transaction, 1981), especially pp. 386–87.

26. Compare with Lester C. Thurow, *The Zero-Sum Society: Distribution and the Possibilities of Economic Change* (New York: Basic Books, 1980); Richard Rose and Guy Peters, *Can Government Go Bankrupt?* (New York: Basic Books, 1978).

27. For a clear example of the problems in the case of social programs as well as techniques for implementing short cuts, see Light, *Artful Work*, p. 74; Beth C. Fuchs and John F. Hoadley, "Reflections from Inside the Beltway: How Congress and the President Grapple with Health Policy," *PS* 20 (Spring 1987):212–20.

28. See Charles Lockhart, "Institutional Innovation and Cultural Change: The Case of American Social Security," paper presented at the 1985 annual meeting of the American Political Science Association, New Orleans, August 31; Light, *Artful Work*, chap. 7.

29. On the impact of these cataclysms, compare Lewis J. Edinger, *Politics in Germany: Attitudes and Processes* (Boston: Little, Brown, 1968), p. 72, with his *Politics in West Germany*, 2d ed. (Boston: Little, Brown, 1977), p. 46.

30. Paul Starr, *The Social Transformation of American Medicine: The Rise of a Sovereign Profession and the Making of a Vast Industry* (New York: Basic Books, 1982), pp. 289, 310–11.

31. Theodore Marmor, *The Politics of Medicare* (Chicago: Aldine, 1970), pp. 164–66; and Mary Weaver, "The Food Stamp Program: A Very Expensive Orphan," in Champagne and Harpham, *Attack on the Welfare State*, pp. 111–29.

Index

Compositor:	G & S Typesetters
Text:	11/13 Sabon
Display:	Sabon
Printer:	Maple-Vail Book Mfg. Group
Binder:	Maple-Vail Book Mfg. Group